Advanced History of Buddhism: Monasteries and Temples

Advanced History of Buddhism: Monasteries and Temples

Sameer Das Gupta

2008

CYBER TECH PUBLICATIONS
4264/3, Ansari Road, Daryaganj, New Delhi-110002 (India)
Ph.: 011-23244078. Fax: 011-23280028
E-Mail: cyberpublicationsdelhi@yahoo.com

ADVANCED HISTORY OF BUDDHISM: MONASTERIES AND TEMPLES

Sameer Das Gupta

First Edition 2008

Published by :

G.S. Rawat for **Cyber Tech Publications**
4264/3, Ansari Road, Daryaganj, New Delhi-110002 (India)
Ph.: 011-23244078. Fax: 011-23280028
E-Mail: cyberpublicationsdelhi@yahoo.com

Printed at : **Amit Enterprises**, Maujpur, Delhi, (9810878184)

Preface

The history of Buddhism is also characterized by the development of numerous movements and schisms, foremost among them the Theravada, Mahayana and Vajrayana traditions, punctuated by contrasting periods of expansion and retreat. The history of Buddhism spans from the 6th century BC to the present, starting with the birth of the Buddha Siddhartha Gautama. This makes it one of the oldest religions practised today. Throughout this period, the religion evolved as it encountered various countries and cultures, adding to its original Indian foundation Hellenistic as well as Central Asian, East Asian and Southeast Asian cultural elements. In the process, its geographical extent became considerable so as to affect at one time or another most of the Asian continent.

According to the Buddhist tradition, the historical Buddha Siddhartha Gautama was born to the Shakya clan, at the beginning of the Magadha period (546-324 BC), in the plains of Lumbini, Southern Nepal. He is also known as the Shakyamuni literally "The sage of the Shakya clan".

—*Author*

Contents

1

INTRODUCTION

History of Buddhism : The history of Buddhism is also characterized by the development of numerous movements and schisms, foremost among them the Theravada, Mahayana and Vajrayana traditions, punctuated by contrasting periods of expansion and retreat. The history of Buddhism spans from the 6th century BC to the present, starting with the birth of the Buddha Siddhartha Gautama. This makes it one of the oldest religions practised today. Throughout this period, the religion evolved as it encountered various countries and cultures, adding to its original Indian foundation Hellenistic as well as Central Asian, East Asian and Southeast Asian cultural elements. In the process, its geographical extent became considerable so as to affect at one time or another most of the Asian continent.

Life of the Buddha

According to the Buddhist tradition, the historical Buddha Siddhartha Gautama was born to the Shakya clan, at the beginning of the Magadha period (546-324 BC), in the plains of Lumbini, Southern Nepal. He is also known as the Shakyamuni (literally "The sage of the Shakya clan").

After an early life of luxury under the protection of his father, Suddhodana, the ruler of Kapilavastu (later to be incorporated into the state of Magadha), Siddhartha entered into contact with the realities of the world and concluded that real life was about inescapable suffering and sorrow. Siddhartha renounced his meaningless life of luxury to become an ascetic.

He ultimately decided that asceticism was also meaningless and instead chose a middle way, a path of moderation away from the extremes of self-indulgence and self-mortification.

Under a fig tree, now known as the Bodhi tree, he vowed never to leave the position until he found Truth. At the age of 35, he attained Enlightenment. He was then known as Gautama Buddha, or simply "The Buddha", which means "the enlightened one".

For the remaining 45 years of his life, he travelled the Gangetic Plain of central India (region of the Ganges/Ganga river and its tributaries), teaching his doctrine and discipline to an extremely diverse range of people. The Buddha's reluctance to name a successor or to formalise his doctrine led to the emergence of many movements during the next 400 years: first the schools of Nikaya Buddhism, of which only Theravada remains today and then the formation of Mahayana, a pan-Buddhist movement based on the acceptance of new scriptures.

Rise of Mahayana (1st c.BC-2nd c.AD)

The rise of Mahayana Buddhism from the 1st century BC was accompanied by complex political changes in northwestern India. The Indo-Greek kingdoms were gradually overwhelmed and their culture assimilated by the Indo-Scythians and then the Yuezhi, who founded the Kushan Empire from around 12 BC.

The Kushans were supportive of Buddhism and a fourth Buddhist council was convened by the Kushan emperor Kanishka, around 100 AD at Jalandhar or in Kashmir and is usually associated with the formal rise of Mahayana Buddhism and its secession from Theravada Buddhism. Theravada Buddhism does not recognize the authenticity of this council and it is sometimes called the "council of heretical monks".

It is said that Kanishka gathered 500 bhikkhus in Kashmir, headed by Vasumitra, to edit the Tripitaka and make references and remarks. Allegedly, during the council there were all together three hundred thousand verses and over nine million statements compiled and it took twelve years to complete. This council did not rely on the original Pali canon (the Tipitaka). Instead, a set of new scriptures was approved, as well as fundamental principles of Mahayana doctrine. The new scriptures, usually in the Gandhari vernacular and the Kharosthi script, were rewritten in the classical language of Sanskrit, to many scholars a turning point in the propagation of Buddhist thought.

The new form of Buddhism was characterized by an almost God-like treatment of the Buddha, by the idea that all beings have a Buddha-nature and should aspire to Buddhahood and by a syncretism due to the various cultural influences within northwestern India and the Kushan Empire.

Mahayana Expansion (1st c.AD-10th c.AD)

From that point on and in the space of a few centuries, Mahayana was to flourish and spread in the East from India to South-East Asia and towards the north to Central Asia, China, Korea and finally to Japan in 538 AD.

India

After the end of the Kushans, Buddhism flourished in India during the dynasty of the Guptas (4th-6th century). Mahayana centres of learning were established, especially at Nalanda in northeastern India, which was to become the largest and most influential Buddhist university for many centuries, with famous teachers such as Nagarjuna. The Gupta style of Buddhist art became very influential from South-East Asia to China as the faith was spreading there.

Indian Buddhism had weakened in the 6th century following the White Hun invasions and Mihirkulas persecution.

Xuanzang reports in his travels across India during the 7th century of Buddhism being popular in Andhra, Dhanyakataka and Dravida which today roughly correspond to the modern day Indian states of Andhra Pradesh and Tamil Nadu. While reporting many deserted stupas in the area around modern day

Nepal and the persecution of Buddhists by Sanka in the Kingdom of Gouda. (In modern day West Bengal.) Xuanzang compliments the patronage of Harshavardana during the same period. After Harshavardanas kingdom, the rise of many small kingdoms that lead to the rise of the Rajputs across the gangetic plains and marked the end of Buddhist ruling clans along with a sharp decline in royal patronage until a revival under the Pala Empire in the Bengal region. Here Mahayana Buddhism flourished and spread to Bhutan and Sikkim between the 8th and the 12th century before the Palas collapsed under the assault of the Hindu Sena dynasty. The Palas created many temples and a distinctive school of Buddhist art. Xuanzang noted in his travels that in various regions Buddhism was giving way to Jainism and Hinduism. By the 10th century Buddhism had experienced a sharp decline beyond the Pala realms in Bengal under a resurgent Hinduism and the incorporation in Vaishnavite Hinduism of Buddha as the 9th incarnation of Vishnu.

A milestone in the decline of Indian Buddhism in the North occurred in 1193 when Turkic Islamic raiders under Muhammad Khilji burnt Nalanda. By the end of the 12th century, following the Islamic conquest of the Buddhist strongholds in Bihar and the loss of political support coupled with social and caste pressures, the practice of Buddhism retreated to the Himalayan foothills in the North and Sri Lanka in the south. Additionally, the influence of Buddhism also waned due to Hinduism's revival movements such as Advaita, the rise of the bhakti movement and the missionary work of Sufis.

Central and Northern Asia

Central Asia: Central Asia had been influenced by Buddhism probably almost since the time of the Buddha. According to a legend preserved in Pali, the language of the Theravada canon, two merchant brothers from Bacteria, named Tapassu and Bhallika, visited the Buddha and became his disciples. They then returned to Bacteria and built temples to the Buddha (Foltz).

Central Asia long played the role of a meeting place between China, India and Persia. During the 2nd century BC, the expansion of the Former Han to the west brought them into contact with the Hellenistic civilizations of Asia, especially the Greco-Bactrian Kingdoms. Thereafter, the expansion of Buddhism to the north led to the formation of Buddhist communities and even Buddhist kingdoms in the oases of Central Asia. Some Silk Road cities consisted almost entirely of Buddhist stupas and monasteries and it seems that one of their main objectives was to welcome and service travellers between east and west.

The Hinayana traditions first spread among the Turkic tribes before combining with the Mahayana forms during the 2nd and 3rd centuries BC to cover modern-day Pakistan, Kashmir, Afghanistan, eastern and coastal Iran, Uzbekistan, Turkmenistan and Tajikistan. These were the ancient states of Gandhara, Bacteria, Parthia and Sogdia from where it spread to China. Among the first of these Turkic tribes to adopt Buddhism was the Turki-Shahi who adopted Buddhism as early as the 3rd century BC. It was not, however, the exclusive faith of this region. There were also Zoroastrians, Hindus, Nestorian Christians, Jews, Manichaeans and followers of shamanism, Tengrism and other indigenous, nonorganized systems of belief.

Various Nikaya schools persisted in Central Asia and China until around the 7th century AD. Mahayana started to become dominant during the period, but since the faith had not developed a Nikaya approach, Sarvastivadin and Dharmaguptakas remained the Vinayas of choice in Central Asian monasteries. Various Buddhism kingdoms rose and prospered in both the Central Asian region and downwards into the Indian sub-continent such as Kushan Empire prior to the White Hun invasion in the 5th century where under the King Mihirkula they were heavily persecuted.

Buddhism in Central Asia started to decline with the expansion of Islam and the destruction of many stupas in war from the 7th century. The Muslims accorded them the status of dhimmis as "people of the Book", such as Christianity or Judaism and Al-Biruni wrote of Buddha as prophet "burxan".

Buddhism saw a surge during the reign of Mongols following the invasion of Genghis Khan and the establishment of the II Khanate and the Chagatai Khanate who brought their Buddhist influence with them during the 13th century, however within a 100 years the Mongols would convert to Islam and spread Islam across all the regions across central Asia.

Parthia: Buddhism expanded westward into Arsacid Parthia, at least to the area of Merv, in ancient Margiana, today's territory of Turkmenistan. Soviet archeological teams have excavated in Giaur Kala, near Merv, a Buddhist chapel, a gigantic Buddha statue, as well as a monastery. Parthians were directly involved in the propagation of Buddhism: An Shigao (c. 148 AD), a Parthian prince, went to China and is the first known translator of Buddhist scriptures into Chinese.

Tarim Basin: The eastern part of central Asia (Chinese Turkestan, Tarim Basin, Xinjiang) has revealed extremely rich Buddhist works of art (wall paintings and reliefs in numerous caves, portable paintings on canvas, sculpture, ritual objects), displaying multiple influences from Indian and Hellenistic cultures. Serindian art is highly reminiscent of the Gandharan style and scriptures in the Gandhari script Kharosthi have been found.

Central Asians seem to have played a key role in the transmission of Buddhism to the East. The first translators of Buddhists scriptures into Chinese were either Parthian (Ch: Anxi) like An Shigao (c. 148 AD) or An Hsuan, Kushan of Yuezhi ethnicity like Lokaksema (c. 178 AD), Zhi Qian and Zhi Yao, or Sogdians like Kang Sengkai. Thirty-seven early translators of Buddhist texts are known and the majority of them have been identified as Central Asians.

Central Asian and East Asian Buddhist monks appear to have maintained strong exchanges until around the 10th century, as shown by frescoes from the Tarim Basin.

These influences were rapidly absorbed however by the vigorous Chinese culture and a strongly Chinese particularism develops from that point.

China

Buddhism probably arrived in China around the 1st century AD from Central Asia (although there are some traditions about a monk visiting China during Ashoka's reign) and through to the 8th century it became an extremely active centre of Buddhism. The year 67 AD saw Buddhism's official introduction to China with the coming of the two monks Moton and Chufarlan. In 68 AD, under imperial patronage, they established the White Horse Temple, which still exists today, close to the imperial capital at Luoyang. By the end of the second century, a prosperous community had been settled at Pengcheng (modern Xuzhou, Jiangsu).

The first known Mahayana scriptural texts are translations made into Chinese by the Kushan monk Lokaksema in Luoyang, between 178 and 189 AD. Some of the earliest known Buddhist artifacts found in China are small statues on "money trees", dated circa 200 AD, in typical Gandharan style (drawing): "That the imported images accompanying the newly arrived doctrine came from Gandhara is strongly suggested by such early Gandhara characteristics on this "money tree" Buddha as the high ushnisha, vertical arrangement of the hair, moustache, symmetrically looped robe and parallel incisions for the folds of the arms." ("Crossroads of Asia" p209)

Buddhism flourished during the beginning of the Tang Dynasty (618-907). The dynasty was initially characterized by a strong openness to foreign influences and renewed exchanges with Indian culture due to the numerous travels of Chinese Buddhist monks to India from the 4th to the 11th century. The Tang capital of Chang'an (today's Xi'an) became an important centre for Buddhist thought. From there Buddhism spread to Korea and Japanese embassies of Kentoshi helped gain footholds in Japan.

However foreign influences came to be negatively perceived towards the end of the Tang Dynasty. In the year 845, the Tang emperor Wu-Tsung outlawed all "foreign" religions (including Christian Nestorianism, Zoroastrianism and Buddhism) in order to support the indigenous Taoism. Throughout his territory, he confiscated Buddhist possessions, destroyed monasteries and temples and executed Buddhist monks, ending Buddhism's cultural and intellectual dominance. Pure Land and Chan Buddhism, however, continued to prosper for some centuries, the latter giving rise to Japanese Zen. In China, Chan flourished particularly under the Song dynasty (1127-1279), when its monasteries were great centres of culture and learning.

Today, China boasts one of the richest collections of Buddhist arts and heritages in the world. UNESCO World Heritage Sites such as the Mogao Caves near Dunhuang in Gansu province, the Longmen Grottoes near Luoyang in Henan province, the Yungang Grottoes near Datong in Shanxi province and the Dazu Rock Carvings near Chongqing are among the most important and renowned Buddhist sculptural sites. The Leshan Giant Buddha, carved out of a hillside in the 8th century during Tang Dynasty and looking down on the confluence of three rivers, is still the largest stone Buddha statue in the world.

Korea

Buddhism was introduced around 372 AD, when Chinese ambassadors visited the Korean kingdom of Goguryeo, bringing scriptures and images. Buddhism prospered in Korea and in particular Seon (Zen) Buddhism from the 7th century onward. However, with the beginning of the Confucean Yi Dynasty of the Joseon period in 1392, Buddhism was strongly discriminated against until it was almost completely eradicated, except for a remaining Seon movement.

Japan

Japan discovered Buddhism in the 6th century when Korean monks travelled to the islands together with numerous scriptures and works of art. The Buddhist religion was adopted by the state in the following century.

Being geographically at the end of the Silk Road, Japan was able to preserve many aspects of Buddhism at the very time it was disappearing in India and being suppressed in Central Asia and China.

From 710 AD numerous temples and monasteries were built in the capital city of Nara, such as the five-story pagoda and Golden Hall of the Horyuji, or the Kofuku-ji temple. Countless paintings and sculptures were made, often under governmental sponsorship. The creation of Japanese Buddhist art was especially rich between the 8th and 13th century during the periods of Nara, Heian and Kamakura.

From the 12th and 13th, a further development was Zen art, following the introduction of the faith by Dogen and Eisai upon their return from China. Zen art is mainly characterized by original paintings (such as sumi-e and the Enso) and poetry (especially haikus), striving to express the true essence of the world through impressionistic and unadorned "non-dualistic" representations. The search for enlightenment "in the moment" also led to the development of other important derivative arts such as the Chanoyu tea ceremony or the Ikebana art of flower arrangement. This evolution went as far as considering almost any human activity as an art with a strong spiritual and aesthetic content, first and foremost in those activities related to combat techniques (martial arts).

Buddhism remains very active in Japan to this day. Around 80,000 Buddhist temples are preserved and regularly restored.

South-East Asia

During the 1st century AD, the trade on the overland Silk Road tended to be restricted by the rise in the Middle-East of the Parthian empire, an unvanquished enemy of Rome, just as Romans were becoming extremely wealthy and their demand for Asian luxury was rising. This demand revived the sea connections between the Mediterranean and China, with India as the intermediary of choice. From that time, through trade connection, commercial settlements and even political interventions, India started to strongly influence Southeast Asian countries. Trade routes linked India with southern Burma, central and southern Siam, lower Cambodia and southern Vietnam and numerous urbanized coastal settlements were established there.

For more than a thousand years, Indian influence was therefore the major factor that brought a certain level of cultural unity to the various countries of the region. The Pali and Sanskrit languages and the Indian script, together with Theravada and Mahayana Buddhism, Brahmanism and Hinduism, were transmitted from direct contact and through sacred texts and Indian literature such as the Ramayana and the Mahabharata.

From the 5th to the 13th century, South-East Asia had very powerful empires and became extremely active in Buddhist architectural and artistic creation. The main Buddhist influence now came directly by sea from the Indian subcontinent, so that these empires essentially followed the Mahayana faith. The Sri Vijaya Empire to the south and the Khmer Empire to the north competed for influence and their art expressed the rich Mahayana pantheon of the Bodhisattvas.

Vietnam

Srivijayan empire (5th-15th century): Srivijaya, a maritime empire centred at Palembang on the island of Sumatra in Indonesia, adopted Mahayana and Vajrayana Buddhism under a line of rulers named the Sailendras. Yijing described Palembang as a great centre of Buddhist learning where the emperor supported over a thousand monks at his court. Atisha studied there before travelling to Tibet as a missionary.

Sriviijaya spread Buddhist art during its expansion in Southeast Asia. Numerous statues of Bodhisattvas from this period are characterized by a very strong refinement and technical sophistication and are found throughout the region. Extremely rich architectural remains are visible at the temple of Borobudur (the largest Buddhist structure in the world, built from around 780 AD), in Java, which has 505 images of the seated Buddha. Srivijaya declined due to conflicts with the Chola rulers of India, before being destabilized by the Islamic expansion from the 13th century.

Khmer Empire (9th-13th century): Later, from the 9th to the 13th century, the Mahayana Buddhist and Hindu Khmer Empire dominated much of the South-East Asian peninsula. Under the Khmer, more than 900 temples were built in Cambodia and in neighbouring Thailand. Angkor was at the centre of this development, with a temple complex and urban organization able to support around one million urban dwellers. One of the greatest Khmer kings, Jayavarman VII (1181-1219), built large Mahayana Buddhist structures at Bayon and Angkor Thom.

Following the destruction of Buddhism in mainland India during the 11th century, Mahayana Buddhism declined in Southeast Asia, to be replaced by the introduction of Theravada Buddhism from Sri Lanka.

Emergence of the Vajrayana (5th Century): Vajrayana Buddhism, also called Tantric Buddhism, first emerged in eastern India between the 5th and 7th centuries AD. It is sometimes considered a sub-school of Mahayana and sometimes a third major "vehicle" (Yana) of Buddhism in its own right. The Vajrayana is an extension of Mahayana Buddhism in that it does not offer new philosophical perspectives, but rather introduces additional techniques (upaya, or 'skilful means'), including the use of visualizations and other yogic practices. Many of the practices of Tantric Buddhism are also derived from Hinduism (the usage of mantras, yoga, or the burning of sacrificial offerings). This school of thought was founded by the Brahmin Padmasambhava.

Early Vajrayana practitioners were forest-dwelling mahasiddas who lived on the margins of society, but by the 9th century Vajrayana had won acceptance at major Mahayana monastic universities such as Nalanda and Vikramshila. Along with much of the rest of Indian Buddhism, the Vajrayana was eclipsed in the wake of the late 12th century Muslim invasions. It has persisted in Tibet, where it was wholly transplanted from the 7th to 12th centuries and became the dominant form of Buddhism to the present day and on a limited basis in Japan as well where it evolved into Shingon Buddhism.

Theravada Renaissance (11th Century AD): From the 11th century, the destruction of Buddhism in the Indian mainland by Islamic invasions led to the decline of the Mahayana faith in South-East Asia. Continental routes through the Indian subcontinent being compromised, direct sea routes between the Middle-East through Sri Lanka and to China developed, leading to the adoption of the Theravada Buddhism of the Pali canon, introduced to the region around the 11th century AD from Sri Lanka.

King Anawrahta (1044-1077); the historical founder of the Burmese empire, unified the country and adopted the Theravada Buddhist faith. This initiated the creation of thousands of Buddhist temples at Pagan, the capital, between the 11th and 13th century. Around 2,000 of them are still standing. The power of the Burmese waned with the rise of the Thai and with the seizure of the capital Pagan by the Mongols in 1287, but Theravada Buddhism remained the main Burmese faith to this day. The Theravada faith was also adopted by the newly founded ethnic Thai kingdom of Sukhothai around 1260. Theravada Buddhism was further reinforced during the Ayutthaya period (14th-18th century), becoming an integral part of the Thai society.

In the continental areas, Theravada Buddhism continued to expand into Laos and Cambodia in the 13th century. However, from the 14th century, on the coastal fringes and in the islands of South-East Asia, the influence of Islam proved stronger, expanding into Malaysia, Indonesia and most of the islands as far as the southern Philippines.

However, since 1966 with Soeharto's rise of power in the aftermath of the bloody events after the so called "September 30th, 1965 murders", allegedly executed by the Communists Party, there has been a remarkable renaissance of Buddhism in Indonesia. This is partly due to the Soeharto's New Order's requirements for the people of Indonesia to adopt one of the five official religions: Islam, Protestantism, Catholicism, Hinduism or Buddhism. Today it is estimated there are some 10 millions Buddhists in Indonesia. A large part of them are people of Chinese ancestry.

Expansion of Buddhism to the West: After the Classical encounters between Buddhism and the West recorded in Greco-Buddhist art, information and legends about Buddhism seem to have reached the West sporadically. During the 8th century, Buddhist Jataka stories were translated into Syriac and Arabic as Kalilag and Damnag. An account of Buddha's life was translated in to Greek by John of Damascus and widely circulated to Christians as the story of Barlaam and Josaphat. By the 1300s this story of Josaphat had become so popular that he was made a Catholic saint.

The next direct encounter between Europeans and Buddhism happened in Medieval times when the Franciscan friar William of Rubruck was sent on an embassy to the Mongol court of Mongke by the French king Saint Louis in 1253. The contact happened in Cailac (today's Qayaliq in Kazakhstan) and William originally thought they were wayward Christians (Foltz, "Religions of the Silk Road").

Major interest for Buddhism emerged during colonial times, when Western powers were in a position to witness the faith and its artistic manifestations in detail. European philosophy was strongly influenced by the study of oriental religions during that period.

The opening of Japan in 1853 also created a considerable interest for the arts and culture of Japan and provided access to one of the most thriving Buddhist cultures in the world. Buddhism started to enjoy a strong interest from the general population in the West during the 20th century, following the perceived failure of social utopias, from Fascism to Marxism. After the Second World War, the focus of progress tended to shift to personal self-realization, on the material as well as spiritual plane.

In this context, Buddhism has been displaying a strong power of attraction, due to its tolerance, its lack of deist authority and determinism and its focus on understanding reality through self inquiry. According to the latest census it is now the fastest growing religion in Britain.

Theravada Buddhist Council in 1871 (5th Buddhist Council)

Another Buddhist Council, this time presided by Theravada monks took place in Mandalay Burma now known as Myanmar in 1871 in the reign of King Mindon. The chief objective of this meeting was to recite all the teachings of the Buddha and examine them in minute detail to see if any of them had been altered, distorted or dropped.

It was presided over by three Elders, the Venerable Mahathera Jagarabhivamsa, the Venerable Narindabhidhaja and the Venerable Mahathera Sumangalasami in the company of some two thousand four hundred monks (2,400). Their joint Dhamma recitation lasted for five months. It was also the work of this council to cause the entire Tripitaka to be inscribed for posterity on seven hundred and twenty-nine marble slabs in the Myanmar script after its recitation had been completed and unanimously approved.

This monumental task was done by some two thousand four hundred (2,400) erudite monks and many skilled craftsmen who upon completion of each slab had them housed in beautiful miniature 'pitaka' pagodas on a special site in the grounds of King Mindon's Kuthodaw Pagoda at the foot of Mandalay Hill where it and the so called 'largest book in the world', stands to this day.

Early Buddhism

Before the royal sponsorship of Ashoka the Great in the 3rd century BC, Buddhism seems to have remained a relatively minor phenomenon and the historicity of its formative events is poorly established. Two formative councils are supposed to have taken place, although our knowledge of them is based on much later accounts. The councils tend to explain the formalization of the Buddhist doctrine and the various subsequent schisms inside the Buddhist movement.

Asian Expansion

In the areas east of the Indian subcontinent (today's Burma), Indian culture strongly influenced the Mons. The Mons are said to have been converted to Buddhism around 200 BC under the proselytizing of the Indian king Ashoka, before the fission between Mahayana and Hinayana Buddhism. Early Mon Buddhist temples, such as Peikthano in central Burma, have been dated between the 1st and the 5th century AD.

The Buddhist art of the Mons was especially influenced by the Indian art of the Gupta and post-Gupta periods and their mannerist style spread widely in South-East Asia following the expansion of the Mon kingdom between the 5th and 8th centuries. The Theravada faith expanded in the northern parts of Southeast Asia under Mon influence, until it was progressively displaced by Mahayana Buddhism from around the 6th century AD.

Sri Lanka was allegedly proselytized by Ashoka's son Mahinda and six companions during the 2nd century BC. They converted the king Devanampiya Tissa and many of the nobility. This is when the Mahavihara monastery, a centre of Sinhalese orthodoxy, was built. The Pali Canon was put in writing in Sri Lanka during the reign of king Vittagamani (r. 29-17 BC) and the Theravada tradition flourished there, harbouring some great commentators such as Buddhaghosa (4th-5th century). Although Mahayana Buddhism gained some influence at that time, Theravada ultimately prevailed and Sri Lanka turned out to be the last stronghold of Theravada Buddhism, from where it would expand again to South-East Asia from the 11th century.

There is also a legend, not directly validated by the edicts, that Ashoka sent a missionary to the north, through the Himalayas, to Khotan in the Tarim Basin, then the land of the Tocharians, speakers of an Indo-European language.

In the areas west of the Indian subcontinent, neighbouring Greek kingdoms had been in place in Bactria (today's northern Afghanistan) since the time of the conquests of Alexander the Great around 326 BC: first the Seleucids from around 323 BC, then the Greco-Bactrian kingdom from around 250 BC.

The Greco-Bactrian king Demetrius I invaded India in 180 BC as far as Pataliputra, establishing an Indo-Greek kingdom that was to last in various part of northern India until the end of the 1st century BC. Buddhism flourished under the Indo-Greek kings and it has been suggested that their invasion of India was intended to show their support for the Mauryan empire and to protect the Buddhist faith from the alleged religious persecutions of the Sungas (185-73 BC), accounts which are disputed by historians.

One of the most famous Indo-Greek kings is Menander (reigned c. 160-135 BC). He apparently converted to Buddhism and is presented in the Mahayana tradition as one of the great benefactors of the faith, on a par with king Ashoka or the later Kushan king Kanishka. Menander's coins bear the mention "Saviour king" in Greek and sometimes designs of the eight-spoked wheel. Direct cultural exchange is also suggested by the dialogue of the Milinda Panha between Menander and the monk Nagasena around 160 BC.

Upon his death, the honour of sharing his remains was claimed by the cities under his rule and they were enshrined in stupas, in a parallel with the historic Buddha (Plutarch, Praec. reip. ger. 28, 6). Several of Menander's Indo-Greek successors inscribed the mention "Follower of the Dharma" in the Kharoshthi script on their coins and depicted themselves or their divinities forming the vitarka mudra.

The interaction between Greek and Buddhist cultures may have had some influence on the evolution of Mahayana, as the faith developed its sophisticated philosophical approach and a man-god treatment of the Buddha somewhat reminiscent of Hellenic gods.

It is also around that time that the first anthropomorphic representations of the Buddha are found, often in realistic Greco-Buddhist style: "One might regard the classical influence as including the general idea of representing a man-god in this purely human form, which was of course well familiar in the West and it is very likely that the example of westerner's treatment of their gods was indeed an important factor in the innovation" (Boardman, "The Diffusion of Classical Art in Antiquity").

2

BUDDHIST COSMOLOGY

INTRODUCTION

The picture of the world presented in Buddhist cosmological descriptions cannot be taken as a literal description of the shape of the universe. The self-consistent Buddhist cosmology which is presented in commentaries and works of Abhidharma in both Theravada and Mahayana traditions, is the end-product of an analysis and reconciliation of cosmological comments found in the Buddhist sutra and vinaya traditions. No single sutra sets out the entire structure of the universe. However, in several sutras the Buddha describes other worlds and states of being and other sutras describe the origin and destruction of the universe. The synthesis of these data into a single comprehensive system must have taken place early in the history of Buddhism, as the system described in the Pali Vibhajyavada tradition (represented by today's Theravadins) agrees, despite some trivial inconsistencies of nomenclature, with the Sarvastivada tradition which is preserved by Mahayana Buddhists. Buddhist cosmology is the description of the shape and evolution of the universe according to the canonical Buddhist scriptures and commentaries.

It is inconsistent and cannot be made consistent, with astronomical data that were already known in ancient India. However, it is not intended to be a description of how humans perceive their world; rather, it is the universe as seen through the divyacakrus, the "divine eye" by which a Buddha or an arhat who has cultivated this faculty can perceive all of the other worlds and the beings arising (being born) and passing away (dying) within them and can tell from what state they have been reborn and into what state they will be reborn.

Cosmology of Buddhist can accordingly be divided into two related kinds: spatial cosmology, which describes the arrangement of the various worlds within the universe and temporal cosmology, which describes how those worlds come into existence and how they pass away.

VERTICAL COSMOLOGY

The universe exists of many worlds-one might say "planes"- stacked one upon the next in layers. Each world corresponds to a mental state or a state of being. A world is not, however, a location so much as it is the beings which compose it; it is sustained by their karma and if the beings in a world all die or disappear, the world disappears too. Likewise, a world comes into existence when the first being is born into it. The physical separation is not so important as the difference in mental state; humans and animals, though they partially share the same physical environments, still belong to different worlds because their minds perceive and react to those environments differently. The vertical cosmology is divided into three realms, or dhatus, each corresponding to a different type of mentality.

These three (Tridhatu) are the Arupyadhatu, the Rupadhatu and the Kamadhatu. This technical division does not correspond to the more informal categorization of the "six realms". In the latter scheme, all of the beings born in the Arupyadhatu and the Rupadhatu may be classified as "gods" or "deities" (deva), as can a considerable fraction of the beings born in the Kamadhatu, even though the deities of the Kamadhatu differ more from those of the Arupyadhatu than they do from humans.

It is to be understood that deva is an imprecise term referring to any being living in a longer-lived and generally more blissful state than humans. Most of them are not "gods" in the common sense of the term, having little or no concern with the human world and rarely if ever interacting with it; only the lowest deities of the Kamadhatu correspond to the gods described in many polytheistic religions.

The term "brahma" is used both as a name and as a generic term for one of the higher devas. In its broadest sense, it can refer to any of the inhabitants of the Arupyadhatu and the Rupadhatu. In more restricted senses, it can refer to an inhabitant of one of the nine lower worlds of the Rupadhatu, or in its narrowest sense, to the three lowest worlds of the Rupadhatu. A large number of devas use the name "Brahma", *e.g.* Brahma Sahampati, Brahma Sanatkumara, Baka Brahma, etc. It is not always clear which world they belong to, although it must always be one of the worlds of the Rupadhatu below the Suddhavasa worlds.

Spatial Cosmology

Spatial cosmology can also be divided into two branches. The vertical cosmology describes the arrangement of worlds in a vertical pattern, some being higher and some lower. The sahasra cosmology describes the grouping of these vertical worlds into sets of thousands, millions or billions.

Arupyadhatu

The Arupyadhatu (Sanskrit) or Arupaloka (Pali) or "Formless realm" would have no place in a purely physical cosmology, as none of the beings inhabiting it has either shape or location; and correspondingly, the realm has no location either.

This realm belongs to those devas who attained and remained in the Four Formless Absorptions of the arupadhyanas in a previous life and now enjoys the fruits (vipaka) of the good karma of that accomplishment. Bodhisattvas, however, are never born in the Arupyadhatu even when they have attained the arupadhyanas.

There are four types of Arupyadhatu devas, corresponding to the four types of arupadhyanas:

- Naivasamjnanasamjnayatana or Nevasannanasannayatana "Sphere of neither perception nor non-perception". In this sphere the formless beings have gone beyond a mere negation of perception and have attained a liminal state where they do not engage in "perception" (samjna, recognition of particulars by their marks) but are not wholly unconscious. This was the sphere reached by Udraka Ramaputra (Pali: Uddaka Ramaputta), the second of the Buddha's two teachers, who considered it equivalent to enlightenment.
- Akimcanyayatana or Akincannayatana "Sphere of Nothingness" (literally "lacking anything"). In this sphere formless beings dwell contemplating upon the thought that "there is no thing". This is considered a form of perception, though a very subtle one. This was the sphere reached by Arara Kalama, the first of the Buddha's two teachers; he considered it to be equivalent to enlightenment.
- Vijnanantyayatana or Vinnananancayatana "Sphere of Infinite Consciousness". In this sphere formless beings dwell meditating on their consciousness (vijnana) as infinitely pervasive.
- Akasanantyayatana or Akasanancayatana "Sphere of Infinite Space". In this sphere formless beings dwell meditating upon space or extension (akasa) as infinitely pervasive.

Rupadhatu

The Rupadhatu or "Form realm" is, as the name implies, the first of the physical realms; its inhabitants all have a location and bodies of a sort, though those bodies are composed of a subtle substance which is of itself invisible to the inhabitants of the Kamadhatu. According to the Janavasabha Sutta, when a brahma (a being from the Brahma-world of the Rupadhatu) wishes to visit a deva of the Trayastrinsa heaven (in the Kamadhatu), he has to assume a "grosser form" in order to be visible to them.

The beings of the Form realm are not subject to the extremes of pleasure and pain, or governed by desires for things pleasing to the senses, as the beings of the Kamadhatu are. The bodies of Form realm beings do not have sexual distinctions.

Like the beings of the Arupyadhatu, the dwellers in the Rupadhatu have minds corresponding to the dhyanas (Pali: jhanas). In their case it is the four lower dhyanas or rupadhyanas. However, although the beings of the Rupadhatu can be divided into four broad grades corresponding to these four dhyanas, each of them is subdivided into further grades, three for each of the four dhyanas and five for the Suddhavasa devas, for a total of seventeen grades (the Theravada tradition counts one less grade in the highest dhyana for a total of sixteen).

Physically, the Rupadhatu consists of a series of planes stacked on top of each other, each one in a series of steps half the size of the previous one as one descends. In part, this reflects the fact that the devas are also thought of as physically larger on the higher planes. The highest planes are also broader in extent than the ones lower down, as discussed in the section on Sahasra cosmology. The height of these planes is expressed in yojanas, a measurement of very uncertain length, but sometimes taken to be about 4,000 times the height of a man and so approximately 4.54 miles or 7.32 kilometers.

Suddhavasa Worlds

The Suddhavasa worlds, or "Pure Abodes", are distinct from the other worlds of the Rupadhatu in that they do not house beings who have been born there through ordinary merit or meditative attainments, but only those Anagamins ("Non-returners") who are already on the path to Arhat-hood and who will attain enlightenment directly from the Suddhavasa worlds without being reborn in a lower plane (Anagamins can also be born on lower planes). Every Suddhavasa deva is therefore a protector of Buddhism. Because a Suddhavasa deva will never be reborn outside the Suddhavasa worlds, no Bodhisattva is ever born in these worlds, as a Bodhisattva must ultimately be reborn as a human being.

Since these devas rise from lower planes only due to the teaching of a Buddha, they can remain empty for very long periods if no Buddha arises. However, unlike the lower worlds, the Suddhavaṣa worlds are never destroyed by natural catastrophe. The Suddhavaśa devas predict the coming of a Buddha and, taking the guise of Brahmins, reveal to human beings the signs by which a Buddha can be recognized. They also ensure that a Bodhisattva in his last life will see the four signs that will lead to his renunciation.

The five Suddhavasa worlds are:

- *Akanistha or Akanittha:* World of devas "equal in rank" (literally: having no one as the youngest). The highest of all the Rupadhatu worlds, it is often used to refer to the highest extreme of the universe. The current Sakra will eventually be born there. The duration of life in Akanistha is 16,000 kalpas (Vibhajyavada tradition). The height of this world is 167,772,160 yojanas above the Earth.
- *Sudarsana or Sudassi:* The "clear-seeing" devas live in a world similar to and friendly with the Akanistha world. The height of this world is 83,886,080 yojanas above the Earth.
- *Sudrsa or Sudassa:* The world of the "beautiful" devas are said to be the place of rebirth for five kinds of anagamins. The height of this world is 41,943,040 yojanas above the Earth.
- *Aṭapa or Atappa:* The world of the "untroubled" devas, whose company those of lower realms wish for. The height of this world is 20,971,520 yojanas above the Earth.
- *Avrha or Aviha:* The world of the "not falling" devas, perhaps the most common destination for reborn Anagamins. Many achieve arhatship directly in this

world, but some pass away and are reborn in sequentially higher worlds of the Pure Abodes until they are at last reborn in the Akanistha world. These are called in Pali uddhatsotas, "those whose stream goes upward". The duration of life in Avaha is 1,000 kalpas (Vibhajyavada tradition). The height of this world is 10,485,760 yojanas above the Earth.

Brhatphala Worlds

The mental state of the devas of the Brhatphala worlds corresponds to the fourth dhyana and is characterized by equanimity (upeksa). The Brhatphala worlds form the upper limit to the destruction of the universe by wind at the end of a mahakalpa, that is, they are spared such destruction.

- *Asannasatta:* "Unconscious beings", devas who have attained a high dhyana (similar to that of the Formless Realm) and, wishing to avoid the perils of perception, have achieved a state of non-perception in which they endure for a time. After a while, however, perception arises again and they fall into a lower state.
- *Brhatphala or Vehapphala*: Devas "having great fruit". Their lifespan is 500 mahakalpas. (Vibhajyavada tradition). Some Anagamins are reborn here. The height of this world is 5,242,880 yojanas above the Earth.
- *Punyaprasava:* The world of the devas who are the "offspring of merit". The height of this world is 2,621,440 yojanas above the Earth.
- *Anabhraka:* The world of the "cloudless" devas. The height of this world is 1,310,720 yojanas above the Earth.

Subhakrtsna Worlds

The mental state of the devas of the Subhaktsna worlds corresponds to the third dhyana and is characterized by a quiet joy (sukha). These devas have bodies that radiate a steady light. The Subhakatsna worlds form the upper limit to the destruction of the universe by water at the end of a mahakalpa, that is, the flood of water does not rise high enough to reach them.

- *Subhakrtsna:* The world of devas of "total beauty". Their lifespan is 64 mahakalpas (some sources: 4 mahakalpas) according to the Vibhajyavada tradition. 64 mahakalpas is the interval between destructions of the universe by wind, including the Subhakstsna worlds. The height of this world is 655,360 yojanas above the Earth.
- *Apramanasubha:* The world of devas of "limitless beauty". Their lifespan is 32 mahakalpas (Vibhajyavada tradition). They possess "faith, virtue, learning, munificence and wisdom". The height of this world is 327,680 yojanas above the Earth.
- *Parittasubha:* The world of devas of "limited beauty". Their lifespan is 16 mahakalpas. The height of this world is 163,840 yojanas above the Earth.

Abhasvara Worlds

The mental state of the devas of the Abhasvara worlds corresponds to the second dhyana and is characterized by delight (priti) as well as joy (sukha); the Abhasvara devas are said to shout aloud in their joy, crying aho sukham! ("Oh joy!"). These devas have bodies that emit flashing rays of light like lightning. They are said to have similar bodies (to each other) but diverse perceptions.

The Abhasvara worlds form the upper limit to the destruction of the universe by fire at the end of a mahakalpa, that is, the column of fire does not rise high enough to reach them. After the destruction of the world, at the beginning of the vivartakalpa, the worlds are first populated by beings reborn from the Abhasvara worlds.

- *Abhasvara or Abhassara:* The world of devas "possessing splendor". The lifespan of the Abhasvara devas is 8 mahakalpas (others: 2 mahakalpas). Eight mahakalpas is the interval between destructions of the universal by water, which includes the Abhasvara worlds. The height of this world is 81,920 yojanas above the Earth.

- *Apramanabha or Appamanabha:* The world of devas of "limitless light", a concept on which they meditate. Their lifespan is 4 mahakalpas. The height of this world is 40,960 yojanas above the Earth.
- *Parittabha or Parittabha:* The world of devas of "limited light". Their lifespan is 2 mahakalpas. The height of this world is 20,480 yojanas above the Earth.

Brahma Worlds

The mental state of the devas of the Brahma worlds corresponds to the first dhyana and is characterized by observation (vitarka) and reflection (vicara) as well as delight (priti) and joy (sukha). The Brahma worlds, together with the other lower worlds of the universe, are destroyed by fire at the end of a mahakalpa.

- Mahabrahma-the world of "Great Brahma", believed by many to be the creator of the world and having as his titles "Brahma, Great Brahma, the Conqueror, the Unconquered, the All-Seeing, All-Powerful, the Lord, the Maker and Creator, the Ruler, Appointer and Orderer, Father of All That Have Been and Shall Be." According to the Brahmajala Sutta (DN.1), a Mahabrahma is a being from the Abhasvara worlds who falls into a lower world through exhaustion of his merits and is reborn alone in the Brahma-world; forgetting his former existence, he imagines himself to have come into existence without cause. Note that even such a high-ranking deity has no intrinsic knowledge of the worlds above his own. Mahabrahma is 1 1/2 yojanas tall. His lifespan variously said to be 1 kalpa (Vibhajyavada tradition) or 1 1/2 kalpas long (Sarvastivada tradition), although it would seem that it could be no longer than 3/4 of a mahakalpa, *i.e.*, all of the mahakalpa except for the Sanvartasthayikalpa, because that is the total length of time between the rebuilding of the lower world and its destruction. It is unclear what period of time "kalpa" refers to in this case. The height of this world is 10,240 yojanas above the Earth.

- Brahmapurohita-the "Ministers of Brahma" are beings, also originally from the Abhasvara worlds, that are born as companions to Mahabrahma after he has spent some time alone. Since they arise subsequent to his thought of a desire for companions, he believes himself to be their creator and they likewise believe him to be their creator and lord. They are 1 yojana in height and their lifespan is variously said to be 1/2 of a kalpa (Vibhajyavada tradition) or a whole kalpa (Sarvastivada tradition). If they are later reborn in a lower world and come to recall some part of their last existence, they teach the doctrine of Brahma as creator as a revealed truth. The height of this world is 5,120 yojanas above the Earth.
- Brahmaparisadya-the "Councilors of Brahma" or the devas "belonging to the assembly of Brahma". They are also called Brahmakayika, but this name can be used for any of the inhabitants of the Brahma-worlds. They are half a yojana in height and their lifespan is variously said to be 1/3 of a kalpa (Vibhajyavada tradition) or 1/2 of a kalpa (Sarvastivada tradition). The height of this world is 2,560 yojanas above the Earth.

Kamadhatu

The beings born in the Kamadhatu differ in degree of happiness, but they are all, other than arhats and Buddhas, under the domination of Mara and are bound by desire, which causes them suffering.

Heavens

The following four worlds are bounded planes, each 80,000 yojanas square, which float in the air above the top of Mount

Sumeru. Although all of the worlds inhabited by devas (that is, all the worlds down to the Caturmaharajikakayika world and sometimes including the Asuras) are sometimes called "heavens", in the western sense of the word the term best applies to the four worlds listed below:

- *Parinirmita-vasavartin*: The heaven of devas "with power over (others') creations". These devas do not create pleasing forms that they desire for themselves, but their desires are fulfilled by the acts of other devas who wish for their favor. The ruler of this world is called Vasavartin (Pali: Vasavatti), who has longer life, greater beauty, more power and happiness and more delightful sense-objects than the other devas of his world. This world is also the home of the devaputra (being of divine race) called Mara, who endeavors to keep all beings of the Kamadhatu in the grip of sensual pleasures. Mara is also sometimes called Vasavartin, but in general these two dwellers in this world are kept distinct. The beings of this world are 4,500 feet tall and live for 9,216,000,000 years (Sarvastivada tradition). The height of this world is 1,280 yojanas above the Earth.
- *Nirmanarati*: The world of devas "delighting in their creations". The devas of this world are capable of making any appearance to please themselves. The lord of this world is called Sunirmita (Pali Sunimmita); his wife is the rebirth of Visakha, formerly the chief of the upasikas (female lay devotees) of the Buddha. The beings of this world are 3,750 feet tall and live for 2,304,000,000 years (Sarvastivada tradition). The height of this world is 640 yojanas above the Earth.
- *Tusita*: The world of the "joyful" devas. This world is best known for being the world in which a Bodhisattva lives before being reborn in the world of humans. Until a few thousand years ago, the Bodhisattva of this world was Svetaketu (Pali: Setaketu), who was reborn as Siddhartha, who would become the Buddha Sakyamuni;

since then the Bodhisattva has been Natha (or Nathadeva) who will be reborn as Ajita and will become the Buddha Maitreya (Pali Metteyya). While this Bodhisattva is the foremost of the dwellers in Turita, the ruler of this world is another deva called Santusita. The beings of this world are 3,000 feet tall and live for 576,000,000 years (Sarvastivada tradition). The height of this world is 320 yojanas above the Earth.

- *Yama*: Sometimes called the "heaven without fighting", because it is the lowest of the heavens to be physically separated from the tumults of the earthly world. Its ruler is the deva Suyama; according to some, his wife is the rebirth of Sirima, a courtesan of Rajagrha in the Buddha's time who was generous to the monks. The beings of this world are 2,250 feet tall and live for 144,000,000 years (Sarvastivada tradition). The height of this world is 160 yojanas above the Earth.

Worlds of Sumeru

The world-mountain of Sumeru is an immense, strangely shaped peak which arises in the centre of the world and around which the Sun and Moon revolve. Its base rests in a vast ocean and it is surrounded by several rings of lesser mountain ranges and oceans. The three worlds listed below are all located on or around Sumeru: the Trayastrinsa devas live on its peak, the Caturmaharajikakayika devas live on its slopes and the Asuras live in the ocean at its base. Sumeru and its surrounding oceans and mountains are the home not just of these deities, but also vast assemblies of beings of popular mythology who only rarely intrude on the human world.

- *Trayastrimsa*: The world "of the Thirty-three (devas)" is a wide flat space on the top of Mount Sumeru, filled with the gardens and palaces of the devas. Its ruler is Sakra devanam indra, "lord of the devas". Besides the eponymous Thirty-three devas, many other devas and supernatural beings dwell here, including the attendants of the devas and many apsarases (nymphs). The beings of this world are 1,500 feet tall and live for 36,000,000 years (Sarvastivada tradition) or 3/4 of a yojana tall and live for 30,000,000 years (Vibhajyavada tradition). The height of this world is 80 yojanas above the Earth.

- *Caturmaharajikakayika*: The world "of the Four Great Kings" is found on the lower slopes of Mount Sumeru, though some of its inhabitants live in the air around the mountain. Its rulers are the four Great Kings of the name, Virushaka, Virupakna and their leader Vaisravasa. The devas who guide the Sun and Moon are also considered part of this world, as are the retinues of the four kings, composed of Kumbhashas (dwarfs), Gandharvas (fairies), Nagas (dragons) and Yakhas (goblins). The beings of this world are 750 feet tall and live for 9,000,000 years (Sarvastivada tradition) or 90,000 years (Vibhajyavada tradition). The height of this world is from sea level up to 40 yojanas above the Earth.
- *Asura*: The world of the Asuras is the space at the foot of Mount Sumeru, much of which is a deep ocean. It is not the Asuras' original home, but the place they found themselves after they were hurled, drunken, from Trayastrinsa where they had formerly lived. The Asuras are always fighting to regain their lost kingdom on the top of Mount Sumeru, but are unable to break the guard of the Four Great Kings. The Asuras are divided into many groups and have no single ruler, but among their leaders are Vemacitrin (Pali: Vepacitti) and Rahu.

Earthly Realms

- *Manusyaloka*: This is the world of humans and human-like beings who live on the surface of the earth. The mountain-rings that engird Sumeru are surrounded by a vast ocean, which fills most of the world. The ocean is in turn surrounded by a circular mountain wall called Cakravara which marks the horizontal limit of the world. In this ocean there are four continents which are, relatively speaking, small islands in it. Because of the immenseness of the ocean, they cannot be reached from each other by ordinary sailing vessels, although in the past, when the cakravartin kings ruled, communication between the continents was possible by means of the treasure called the cakraratna (Pali cakkaratana), which a cakravartin and his retinue could use to fly through the air between the continents. The four continents are:

- Jambudvipa or Jambudipa is located in the south and is the dwelling of ordinary human beings. It is said to be shaped "like a cart", or rather a blunt-nosed triangle with the point facing south. (This description probably echoes the shape of the coastline of southern India.) It is 10,000 yojanas in extent (Vibhajyavada tradition) or has a perimeter of 6,000 yojanas (Sarvastivada tradition) to which can be added the southern coast of only 3 1/2 yojanas' length. The continent takes its name from a giant Jambu tree (Syzygium cumini), 100 yojanas tall, which grows in the middle of the continent. Every continent has one of these giant trees. All Buddhas appear in Jambudvipa. The people here are five to six feet tall and their length of life varies between 80,000 and 10 years.
- Purvavideha or Pubbavideha is located in the east and is shaped like a semicircle with the flat side pointing westward (*i.e.*, towards Sumeru). It is 7,000 yojanas in extent (Vibhajyavada tradition) or has a perimeter of 6,350 yojanas of which the flat side is 2,000 yojanas long (Sarvastivada tradition). Its tree is the acacia. The people here are about 12 feet tall and they live for 250 years.
- Aparagodaniya or Aparagoyana is located in the west and is shaped like a circle with a circumference of about 7,500 yojanas (Sarvastivada

tradition). The tree of this continent is a giant Kadambu tree. The human inhabitants of this continent do not live in houses but sleep on the ground. They are about 24 feet tall and they live for 500 years.

- o Uttarakuru is located in the north and is shaped like a square. It has a perimter of 8,000 yojanas, being 2,000 yojanas on each side. This continent's tree is called a kalpavkkha (Pali: kapparukkha) or kalpa-tree, because it lasts for the entire kalpa. The inhabitants of Uttarakuru are said to be extraordinarily wealthy. They do not need to labor for a living, as their food grows by itself and they have no private property. They have cities built in the air. They are about 48 feet tall and live for 1,000 years and they are under the protection of Vaisravana.

- *Tiryagyoni-loka*: This world comprises all members of the animal kingdom that are capable of feeling suffering, from the smallest insect to the elephant.
- *Pretaloka*: The pretas, or "hungry ghosts", are mostly dwellers on earth, though due to their mental state they perceive it very differently from humans. They live for the most part in desert and waste places.

Narakas

Naraka or Niraya is the name given to one of the worlds of greatest suffering, usually translated into English as "hell" or "purgatory". As with the other realms, a being is born into one of these worlds as a result of his karma and resides there for a finite length of time until his karma has achieved its full result, after which he will be reborn in one of the higher worlds as the result of an earlier karma that had not yet ripened. The mentality of a being in the hells corresponds to states of extreme fear and helpless anguish in humans. Physically, Naraka is thought of as a series of layers extending below Jambudvipa into the earth. There are several schemes for counting these Narakas and enumerating their torments. One of the more common is that of the Eight Cold Narakas and Eight Hot Narakas.

Cold Narakas

- Arbuda-the "blister" Naraka
- Nirarbuda-the "burst blister" Naraka
- Atata-the Naraka of shivering
- Hahava-the Naraka of lamentation
- Huhuva-the Naraka of chattering teeth
- Utpala-the "blue lotus" Naraka
- Padma-the "lotus" Naraka
- Mahapadma-the "great lotus" Naraka

Each lifetime in these Narakas is twenty times the length of the one before it.

Hot Narakas

- Sanjiva-the "reviving" Naraka. Life in this Naraka is 162×10^{10} years long.
- Kalasutra-the "black thread" Naraka. Life in this Naraka is 1296×10^{10} years long.
- Samghata-the "crushing" Naraka. Life in this Naraka is $10{,}368 \times 10^{10}$ years long.
- Raurava-the "screaming" Naraka. Life in this Naraka is $82{,}944 \times 10^{10}$ years long.
- Maharaurava-the "great screaming" Naraka. Life in this Naraka is $663{,}552 \times 10^{10}$ years long.
- Tapana-the "heating" Naraka. Life in this Naraka is $5{,}308{,}416 \times 10^{10}$ years long.
- Pratapana-the "great heating" Naraka. Life in this Naraka is $42{,}467{,}328 \times 10^{10}$ years long.
- Avici-the "uninterrupted" Naraka. Life in this Naraka is $339{,}738{,}624 \times 10^{10}$ years long.

The Foundations of the Earth

All of the structures of the earth, Sumeru and the rest, extend downward to a depth of 80,000 yojanas below sea level-the same as the height of Sumeru above sea level. Below this is a layer of "golden earth", a substance compact and firm enough to support the weight of Sumeru. It is 320,000 yojanas in depth and so extends to 400,000 yojanas below sea level. The layer of golden earth in turn rests upon a layer of water, which is 8,000,000 yojanas in depth, going down to 8,400,000 yojanas below sea level. Below the layer of water is a "circle of wind", which is 16,000,000 yojanas in depth and also much broader in extent, supporting 1,000 different worlds upon it.

Sahasra Cosmology

While the vertical cosmology describes the arrangement of the worlds vertically, the sahasra (Sanskrit: "thousand") cosmology describes how they are grouped horizontally. The four heavens of the Kamadhatu, as mentioned, occupy a limited space no bigger than the top of Mount Sumeru. The three Brahma-worlds, however, stretch out as far as the mountain-wall of Cakravana, filling the entire sky. This whole group of worlds, from Mahabrahma down to the foundations of water, constitutes a single world-system. It corresponds to the extent of the universe that is destroyed by fire at the end of one mahakalpa.

Above Mahabrahma are the Abhasvara worlds. These are not only higher but also wider in extent; they cover 1,000 separate world-systems, each with its own Sumeru, Cakravana, Sun, Moon and four continents. This system of 1,000 worlds is called a sahasra-cunika-lokadhatu, or "small chiliocosm". It corresponds to the extent of the universe that is destroyed by water at the end of 8 mahakalpas. Above the Abhasvara worlds are the Subhakstsna worlds, which cover 1,000 chiliocosms, or 1,000,000 world-systems. This larger system is called a dvisahasra-madhyama-lokadhatu, or "medium dichiliocosm". It corresponds to the extent of the universe that is destroyed by wind at the end of 64 mahakalpas.

Likewise, above the Subhakhtsna worlds, the Suddhavasa and Brhatphala worlds cover 1,000 dichiliocosms, or 1,000,000,000 world-systems. This largest grouping is called a trisahasra-mahasahasra-lokadhatu or "great trichiliocosm".

Temporal Cosmology

Buddhist temporal cosmology describes how the universe comes into being and is dissolved. Like other Indian cosmologies, it assumes an infinite span of time and is cyclical. This does not mean that the same events occur in identical form with each cycle, but merely that, as with the cycles of day and night or summer and winter, certain natural events occur over and over to give some structure to time.

The basic unit of time measurement is the mahakalpa or "Great Eon". The exact length of this time in human years is never defined exactly, but it is meant to be very long, to be measured in billions of years if not longer.

A mahakalpa is divided into four kalpas or "eons", each distinguished from the others by the stage of evolution of the universe during that kalpa. The four kalpas are:

- Vivartakalpa "Eon of evolution"-during this kalpa the universe comes into existence.
- Vivartasthayikalpa "Eon of evolution-duration"-during this kalpa the universe remains in existence in a steady state.
- Samvartakalpa "Eon of dissolution"-during this kalpa the universe dissolves.
- Samvartasthayikalpa "Eon of dissolution-duration"-during this kalpa the universe remains in a state of emptiness.

Each one of these kalpas is divided into twenty antarakalpas (Pali antarakappa, "inside eons") each of about the same length. For the Sarvartasthayikalpa this division is merely nominal, as nothing changes from one antarakalpa to the next; but for the other three kalpas it marks an interior cycle within the kalpa.

Vivartakalpa

The Vivartakalpa begins with the arising of the primordial wind, which begins the process of building up the structures of the universe that had been destroyed at the end of the last mahakalpa. As the extent of the destruction can vary, the nature of this evolution can vary as well, but it always takes the form of beings from a higher world being born into a lower world.

The example of a Mahabrahma being the rebirth of a deceased Abhasvara deva is just one instance of this, which continues throughout the Vivartakalpa until all the worlds are filled from the Brahmaloka down to Naraka. During the Vivartakalpa the first humans appear; they are not like present-day humans, but are beings shining in their own light, capable of moving through the air without mechanical aid, living for a very long time and not requiring sustenance; they are more like a type of lower deity than present-day humans are.

Over time, they acquire a taste for physical nutriment and as they consume it, their bodies become heavier and more like human bodies; they lose their ability to shine and begin to acquire differences in their appearance and their length of life decreases. They differentiate into two sexes and begin to become sexually active. Then greed, theft and violence arise among them and they establish social distinctions and government and elect a king to rule them, called Mahasammata, "the great appointed one". Some of them begin to hunt and eat the flesh of animals, which have by now come into existence. These developments are described in the Agganna Sutta (DN.27).

Vivartasthayikalpa

First Antarakalpa: The Vivartasthayikalpa begins when the first being is born into Naraka, thus filling the entire universe with beings. During the first antarakalpa of this eon, human lives are declining from a vast but unspecified number of years (but at least several tens of thousands of years) toward the modern lifespan of less than 100 years. At the beginning of the antarakalpa, people are still generally happy. They live under the rule of a universal monarch or "wheel-turning king" (cakravartin), who conquer. The Mahasudassana-sutta (DN.17) tells of the life of a cakravartin king, Mahasudassana (Sanskrit: Mahasudarsana) who lived for 336,000 years.

The Cakkavatti-sihanada-sutta (DN.26) tells of a later dynasty of cakravartins, Darhanemi and five of his descendants, who had a lifespan of over 80,000 years. The seventh of this line of cakravartins broke with the traditions of his forefathers, refusing to abdicate his position at a certain age, pass the throne on to his son and enter the life of a sramara. As a result of his subsequent misrule, poverty increased; as a result of poverty, theft began; as a result of theft, capital punishment was instituted; and as a result of this contempt for life, murders and other crimes became rampant.

The human lifespan now quickly decreased from 80,000 to 100 years, apparently decreasing by about half with each generation (this is perhaps not to be taken literally), while with each generation other crimes and evils increased: lying, adultery, evil speech, greed and hatred, wrong views, incest and other sorts of sexual abnormalities, disrespect for parents and elders.

During this period, according to the Mahapadana-sutta (DN.14) three of the four Buddhas of this antarakalpa lived: Krakucchanda Buddha (Pali: Kakusandha), at the time when the lifespan was 40,000 years; Kanakamuni Buddha (Pali: Konagamana) when the lifespan was 30,000 years; and Kasyapa Buddha (Pali: Kassapa) when the lifespan was 20,000 years.

Our present time is taken to be toward the end of the first antarakalpa of this Vivartasthayikalpa, when the lifespan is less than 100 years, after the life of Sakyamuni Buddha, who lived to the age of 80.

The remainder of the antarakalpa is prophesied to be miserable: lifespans will continue to decrease and all the evil tendencies of the past will reach their ultimate in destructiveness. People will live no longer than ten years and will marry at five; foods will be poor and tasteless; no form of morality will be acknowledged. The most contemptuous and hateful people will become the rulers. Incest will be rampant. Hatred between people, even members of the same family, will grow until people think of each other as hunters do of their prey.

Eventually a great war will ensue, in which the most hostile and aggressive will arm themselves and go out to kill each other. The less aggressive will hide in forests and other secret places while the war rages. This war marks the end of the first antarakalpa.

Second Antarakalpa: At the end of the war, the survivors will emerge from their hiding places and repent their evil habits. As they begin to do good, their lifespan increases and the health and welfare of the human race will also increase with it. After a long time, the descendants of those with a 10-year lifespan will live for 80,000 years and at that time there will be a cakravartin king named Sarkha. During his reign, the current bodhisattva in the Ṭunita heaven will descend and be reborn under the name of Ajita. He will enter the life of a sramara and will gain perfect enlightenment as a Buddha; and he will then be known by the name of Maitreya.

After Maitreya's time, the world will again worsen and the lifespan will gradually decrease from 80,000 years to 10 years again, each antarakalpa being separated from the next by devastating war, with peaks of high civilization and morality in the middle. After the 19th antarakalpa, the lifespan will increase to 80,000 and then not decrease, because the Vivartasthayikalpa will have come to an end.

Sarvartakalpa

The Sarvartakalpa begins when beings cease to be born in Naraka. This cessation of birth then proceeds in reverse order up the vertical cosmology, *i.e.* pretas then cease to be born, then animals, then humans and so on up to the realms of the deities. When these worlds as far as the Brahmaloka are devoid of inhabitants, a great fire consumes the entire physical structure of the world. It burns all the worlds below the Abhasvara worlds. When they are destroyed, the Sarvartasthayikalpa begins.

Sarvartasthayikalpa

There is nothing to say about the Sarvartasthayikalpa, since nothing happens in it below the Abhasvara worlds. It ends when the primordial wind begins to blow and build the structure of the worlds up again.

Other Destructions: The destruction by fire is the normal type of destruction that occurs at the end of the Sarvartakalpa. But every eighth mahakalpa, after seven destructions by fire, there is a destruction by water. This is more devastating, as it eliminates not just the Brahma worlds but also the Abhasvara worlds. Every sixty-fourth mahakalpa, after 56 destructions by fire and 7 destructions by water, there is a destruction by wind. This is the most devastating of all, as it also destroys the Subhakhtsna worlds. The higher worlds are never destroyed.

DHARMA

Dharma or Dhamma in Buddhism has two primary meanings:

- the teachings of the Buddha which lead to enlightenment
- the constituent factors of the experienced world

In East Asia, the character for Dharma is pronounced fa in Mandarin and ho in Japanese. The Tibetan translation of this term is chos (cho).

Buddha's Teachings

What is called Buddhism in the west has been referred to in India (the teachings' place of origin) and the east generally for many centuries as buddha-dharma. This term has no sectarian connotations but simply means "Path of Awakening" and thus conforms to a universal understanding of dharma.

The status of dharma is regarded variably by different traditions. Some regard it as an ultimate and transcendent truth which is utterly beyond worldly things, somewhat like the Christian logos. Others, who regard the Buddha as simply an enlightened human being, see dharma as the 84,000 different teachings that the Buddha gave to various types of people based on their needs. The teachings are expedient means of raising doubt in the hearer's own cherished beliefs and view of life; when doubt has opened the door to the truth, the teaching can be put aside.

"Dharma" usually refers inclusively not just to the sayings of the Buddha but to the later traditions of interpretation and addition that the various schools of Buddhism have developed to help explain and expand upon the Buddha's teachings. For others still, they see the dharma as referring to the "truth" or ultimate reality or "the way things are".

The dharma is one of the Three Jewels of Buddhism of which practitioners of Buddhism seek refuge in (what one relies on for his/her lasting happiness). The three jewels of Buddhism are the Buddha (mind's perfection of enlightenment), the dharma (teachings and methods) and the Sangha (awakened beings who provide guidance and support).

Buddha's Dharma Body

The qualities of the Dharma (Law, truth) is the same as the qualities of the Buddha and forms his "truth body" or "Dhamma Kaya": In the Samyutta Nikaya, Vakkali Sutta, Buddha said to his disciple Vakkali that,

> *"Yo kho Vakkali dhammam passati so mam passati"*
>
> *Vakkali, whoever sees Dhamma, sees me [the Buddha]*

Another reference from the Agganna Sutta of the Digha Nikaya, says to his disciple Vasettha:

> *"Tathagatassa h'etam Vasettha adivacanam Dhammakayo iti pi...":*
>
> *O Vasettha! The Word of Dhammakaya is indeed the name of the Tathagata*

Qualities of Buddha Dharma

The Teaching of the Buddha also has six supreme qualities:

1. *Svakkhato:* The Dhamma is not a speculative philosophy, but is the Universal Law found through enlightenment and is preached precisely. Therefore it is excellent in the beginning (sila-Sanskrit sila-moral principles), excellent in the middle (samadhi-concentration) and excellent in the end (panna-Sanskrit prajna... Wisdom),
2. *Sanditthiko*: The Dhamma can be tested by practice and therefore he who follows it will see the result by himself through his own experience.
3. *Akaliko:* The Dhamma is able to bestow timeless and immediate results here and now, for which there is no need to wait until the future or next existence.
4. *Ehipassiko*: The Dhamma welcomes all beings to put it to the test and come see for themselves.
5. *Opanayiko*: The Dhamma is capable of being entered upon and therefore it is worthy to be followed as a part of one's life.
6. *Paccattam Veditabbo Vinnuhi*: The Dhamma can be perfectly realized only by the noble disciples (Ariyas) who have matured and enlightened enough in supreme wisdom.

Knowing these attributes, Buddhists believe that they will attain the greatest peace and happiness through the practice of the Dhamma. Each person is therefore fully responsible for himself to put it in the real practice.

Here the Buddha is compared to an experienced and skilful doctor and the Dhamma to proper medicine. However efficient the doctor or wonderful the medicine may be, the patients cannot be cured unless they take the medicine properly. So the practice of the Dhamma is the only way to attain the final deliverance of Nibbana.

These teachings ranged from understanding karma (Pali: kamma) (cause and effect) and developing good impressions in one's mind, to reach full enlightenment by recognizing the nature of mind.

Dharmas in Buddhist Phenomenology

Other uses include dharma, normally spelled with a small "d" (to differentiate), which refers to a phenomenon or constituent factor of human experience. This was gradually expanded into a classification of constituents of the entire material and mental world. Rejecting the substantial existence of permanent entities which are qualified by possibly changing qualities, Buddhist Abhidharma philosophy, which enumerated seventy-five dharmas, came to propound that these "constituent factors" are the only type of entity that truly exists. This notion is of particular importance for the analysis of human experience: Rather than assuming that mental states inhere in a cognizing subject, or a soul-substance, Buddhist philosophers largely propose that mental states alone exist as "momentary elements of consciousness" and that a subjective perceiver is assumed.

One of the central tenets of Buddhism, is the denial of a separate permanent "I" and is outlined in the three marks of existence. The three signs: 1. Dukkha (Pali: Dukkha)-Suffering, 2. Anitya (Pali: Anicca)-Change/Impermanence, 3. Anatman (Pali: Anatta)-Non-self. At the heart of Buddhism, is the denial of a "self" or "I" (and hence the delusion) as a separate self-existing entity.

Later, Buddhist philosophers like Nagarjuna would question whether the dharmas (momentary elements of consciousness) truly have a separate existence of their own. (*i.e.* Do they exist apart from anything else?) Rejecting any inherent reality to the dharmas, he asked (rhetorically):

> *When all dharmas are empty, what is endless? What has an end?*
>
> *What is endless and with an end? What is not endless and not with an end?*

What is it? What is other? What is permanent? What is impermanent?

What is impermanent and permanent? What is neither?

Auspicious is the pacification of phenomenal metastasis, the pacification of all apprehending;

There is no dharma whatsoever taught by the Buddha to whomever, whenever, wherever.--Mulamadhyamakakarika, nirvanaparikna, 25:22-24

Dharma as Righteousness

According to S. N. Goenka, teacher of Vipassana Meditation, the original meaning of dhamma is "dhareti ti dhamma', or "that which is contained". Dharma in the Buddhist scriptures has a variety of meanings, including "phenomenon" and "nature" or "characteristic". Dharma also means 'mental contents' and is paired with citta, which means heart/mind. The pairing is paralleled with the pairing of kaya (body) and vedana (feelings or sensations, that which arise within the body but experienced through the mind), in major sutras such as the Mahasatipatthana sutra. Dharma is also used to refer to the teachings of the Buddha, not in the context of the words of one man, even an enlightened man, but as a reflection of natural law which was re-discovered by this man and shared with the world. A person who lives their life with an understanding of this natural law, is a "dhammic" person, which is often translated as "righteous".

3

PHILOSOPHY OF BUDDHIST

INTRODUCTION

They are among the truths the Buddha realised during his enlightenment experience. Why the Buddha taught in this way is illuminated by the social context of the time in which he lived. The Buddha was a Sramaa, a wandering ascetic whose "aim was to discover the truth and attain happiness". The Buddha claimed to have achieved this aim while under a bodhi tree near the Ganges River; the Four Noble Truths are a formulation of his understanding of "suffering", the fundamental cause of all suffering, the escape from suffering and what effort a person can go to so that they themselves can "attain happiness." The four Noble Truths are one of the most fundamental Buddhist teachings, they appear many times throughout the most ancient Buddhist texts, the Pali Canon. These truths are not expressed as a theory or tentative idea, rather the Buddha says:

> *"These Four Noble Truths, monks, are actual, unerring, not otherwise. Therefore, they are called noble truths."*

The Buddha said that he taught them...

> *"...because it is beneficial, it belongs to the fundamentals of the holy life, it leads to disenchantment, to dispassion, to cessation, to peace, to direct knowledge, to enlightenment, to Nirvana. That is why I have declared it."*

This teaching was the basis of the Buddha's first discourse after his enlightenment.

Mahayana Buddhism contains within itself an alternative version of the Four Noble Truths, in which the immortality of the Buddha occupies a central position.

Four Noble Truths

1. *Suffering (Dukkha)*: Now this, monks, is the noble truth of suffering: Birth is suffering, aging is suffering, sickness is suffering, death is suffering; union with what is displeasing is suffering; separation from what is pleasing is suffering; not to get what one wants is suffering; in brief, the five aggregates subject to clinging are suffering.
2. *Source of Suffering (Samudaya)*: Now this, monks, is the noble truth of the origin of suffering: It is this craving which leads to renewed existence, accompanied by delight and lust, seeking delight here and there; that is, craving for sensual pleasures, craving for existence, craving for extermination.
3. *The Cessation of Suffering (Nirodha)*: Now this, monks, is the noble truth of the cessation of suffering: It is the remainder less fading away and cessation of that same craving, the giving up and relinquishing of it, freedom from it and non-reliance on it.
4. *The Way Leading to the Cessation of Suffering (Magga)*: Now this, monks, is the noble truth of the way leading to the cessation of suffering: It is this Noble Eightfold Path; that is, right view, right intention, right speech, right action, right livelihood, right effort, right mindfulness, right concentration."

Variant Four Noble Truths in Mahayana Buddhism

Certain major Mahayana sutras, including the Mahaparinirvana Sutra and the Angulimaliya Sutra, present variant versions of the Four Noble Truths in line with their own metaphysics and soteriology. In the Mahaparinirvana Sutra, the Buddha declares that:

the Truth of Suffering relates to the failure to recognise the eternity of the Buddha;

the Truth of the Cause of Suffering concerns the perversion and distortion of the True Dharma;

The Truth of the Cessation of Suffering relates to the correct meditative cultivation of the tathagatagarbha (indwelling Buddha Essence in all beings) and not erroneously viewing it as non-Self and empty; cessation of suffering also arises with the elimination of inner defilements, when one can then enter into the Buddhic Essence within oneself: "When the afflictions have been eradicated, then one will perceive entry into the tathagata-garbha"; the Truth of the Path to the Cessation of Suffering entails envisioning the Buddha, Dharma and Sangha as eternal, immovable and indestructible.

The Angulimaliya Sutra similarly emphasises the seeing and knowing of the Buddha's eternality, immutability and peace as the key factors in liberation from suffering; failure to see this eternal nature of ultimate reality is said to constitute the primary cause of beings' continued entrapment in the sufferings of samsara.

NIRVANA

Nirvana, is a Sanskrit word from India that literally means extinction (as in a candle flame) and/or extinguishing (*i.e.* of the passions).

It is a mode of being that is free from mind-contaminants (Kilesa) such as lust, anger or craving. It is thus a state of great inner peace and contentment-the end of suffering, or Dukkha. The Buddha in the Dhammapada says of Nirvana that it is "the highest happiness." This is not the transitory, sense-based happiness of everyday life, but rather an enduring, transcendental happiness integral to the calmness attained through enlightenment.

The Buddha describes the abiding in nirvana as 'deathlessness' (Pali: amata or amaravati) or 'the unconditioned' and as the highest spiritual attainment, the natural result that accrues to one who lives a life of virtuous conduct in accordance with Dharma. Such a life (called Brahmacarya in India) dissolves the causes for future becoming (Skt, Karma; Pali, Kamma) that otherwise keep beings forever wandering through realms of desire and form (samsara).

There are many synonyms for Nirvana, as shown by the following passage:

> *World Honoured One, the ground of fruition is bodhi, nirvana, true suchness, the Buddha-nature, the amala-consciousness, the empty treasury of the Thus Come One, the great, perfect mirror-wisdom. But although it is called by these seven names, it is pure and perfect, its substance is durable, like royal vajra, everlasting and indestructible. (Surangama Sutra IV 207)*

Overview: Nirvana (Pali nibbana) in sutra is "bhavanirodha nibbanam" (The cessation of becoming means Nirvana). Nirvana in sutra is never conceived of as a place, but the antinomy of samsara which itself is synonymous with ignorance (avidya, Pali avijja). "This said:

> *'the liberated mind (citta) that no longer clings' means Nibbana" (Majjhima Nikaya 2-Att. 4.68).*

Nibbana is meant specifically as pertains gnosis that which ends the identity of the mind (citta) with empirical phenomena. Doctrinally Nibbana is said of the mind which no "longer is coming (bhava) and going (vibhava)", but which has attained a status in perpetuity, whereby "liberation (vimutta) can be said".

It carries further connotations of stilling, cooling and peace. The realizing of nirvana is compared to the ending of avidya (ignorance) which perpetuates the will (cetana) into effecting the incarnation of mind into biological or other form passing on forever through life after life (samsara). Samsara is caused principally by craving and ignorance. Nirvana, then, is not a place nor a state, it is an absolute truth to be realized and a person can do so without dying. When a person who has realized nirvana dies, his death is referred as his parinirvana, his fully passing away, as his life was his last link to the cycle of death and rebirth (samsara) and he will not be reborn again. Buddhism holds that the ultimate goal and end of samsaric existence (of ever "becoming" and "dying" and never truly being) is realization of nirvana; what happens to a person after his parinirvana cannot be explained, as it is outside of all conceivable experience.

Nirvana and Samsara

In Mahayana Buddhism, calling nirvana the "opposite" of samsara or implying that it is apart from samsara is doctrinally problematic. According to early Mahayana Buddhism, they can be considered to be two aspects of the same perceived reality. By the time of Nagarjuna, there are teachings of the identity of nirvana and samsara. However, even here it is assumed that the natural man suffers from at the very least a confusion regarding the nature of samsara.

The Theravada school makes the antithesis of samsara and Nibbana the starting point of the entire quest for deliverance. Even more, it treats this antithesis as determinative of the final goal, which is precisely the transcendence of samsara and the attainment of liberation in Nibbana.

Where Theravada differs significantly from the Mahayana schools, which also start with the duality of samsara and Nirvana, is in not regarding this polarity as a mere preparatory lesson tailored for those with blunt faculties, to be eventually superseded by some higher realization of non-duality. From the standpoint of the Pali Suttas, even for the Buddha and the Arahants suffering and its cessation, samsara and Nibbana, remain distinct.

In the experience of all, Nirvana is a state which all six bases (Eye, Ear, Nose, Tongue, Body and Mind) cannot feel.

It is probably best to understand the relationship between Nirvana and samsara in terms of the Buddha while on earth. Buddha was both in Samsara while having attained to Nirvana so that he was seen by all and simultaneously free from samsara.

Nirvaṇa in Buddhist Commentaries

Sarvastivadin commentary, Abhidharma-mahavibhasa-sastra, gives the complete context of the possible meanings from its Sanskrit roots:

- Vana, implying the path of rebirth, + nir, meaning leaving off' or 'being away from the path of rebirth.'
- Vana, meaning 'stench', + nir, meaning 'freedom': 'freedom from the stench of distressing kamma.'
- Vana, meaning 'dense forests', + nir, meaning 'to get rid of' = 'to be permanently rid of the dense forest of the five aggregates (panca skandha), or the 'three roots of greed, hate and delusion (lobha, dosa, moha)' or 'three characteristics of existence (impermanence, anitya; unsatisfactoriness, dukkha, soullessness, anatma).
- Vana, meaning 'weaving', + nir, meaning 'knot' = 'freedom from the knot of the distressful thread of kamma.'

Nirvana in the Mahaparinirvana Sutra

The nature of Nirvana assumes a differently aspected Mahayana focus in what alleges to be the final of all Mahayana Sutras, allegedly delivered by the Buddha on his last day of life on earth-the Mahaparinirvana Sutra or Nirvana Sutra. Here, as well as in a number of linked "tathagatagarbha" sutras, in which the Tathagatagarbha is equated with the Buddha's eternal Self or eternal nature, Nirvana is spoken of by the Mahayana Buddha in very "cataphatic", positive terms. Nirvana, or "Great Nirvana", is indicated to be the sphere or domain (vishaya) of the True Self.

It is seen as the state which constitutes the attainment of what is "Eternal, the Self, Bliss and the Pure". Maha-nirvana ("Great Nirvana") thus becomes equivalent to the ineffable, unshakeable, blissful, all-pervading and deathless Selfhood of the Buddha himself-a mystery which no words can adequately reach and which, according to the Nirvana Sutra, can only be fully known by an Awakened Being-a perfect Buddha-directly.

Strikingly, the Buddha of the Mahaparinirvana Sutra gives the following definition of the attributes of Nirvana, which includes the ultimate reality of the Self (not to be confused with the "worldly ego" of the 5 skandhas):

"The attributes of Nirvana are eightfold. What are these eight? Cessation [nirodha], loveliness/ wholesomeness [subha], Truth [satya], Reality [tattva], eternity [nitya], bliss [sukha], the Self [atman] and complete purity [parisuddhi]: that is Nirvana."

He further states: "Non-Self is Samsara [the cycle of rebirth]; the Self (atman) is Great Nirvana."

An important facet of Nirvana in general is that it is not something that comes about from a concatenation of causes, that springs into existence as a result of an act of creation or an agglomeration of causative factors: it was never created; it always was, is and will be. But due to the moral and mental darkness of ordinary, samsarically benighted sentient beings, it remains hidden from unawakened perception. The Buddha of the Mahaparinirvanasutra insists on its eternal nature and affirms its identity with the enduring, blissful Self, saying:

> *"It is not the case that the inherent nature of Nirvana did not primordially exist but now exists. If the inherent nature of Nirvana did not primordially exist but does now exist, then it would not be free from taints (asravas) nor would it be eternally (nitya) present in nature. Regardless of whether there are Buddhas or not, its intrinsic nature and attributes are eternally present... Because of the obscuring darkness of the mental afflictions (kilesas), beings do not see it. The Tathagata, endowed with omniscient awareness (sarvajna-jnana), lights the lamp of insight with his skill-in-means (upaya-kausalya) and causes Bodhisattvas to perceive the Eternal, Bliss, the Self and the Pure of Nirvana."*

Vitally, according to these Mahayana teachings, any being who has reached Nirvana is not blotted out or extinguished: there is the extinction of the impermanent and suffering-prone "worldly self" or ego (comprised of the five changeful skandhas), but not of the immortal "supramundane" Self of the indwelling Buddha Principle [Buddha-dhatu]. Spiritual death for such a Nirvanaed being becomes an utter impossibility. The Buddha states in the "Mahayana Mahaparinirvana Sutra" (Tibetan version): "Nirvana is deathless... Those who have passed into Nirvana are deathless. I say that anybody who is endowed with careful assiduity is not compounded and, even though they involve themselves in compounded things, they do not age, they do not die, they do not perish."

Paths to Nirvana in the Pali Canon

In the Visuddhimagga, Ch. I, v. 6 (Buddhaghosa & Nanamoli, 1999, pp. 6-7), Buddhaghosa identifies various options within the Pali canon for pursuing a path to Nirvana, including:

1. by insight (vipassana) alone
2. by jhana and understanding
3. by deeds, vision and righteousness
4. by virtue, consciousness and understanding
5. by virtue, understanding, concentration and effort
6. by the four foundations of mindfulness

Depending on one's analysis, each of these options could be seen as a reframing of the Buddha's Threefold Training of virtue, mental development and wisdom.

THREE JEWELS

The Three Jewels, also rendered as Three Treasures, Three Refuges or Triple Gem are the three things that Buddhists give themselves to and in return look toward for guidance, in the process known as taking refuge.

Taking refuge in the Three Jewels is central to Buddhist lay and monastic ordination ceremonies, as originated by Gautama Buddha.

Taking refuge in the Triple Gem is generally considered to make one officially a Buddhist. Thus, in many Theravada Buddhist communities, the following Pali chant, the Vandana Ti-sarana is often recited by both monks and lay people:

- Buddham saranaṃ gacchami
  I go for refuge in the Buddha
- Dhammam saranam gacchami
  I go for refuge in the Dharma
- Sangham saranam gacchami
  I go for refuge in the Sangha

The Mahayana Chinese/Japanese version differs only slightly from the Theravada:

> *I take refuge in the Buddha, wishing for all sentient beings to understand the great way and make the greatest vow.*
>
> *I take refuge in the Dharma, wishing for all sentient beings to deeply delve into the Sutra Pitaka, gaining an ocean of knowledge.*
>
> *I take refuge in the Sangha, wishing all sentient beings to lead the congregation in harmony, entirely without obstruction.*

Importance of the Triple Gem

The Triple Gem is important and is one of the major practices of mental "reflection" in Buddhism, we reflect on the true qualities of the Buddha, Dharma and Sangha. These qualities are called the Mirror of the Dharma in the Mahaparinibbana Sutta and help us attain the true "mind like a mirror".

Reflection in the Mirror of the Dharma

The qualities of the Buddha, Dharma and Sangha are frequently repeated in the ancient texts. It is a Buddhist practise to reflect upon them.

- *The Buddha:* "The Blessed One is an Arahant, perfectly enlightened, accomplished in true knowledge and conduct, fortunate, knower of the world, unsurpassed leader of persons to be tamed, teacher of devas and humans, the Enlightened One, the Blessed One."

In some traditions, the Buddha as refuge, is known as the historical Buddha and also 'the full development of mind', in other words, the full development of one's highest potential *i.e.* recognition of mind and the completion or full development of one's inherent qualities and activities.

- *The Dharma:* "The Dhamma is well expounded by the Blessed One, directly visible, immediate, inviting one to come and see, applicable, to be personally experienced by the wise."

  Refuge in the Dharma in the Vajrayana tradition includes reference not only to the words of the Buddha, but to the living experience of realization and teachings of fully realized practitioners. In Tibetan Buddhism, it includes both the Kangyur (the teaching of the Buddha) and the Tengyur (the commentaries by realized practioners) and in an intangible way also includes the living transmission of those masters, which can also be very inspiring.
- *The Sangha:* "The Sangha of the Blessed One's disciples is practising the good way, practising the straight way, practising the true way, practising the proper way; that is, the four pairs of persons, the eight types of individuals-This Sangha of the Blessed One's disciples is worthy of gifts, worthy of hospitality, worthy of offerings, worthy of reverential salutation, the unsurpassed field of merit for the world."

In the Vajrayana, a more liberal definition of Sangha can include all practitioners who are actively using the Buddhas teachings to benefit themselves and/or others. It can be more strictly defined as the 'Realized Sangha' or 'Arya-Sangha', in other words, practitioners and historical students of the Buddha who have fully realized the nature of their mind, also known as realized Boddhisatvas; and 'Ordinary Sangha', which can loosely mean practitioners and students of the Buddha who are using the same methods and working towards the same goal.

In the Vajrayana traditions, there is another very important and expanded aspect of the Refuge, the refuge in the teacher. This can be understood on many levels including what is called the Three Roots-the Root of Blessing, Root of Methods and Root of Protection. Another way to understand this is as the Body (Sangha), Speech (Dharma) and Mind (Buddha) of the Buddha. The teacher has a prominent place in the Vajrayana, as without his personal permission and guidance, a practitioner cannot achieve proper spiritual progress.

Why is it called the Triple Gem?

In Buddhism, the following three are called Gems (Ratna) as they are invaluable:

- Buddha, who, depending on one's interpretation, can mean the Historical Buddha, Shakyamuni, or the Buddha nature or ideal within all beings;
- Dharma, which is the Teachings of the Buddha.
- Sangha, The Community of those great people who have attained Enlightenment. So that those people (Sangha) will help you to attain Enlightenment.

The three gems are so called since amongst all gems, the Buddha gem and Dharma gem are considered incomparable in value as they are not material, so cannot be created, destroyed or changed in any way. Buddha's mind in his earth body or sambhogakaya is frequently associated with the greatest gem of all, the diamond. In the Anguttara Nikaya (3:25), Buddha talks about the diamond mind:

These three types of persons are found in the world: One with a mind like an open sore; one with a mind like a flash of lightning; one with a mind like a diamond.

- One who is irascible and very irritable, displaying anger, hatred and sulkiness; such a one is said to be a person with a mind like an open sore.

- One who understands the Four Noble Truths correctly is said to have a mind like a flash of lightning.
- One who has destroyed the mind-intoxicating defilements and realized the liberation of mind and the liberation by knowledge is said to have a mind like a diamond

With this we understand that to take refuge in the Buddha is to take refuge in the mind like a diamond, the hardest natural substance that can cut through all delusion.

The Three Gems when used in the process of taking refuge, become the Three Refuges.

The expression Three Gems are found in the earliest Buddhist literature of the Pali Canon, besides other works there is one sutta in the Sutta-nipata, called the Ratana-sutta which contains a series of verses on the Jewels in the Buddha, Dharma and Sangha. In the Ratana-sutta, all the qualities of the Sangha mentioned are attributes of the Buddha's enlightened disciples.

The Three Refuges occur very frequently in the ancient Buddhist Texts and here the Sangha is used more broadly to refer to either the Sangha of Bhikkhus, or the Sangha of Bhikkhunis. "I go to Master Gautama for refuge and to the Dhamma and to the Sangha of Bhikkhus."

THREE MARKS OF EXISTENCE

After much meditation, the Buddha concluded that everything in the physical world (plus everything in the phenomenology of psychology) is marked by three characteristics, known as the three characteristics of existence, three signs of being or Dharma Seals. Together the three characteristics of existence are called ti-lakkhana, in Pali; or tri-laksana, in Sanskrit.

- Dukkha (Sanskrit duhkha) or unsatisfactoriness. Nothing found in the physical world or even the psychological realm can bring lasting deep satisfaction.

- Anicca (Sanskrit anitya) or impermanence. This refers not only to the fact that all conditioned things eventually cease to exist, but also that all conditioned things are in a constant state of flux. (Visualize a leaf growing on a tree. It dies and falls off the tree but is soon replaced by a new leaf.)
- Anatta (Sanskrit anatman) impersonality, or non-Self. The human personality, "soul", or Self, is a conventional appellation applied to the assembly of physical and psychological components, each individually subject to constant flux; there is no central core (or essence); this is somewhat similar to a bundle theory of mind or soul.

There is often a fourth Dharma Seal mentioned:

- Nirvana is peace. Nirvana is the 'other shore' from Samsara.

By bringing the three (or four) seals into moment-to-moment experience through concentrated awareness, we are said to achieve Wisdom-the third of the three higher trainings-the way out of Samsara. In this way we can identify that, according to Sutra, the recipe (or formula) for leaving Samsara is achieved by a deep-rooted change to our Weltanschauung.

According to the Buddhist tradition, all phenomena (dharmas) are marked by three characteristics, sometimes referred to as the Dharma seals, that is dukkha (suffering), anicca (impermanence) and anatta (non-Self).

Dukkha

Whatever is impermanent is subject to change. Whatever is subject to change is subject to suffering.
—The Buddha

Striving for what we desire, we may experience stress and suffering-dukkha. Getting what we desired, we may find delight and happiness. Soon after, the novelty may wear out and we may get bored with it. Boredom is a form of dissatisfaction (or suffering) and to escape from it, we divert ourselves from such boredom by indulging in a pursuit of new forms of pleasure. Sometimes not willing to relinquish objects that we are already disinterested in, we start to collect and amass possessions instead of sharing with others who may have better use in it than we do. Boredom is a result of change. Change of our interest in that object of desire that so captivated us in the first place.

If we do not get bored already, then change may instead occur in the object of desire. Silverware may become tarnished, a new dress worn thin or a gadget gone obsolete. Or it may become broken, causing us to grieve. In some cases it may get lost or stolen. In some cases, we may worry about such losses even before they happen. Husbands and wives worry about losing their spouses even though their partners are faithful. Unfortunately, sometimes our very worry and fear drives us to act irrationally, resulting in distrust and breaking up of the very relationship that we cherished so much.

While we like changes such as becoming an adult when we are in our teens, we dislike the change called aging. While we strive for change to become rich, we fear the change of retrenchment. We are selective in our attitude towards the transient nature of our very existence. Unfortunately, this transient nature is unselective. We can try to fight it, just as many have tried since beginningless time, only to have our efforts washed away through the passages of time. As a result, we continually experience dissatisfaction or suffering due to the very impermanence of compounded phenomena.

Only in the realm of Nirvana-so Mahayana Buddhism insists-can true and lasting happiness be found. Nirvana is the opposite of the conditional, the transitory and the painful (dukkha), so it does not result in disappointment or deterioration of the state of bliss. Nirvana is the refuge from the otherwise universal tyranny of change and suffering. In other schools of Buddhism, nirvana is not viewed as the goal, but merely as a projection from the state of samsara. According to these schools samsara (confusion) and nirvana (perfection) are two sides of the same coin that must be transcended through diligent practice of meditation.

Anicca

All compounded phenomena (things and experiences) are inconstant, unsteady and impermanent. (Practically) everything is made up of parts and is dependent on the right conditions for its existence. Everything is in constant flux and so conditions and the thing itself is constantly changing. Things are constantly coming into being and ceasing to be. Nothing lasts.

The important point here is that phenomena arise and cease according to (complex) conditions and not according to our whims and fancy. While we have limited ability to effect change to our possessions and surroundings, experience tells us that our feeble attempts are no guarantee that the results of our efforts will be to our likings. More often than not, the results fall short of our expectations.

In Mahayana Buddhism, a caveat is added: one should indeed always meditate on the impermanence and changefulness of compounded structures and phenomena, but one must guard against extending this to the realm of Nirvana, where impermanence holds no sway and eternity alone obtains. To see Nirvana or the Buddha (in his ultimate Dharmakaya nature) as impermanent would be to indulge in "perverted Dharma" and would be seriously to go astray, according to the Buddha's final Mahayana doctrines. Other schools of Buddhism, however, feel uneasy with such a teaching.

Anatta

In Indian philosophy, the concept of a Self is called atman (that is, "soul" or metaphysical Self), which refers to an unchanging, permanent essence conceived by virtue of existence. This concept and the related concept of Brahman, the Vedantic monistic ideal, which was regarded as an ultimate atman for all beings, were indispensable for mainstream Indian metaphysics, logic and science; for all apparent things there had to be an underlying and persistent reality, akin to a Platonic form. The Buddha rejected all concepts of atman, emphasizing not permanence, but changeability. He taught that all concepts of a substantial personal Self were incorrect and formed in the realm of ignorance.

However, in a number of major Mahayana sutras (*e.g.* the Mahaparinirvana Sutra, the Tathagatagarbha Sutra, the Srimala Sutra, among others), the Buddha is presented as clarifying this teaching by saying that, while the skandhas (constituents of the ordinary body and mind) are not the Self, there does truly exist an eternal, unchanging, blissful Buddha-essence in all sentient beings, which is the uncreated and deathless Buddha-nature ("Buddha-dhatu") or "True Self" of the Buddha himself. This immaculate Buddhic Self (atman) is in no way to be construed as a mundane, impermanent, suffering "ego", of which it is the diametrical opposite. On the other hand, this Buddha-essence or Buddha-nature is also often explained as the potential for achieving Buddhahood, rather than an existing phenomenon one can grasp onto as being me or Self.

It is the opposite of a personalised, samsaric "I" or "mine". The paradox is that as soon as the Buddhist practitioner tries to grasp at this inner Buddha potency and cling to it as though it were his or her ego writ large, it proves elusive. It does not "exist" in the time-space conditioned and finite mode in which mundane things are bodied forth. It is presented by the Buddha in the relevant sutras as ultimately inexplicable, primordially present Reality itself-the living potency for Buddhahood inside all beings. It is finally revealed (in the last of the Buddha's Mahayana sutras, the Nirvana Sutra) not as the circumscribed "non-Self", the clinging ego (which is indeed anatta/anatman), but as the ever-enduring, egoless Great Self or Dharmakaya of the Buddha.

The scriptural evidence of the Nikayas and Agamas is ambivalent with regard to the Buddha's reported views on the existence or otherwise of a permanent Self (atman/atta). Though he is clearly reported to have criticized many of the heterodox concepts concerning an eternal personal Self and to have denied the existence of an eternal Self with regards to any of the constituent elements (skandha) of a being, he is nevertheless not reported to have explicitly denied the existence of a non-personal, permanent Self, contrary to the popular, orthodox view of the Buddha's teachings. Moreover, when the Buddha predicates "anatman" (anatta) with regards to the constituents of a being, there is a grammatical ambivalence in the use of the term.

The most natural interpretation is that he is simply stating that "the constituents are not the Self" rather than "the constituents are devoid of Self". This ambivalence was to prove troublesome to Buddhists after the Buddha's passing. Some of the major schools of Buddhism that developed subsequently maintained the former interpretation, but other influential schools adopted the latter interpretation and took measures to establish their view as the orthodox Buddhist position.

One such proponent of this hard-line "non-Self" position was the monk Nagasena, who appears in the Questions of King Milinda, composed during the period of the Hellenistic Indo-Greek kingdom of the 2nd and 1st centuries BC. In this text, Nagasena demonstrates the concept of absolute 'non-Self' by likening human beings to a chariot and challenges the Greek king "Milinda" (Menander) to find the essence of the chariot. Nagasena states that just as a chariot is made up of a number of things, none of which are the essence of the chariot in isolation, without the other pieces, similarly no one part of a person is a permanent entity; we can be broken up into five constituents-body, sensations, ideation, mental formations and consciousness-the consciousness being closest to the permanent idea of 'Self', but is ever-changing with each new thought according to this viewpoint.

According to some thinkers both in the East and the West, the doctrine of "non-Self", may imply that Buddhism is a form of nihilism or something similar. However, as thinkers like

Nagarjuna have clearly pointed out, Buddhism is not simply a rejection of the concept of existence (or of meaning, etc.) but of the hard and fast distinction between existence and non-existence, or rather between being and no-thingness.

Phenomena are not independent from causes and conditions and do not exist as isolated things as we perceive them to be. Philosophers such as Nagarjuna stress that the lack of a permanent, unchanging, substantial Self in beings and things does not mean that they do not experience growth and decay on the relative level. But on the ultimate level of analysis, one cannot distinguish an object from its causes and conditions, or even object and subject. (This is an idea appearing relatively recently in Western science.) Buddhism thus has much more in common with Western empiricism, pragmatism, anti-foundationalism and even poststructuralism than with nihilism.

In the Nikayas, the Buddha and his disciples are commonly found to ask in question or declare "Is that which is impermanent, subject to change, subject to suffering fit to be considered thus: 'This I am, this is mine, this is my self'?" The question which the Buddha posts to his audience is whether compounded phenomena is fit to be considered as self, in which the audience agrees that it is unworthy to be considered so. And in relinquishing such an attachment to compounded phenomena, such a person gives up delight, desire and craving for compounded phenomena and is unbounded by its change. When completely free from attachments, craving or desire to the five aggregates, such a person experiences then transcends the very causes of suffering.

In this way, the insight wisdom or prajna of non-Self gives rise to cessation of suffering and not an intellectual debate over whether a self exists or not.

It is by realizing (not merely understanding intellectually, but making real in one's experience) the three marks of conditioned existence that one develops prajna, which is the antidote to the ignorance that lies at the root of all suffering. From the "tathagatagarbha-Mahayana" perspective (which diverges from the Theravadin understanding of Buddhism), however, a further step is required if full Buddhahood is to be attained: not only seeing what is impermanent, suffering and non-Self in the samsaric sphere, but equally recognising that which is truly Eternal, Blissful, Self and Pure in the transcendental realm-the realm of Mahaparinirvana.

Interpretations of the Three Marks by Various Schools

Some Buddhist traditions assert that Anatta pervades everything and is not limited to personality, or soul. These traditions assert that Nirvana also has the quality of Anatta, but that Nirvana (by definition) is the cessation of Dukkha and Anicca.

In Nagarjuna's MMK XXV:19, he says

There is not the slightest difference

Between Samsara and Nirvana

This verse points us to an interesting stress between dukkha and nirvana, through an argument based in anatta. This specific stress can be seen to be the key to (and possibly source for the development of) the deity yogas of vajrayana.

The sutra path enjoins us to identify the entire world (internally and externally) as samsara-a continual churning of suffering that nobody wants to be part of. Our practice is that of leaving the shores of samsara. On the other hand, we are told that unconditioned, enlightened activity is not actually different from samsara. Whereas the deity yoga of vajrayana enjoins us to identify the entire world as nirvana-a continual play of enlightening activity that everyone wishes to be a part of. Our practice here is that of arriving at the shores of nirvana.

At this level, the distinction between Sutra and Vajrayana remain that of view (departing vs. arriving), but basically the practitioner remains involved in undergoing a transformative development to his or her Weltanschauung and in this context, these practices remain rooted in psychological change, grounded in the development of Samatha, or training in concentration.

However, there are certain practices in Tantra which are not solely concerned with psychological change; these revolve around the basic idea that it is possible to induce deep levels of concentration through psycho-physical methods as a result of special exercises. The purpose remains the same (to achieve liberating view), but the method involves a 'short cut' for the training in Samatha.

SKANDHA

The five skandhas (Sanskrit) or khandhas (Pali) are the five "aggregates" which categorize or constitute all individual experience according to Buddhist phenomenology. An important corollary in Buddhism is that a "person" is made up of these five aggregates, beyond which there is no "self." In the Theravada tradition, suffering arises when one identifies with or otherwise clings to an aggregate; hence, suffering is extinguished by relinquishing attachments to aggregates. The Mahayana tradition further puts forth that ultimate freedom is realized by deeply penetrating the intrinsically empty nature of all aggregates.

Outside of Buddhist didactic contexts, "skandha" can mean mass, heap, bundle or tree trunk.

Definition

Buddhist doctrine describes five aggregates:

1. "form" or "matter" (Skt., Pali rupa): external and internal matter. Externally, rupa is the physical world. Internally, rupa includes the material body and the physical sense organs.
2. "sensation" or "feeling" (Skt., Pali vedana): sensing an object as either pleasant or unpleasant or neutral.
3. "perception" or "cognition" (Skt. samjna, Pali sanna): registers whether an object is recognized or not (for instance, the sound of a bell or the shape of a tree).
4. "mental formations" or "volition" (Skt. samskara, Pali sankhara): all types of mental habits, thoughts, ideas,

opinions, compulsions and decisions triggered by an object.

5. "consciousness":
   (a) In the Nikayas: cognizance.
   (b) In the Abhidhamma: a series of rapidly changing interconnected discrete acts of cognizance.
   (c) In Mahayana sources: the base that supports all experience.

In this scheme, form, the mental aggregates and consciousness are mutually dependent.

Other Buddhist literature has described the aggregates as arising in a linear or progressive fashion, from form to feeling to perception to mental formations to consciousness.

Theravada Perspectives

Bhikkhu Bodhi (2000b, p. 840) states that an examination of the aggregates has a "critical role" in the Buddha's teaching for multiple reasons, including:

1. *Understanding the Four Noble Truths*: The five aggregates are the "ultimate referent" in the Buddha's elaboration on suffering (dukkha) in his First Noble Truth and "since all four truths revolve around suffering, understanding the aggregates is essential for understanding the Four Noble Truths as a whole."
2. *Future Suffering's Cause*: The five aggregates are the substrata for clinging and thus "contribute to the causal origination of future suffering."
3. *Release*: Clinging must be removed from the five aggregates in order to achieve release.

Below, excerpts from the Pali literature will bear out Bhikkhu Bodhi's assessment.

Suffering's Ultimate Referent

In the Buddha's first discourse, the "Dhammacakkappavattana Sutta" ("The Setting in Motion the Wheel of Truth

Discourse," SN 56:11), he provides a classic elaboration on the first of his Four Noble Truths, "The Truth of Suffering" (Dukkhasacca):

> *"The Noble Truth of Suffering (dukkha), monks, is this: Birth is suffering, aging is suffering, sickness is suffering, death is suffering, association with the unpleasant is suffering, dissociation from the pleasant is suffering, not to receive what one desires is suffering-in brief the five aggregates subject to grasping are suffering." [Boldface added.] (Trans. from the Pali by Piyadassi Thera, 1999.)*

According to Thanissaro (2002):

> *"Prior to the Buddha, the Pali word khandha had very ordinary meanings: A khandha could be a pile, a bundle, a heap, a mass. It could also be the trunk of a tree. In his first sermon, though, the Buddha gave it a new, psychological meaning, introducing the term 'clinging-khandhas' to summarize his analysis of the truth of stress and suffering. Throughout the remainder of his teaching career, he referred to these psychological khandhas time and again."*

In what way are the aggregates suffering? For this we can turn to Khandhavagga suttas.

Future Suffering's Cause

The Samyutta Nikaya contains a book entitled the "Khandhavagga" ("The Book of Aggregates") compiling over a hundred suttas related to the five aggregates. Typical of these suttas is the "Upadaparitassana Sutta" ("Agitation through Clinging Discourse," SN 22:7), which states in part:

> *"...[T]he instructed noble disciple... does not regard form [or other aggregates] as self, or self as possessing form, or form as in self, or self as in form. That form of his changes and alters. Despite the change and alteration of form, his consciousness does not become preoccupied with the change of form.... [T]hrough non-clinging he*

does not become agitated." (Trans. by Bodhi, 2000b, pp. 865-866.)

Put another way, if we were to self-identify with an aggregate then we would cling (upadana) to such; and, given that all aggregates are impermanent (anicca), it would then be likely that at some level we would experience agitation (paritassati) or loss or grief or stress or suffering. Therefore, if we want to be free of suffering, it is wise to experience the aggregates clearly, without clinging or craving (tanha), as apart from any notion of self (anatta).

Many of the suttas in the Khandhavagga express the aggregates in the context of the following sequence:

1. An uninstructed worldling (assutava puthujjana)
   a. regards: form as self; self as possessing form; form as in self; self as in form.
   b. lives obsessed by the notions: I am form; and/or, form is mine
   c. this form changes
   d. with the changes of form, there arises dukkha
2. An instructed noble disciple (sutava ariyasavaka) does not regard form as self, etc. and thus, when form changes, dukkha does not arise.

Example of Aggregate-Clinging

To give a simplistic example, if one believes "this body is mine" or "I exist within this body," then as their body ages, becomes ill and approaches death, such a person will likely experience longing for youth or health or eternal life, will likely dread aging and sickness and death and will likely spend much time and energy lost in fears, fantasies and ultimately futile activities.

In the Nikayas, such is likened to shooting oneself with a second arrow, where the first arrow is a physical phenomenon (such as, in this case, a bodily manifestation associated with aging or illness or dying) and the second is the mental anguish of the undisciplined mind associated with the physical phenomenon.

On the other hand, one with a disciplined mind who is able to see this body as a set of aggregates will be free of such fear, frustration and time-consuming escapism.

But how does one become aware of and then let go of ones own identification with or clinging to the aggregates? Below is an excerpt from the classic Satipatthana Sutta that shows how traditional mindfulness practices can awaken understanding, release and wisdom.

Release through Aggregate-contemplation

In the classic Theravada meditation reference, the "Satipathana Sutta" ("The Foundations of Mindfulness Discourse," MN 10), the Buddha provides four bases for establishing mindfulness: body (kaya), sensations (vedana), mind (citta) and mental objects (dhamma). When discussing mental objects as a basis for meditation, the Buddha identifies five objects, including the aggregates. Regarding meditation on the aggregates, the Buddha states:

> *"How, monks, does a monk live contemplating mental objects in the mental objects of the five aggregates of clinging?*
>
> *"Herein, monks, a monk thinks, 'Thus is material form; thus is the arising of material form; and thus is the disappearance of material form. Thus is feeling; thus is the arising of feeling; and thus is the disappearance of feeling. Thus is perception; thus is the arising of perception; and thus is the disappearance of perception. Thus are formations; thus is the arising of formations; and thus is the disappearance of formations. Thus is consciousness; thus is the arising of consciousness; and thus is the disappearance of consciousness.'*
>
> *"...Or his mindfulness is established with the thought, 'Mental objects exist,' to the extent necessary just for knowledge and mindfulness and he lives detached and*

> *clings to nothing in the world. Thus also, monks, a monk lives contemplating mental objects in the mental objects of the five aggregates of clinging." (Nyanasatta, trans., 1994.)*

Thus, through mindfulness contemplation, one sees an "aggregate as an aggregate"--sees it arising and dissipating. Such clear seeing creates a space between the aggregate and clinging, a space that will prevent or enervate the arising and propagation of clinging, thereby diminishing future suffering.

As clinging disappears, so too notions of a separate "self." In the Mahasunnata Sutta ("The Greater Discourse on Emptiness," MN 122), after reiterating the aforementioned aggregate-contemplation instructions (for instance, "Thus is form; thus is the arising of form; and, thus is the disappearance of form"), the Buddha states:

> *"When he [a monk] abides contemplating rise and fall in these five aggregates affected by clinging, the conceit 'I am' based on these five aggregates affected by clinging is abandoned in him...." (Nanamoli & Bodhi, 2001, p. 975.)*

In a complementary fashion, in the Buddha's second discourse, the Anattalakkhana Sutta ("The Characteristic of Nonself," SN 22:59), the Buddha instructs:

> *"Monks, form is nonself. For if, monks, form were self, this form would not lead to affliction and it would be possible to [manipulate] form [in the following manner]: 'Let my form be thus; let my form not be thus....' [Identical statements are made regarding feeling, perception, volitional formations and consciousness.]*
>
> *"...Seeing thus [for instance, through contemplation], monks, the instructed noble disciple becomes disenchanted with form [and the other aggregates].... Being disenchanted, he becomes dispassionate. Through dispassion [his mind] is liberated." (Bodhi, 2005, pp. 341-2.)*

Mahayana Perspectives

In one of Mahayana Buddhism's most famous declarations, the aggregates are referenced:

> *"Form is emptiness, emptiness is form."*

What does this mean? To what degree is it a departure from the aforementioned Theravada perspective? Moreover, more generally, how are the aggregates used in the Mahayana literature?

The Intrinsic Emptiness of all Things

The classic "Prajnaparamita Hridaya Sutra" ("Heart Sutra") begins:

> *The Bodhisattva Avalokita,*
> *while moving in the deep course of Perfect Understanding,*
> *shed light on the five skandhas*
> *and found them equally empty [of self].*
> *After this penetration, he overcame all pain.*

From its very first verse, the Heart Sutra introduces an alternative practice and worldview to the Theravada perspective of the aggregates:

- *Prajnaparamita:* Whereas Theravada meditation practices with the aggregates generally use change-penetrating vipassana meditation, here the non-dualistic prajnaparamita practice is invoked.
- *Svabhava:* In Theravada texts, when "emptiness of self" is mentioned, the English word "self" is a translation of the Pali word "atta" (Sanskrit, "atman"); in the Heart Sutra, the English word "self" is a translation of the Sanskrit word "sva-bhava". According to Red Pine, "The 'self' (sva)... was more generalized in its application than 'ego' (atman) and referred not only to beings but to any inherent substance that could be identified as existing in time or space as a permanent or independent entity." (Italics added.)

In other words, whereas the Sutta Pitaka typically instructs one to apprehend the aggregates without clinging or self-identification, Prajnaparamita leads one to apprehend the aggregates as having no intrinsic reality.

In the Heart Sutra's second verse, after rising from his aggregate meditation, Avalokiteshvara declares:

> *"Form is emptiness, emptiness is form,*
> *form does not differ from emptiness, emptiness does not differ from form.*
> *The same is true with feelings, perceptions, mental formations and consciousness."*

Thich Nhat Hanh interprets this statement as:

> *"Form is the wave and emptiness is the water.... [W]ave is water, water is wave.... [T]hese five [aggregates] contain each other. Because one exists, everything exists."*

Red Pine comments:

> *"That form is empty was one of the Buddha's earliest and most frequent pronouncements. But in the light of Prajnaparamita, form is not simply empty, it is so completely empty, it is emptiness itself, which turns out to be the same as form itself.... All separations are delusions. But if each of the skandhas is one with emptiness and emptiness is one with each of the skandhas, then everything occupies the same indivisible space, which is emptiness.... Everything is empty and empty is everything.*

Tangibility and Transcendence

Commenting on the Heart Sutra, D.T. Suzuki notes:

> *"When the sutra says that the five Skandhas have the character of emptiness..., the sense is: no limiting qualities are to be attributed to the Absolute; while it is immanent in all concrete and particular objects, it is not in itself definable."*

That is, from the Mahayana perspective, the aggregates convey the relative (or conventional) experience of the world by an individual, although Absolute truth is realized through them.

Vajrayana Perspectives

The Vajrayana tradition further develops the aggregates in terms of mahamudra epistemology and tantric reifications.

The Truth of our Insubstantiality

Referring to mahamudra teachings, Chogyam Trungpa (Trungpa, 2001, pp. 10-12; and, Trungpa, 2002, pp. 124, 133-4) identifies the form aggregate as the "solidification" of ignorance (Pali, avijja; Skt., avidya), allowing one to have the illusion of "possessing" ever dynamic and spacious wisdom (Pali, vijja; Skt. vidya) and thus being the basis for the creation of a dualistic relationship between "self" and "other."

According to Trungpa Rinpoche (1976, pp. 20-22), the five skandhas are "a set of Buddhist concepts which describe experience as a five-step process" and that "the whole development of the five skandhas...is an attempt on our part to shield ourselves from the truth of our insubstantiality," while "the practice of meditation is to see the transparency of this shield." (ibid, p.23)

Bardo Deity Manifestations

Trungpa Rinpoche writes (2001, p. 38):

> *"[S]ome of the details of tantric iconography are developed from abhidharma [that is, in this context, detailed analysis of the aggregates]. Different colours and feelings of this particular consciousness, that particular emotion, are manifested in a particular deity wearing such-and-such a costume, of certain particular colours, holding certain particular sceptres in his hand. Those details are very closely connected with the individualities of particular psychological processes."*

Perhaps it is in this sense that the Tibetan Book of the Dead (Fremantle & Trungpa, 2003) makes the following associations between the aggregates and tantric deities during the bardo after death:

- "The blue light of the skandha of consciousness in its basic purity, the wisdom of the dharmadhatu, luminous, clear, sharp and brilliant, will come towards you from the heart of Vairocana and his consort and pierce you so that your eyes cannot bear it." (p. 63)
- "The white light of the skandha of form in its basic purity, the mirror-like wisdom, dazzling white, luminous and clear, will come towards you from the heart of Vajrasattva and his consort and pierce you so that your eyes cannot bear to look at it." (p. 66)
- "The yellow light of the skandha of feeling in its basic purity, the wisdom of equality, brilliant yellow, adorned with discs of light, luminous and clear, unbearable to the eyes, will come towards you from the heart of Ratnasambhava and his consort and pierce your heart so that your eyes cannot bear to look at it." (p. 68)
- "The red light of the skandha of perception in its basic purity, the wisdom of discrimination, brilliant red, adorned with discs of light, luminous and clear, sharp and bright, will come from the heart of Amitabha and his consort and pierce your heart so that your eyes cannot bear to look at it. Do not be afraid of it." (p. 70)
- "The green light of the skandha of concept [samskara] in its basic purity, the action-accomplishing wisdom, brilliant green, luminous and clear, sharp and terrifying, adorned with discs of light, will come from the heart of Amoghasiddhi and his consort and pierce your heart so that your eyes cannot bear to look at it.

  Do not be afraid of it. It is the spontaneous play of your own mind, so rest in the supreme state free from activity and care, in which there is no near or far, love or hate." (p. 73)

Relation to other Buddhist Concepts

Other fundamental Buddhist concepts associated with the five skandhas include:

- *Samsara:* It is through the five skandhas that the world (samsara) is experienced and nothing is experienced apart from the five skandhas.
- *Three Characteristics:* It is through the five skandhas that impermanence (anicca) is experienced, that suffering (duhkha) arises and that "non-self" (anatta or anatman) can be realized.
- *Twelve Nidanas/Dependent Origination:* The Twelve Nidanas describe twelve phenomenal links by which suffering is perpetuated between and within lives. It is through the five skandhas that clinging (upadana) occurs, a pivotal link in this endless chain of suffering.
- *Eighteen Dhatus:* The eighteen dhatus function through the five aggregates. The eighteen dhatus can be arranged into six triads, where each triad is composed of a sense organ, a sense object and sense consciousness. In regards to the aggregates:
    - o The first five sense organs (eye, ear, nose, tongue, body) are derivates of form. The sixth sense organ (mind) is part of consciousness.
    - o The first five sense objects (visible forms, sound, smell, taste, touch) are also derivatives of form. The sixth sense object (mental object) includes form, sensation, perception and mental formations.
    - o The six sense consciousness are the basis for consciousness.

NOBLE EIGHTFOLD PATH

The Noble Eightfold Path is, in the Buddhist tradition as taught by the Buddha Sakyamuni, considered to be the way that leads to the end of suffering. It forms the fourth part of the Four Noble Truths, which are the most fundamental Buddhist teachings. The Noble Eightfold Path is essentially a practical guide of ethics, mental rehabilitation and mind deconditioning and is believed, by Buddhists, to result in an end to dukkha, or suffering, which is a goal that has informed and driven the entire Buddhist tradition since its inception 2500 years ago. As the name indicates, there are eight elements in the Noble Eightfold Path and these are further subdivided into three basic categories as follows:

- Wisdom (Sanskrit: prajna, Pali: panna)
    1. Right understanding
    2. Right intention
- Ethical conduct (Sanskrit: sila, Pali: sila)
    3. Right speech
    4. Right action
    5. Right livelihood
- Mental discipline (Sanskrit and Pali: samadhi)
    6. Right effort
    7. Right mindfulness
    8. Right concentration

In all of the elements of the Noble Eightfold Path, the word "right" is a translation of the word samyanc (Sanskrit) or samma (Pali), which denotes completion, togetherness and coherence and which can also carry the sense of "perfect" or "ideal".

Though the path is numbered one through eight, it is generally not considered to be a series of linear steps through which one must progress; rather, as the Buddhist monk and scholar Walpola Rahula points out, the eight elements of the Noble Eightfold Path "are to be developed more or less simultaneously, as far as possible according to the capacity of each individual. They are all linked together and each helps the cultivation of the others".

In Buddhist symbology, the Noble Eightfold Path is often represented by means of the Dharma wheel (Sanskrit:

dharmacakra, Pali: dhammacakka), whose eight spokes represent the eight elements of the path.

Wisdom (Prajna-Panna)

The "wisdom" subdivision of the Noble Eightfold Path is constituted by those elements that refer primarily to the mental or cognitive aspect of a Buddhist practitioner's practice.

Right understanding

Right understanding can also be translated as "right view" or "right perspective". This element of the Noble Eightfold Path refers explicitly to the Four Noble Truths of Buddhism, stating that these must be fully understood by the Buddhist practitioner. In the Mahasatipathana Sutta, one of the Buddha Sakyamuni's discourses, right understanding is explained directly in terms of the Four Noble Truths:

> *And what, O bhikkhus, is right understanding? To understand suffering, to understand the origination of suffering, to understand extinction of suffering, to understand the path leading to the extinction of suffering; this is called right understanding.*

Additionally, right understanding is sometimes considered to encompass an understanding of the Buddhist idea of the non-permanence, or even nonexistence, of the self, an idea known as anatman in Sanskrit and anatta in Pali.

There are two stages for every stage of the eightfold path, a preliminary stage and the higher stages gradually obtained through the journey towards enlightenment. The preliminary stage of Right Views or right understanding is the knowledge of the Four Noble Truths.

The higher stage require more than the comprehension of the Four Noble Truths, it also includes the knowledge and understanding of the not-self doctorine, imperminence, dependent origination, the five aggregates, kamma and rebirth and so on.

Right Thought

Right thought can also be translated as "right intention", "right resolve", or "right aspiration". This element of the Noble Eightfold Path deals, fundamentally, with the Buddhist practitioner's reasons for practising Buddhism and with his or her outlook towards the world. It enjoins renunciation of worldly things and an accordant greater commitment to spiritual matters; good will; and a commitment to non-violence, or ahimsa, towards other living beings. In the Magga-vibhanga Sutta, it is simply explained as follows:

> *And what is right thought? Being resolved on renunciation, on freedom from ill will, on harmlessness: This is called right thought.*

Ethical Conduct (Sila-Sila)

The "ethical conduct" (Sila) subdivision of the Noble Eightfold Path is constituted by those elements that are driven by and ultimately conducive to the Buddhist idea of karuga, which is generally translated as compassion and somewhat akin to the Christian notion of agape, or "unconditional love". This aspect of the Noble Eightfold Path is the most outward-oriented aspect of the Noble Eightfold Path insofar as it deals directly with a Buddhist practitioner's relationship with other members of his or her society.

Right Speech

Right speech (samyag-vac, samma-vaca), as the name implies, deals with the way in which a Buddhist practitioner would best make use of his or her words. In the Magga-vibhanga Sutta, this aspect of the Noble Eightfold Path is explained as follows:

> *And what is right speech? Abstaining from lying, abstaining from divisive speech, abstaining from abusive speech, abstaining from idle chatter: This, monks, is called right speech.*

Walpola Rahula glosses this by stating that not engaging in such "forms of wrong and harmful speech" ultimately means that "one naturally has to speak the truth, has to use words that are friendly and benevolent, pleasant and gentle, meaningful and useful".

Right Action

Right action (samyak-karmanta, samma-kammanta) can also be translated as "right conduct" and, as the name implies, deals with the proper way in which a Buddhist practitioner would act in his or her daily life. In the Magga-vibhanga Sutta, this aspect of the Noble Eightfold Path is explained as follows:

> *And what, monks, is right action? Abstaining from taking life, abstaining from stealing, abstaining from unchastity: This, monks, is called right action.*

Together with the idea of ahimsa and right speech, right action constitutes the Five Precepts (Sanskrit: pancasila, Pali: pancasila), which form the fundamental ethical code undertaken by lay followers of Buddhism and which are as follows:

1. To refrain from destroying living beings.
2. To refrain from stealing.
3. To refrain from sexual misconduct (adultery, rape, etc.).
4. To refrain from false speech (lying).
5. To refrain from intoxicants which lead to heedlessness.

Right Livelihood

Right livelihood (samyag-ajiva, samma-ajiva) is based around the concept of ahimsa, or harmlessness and essentially states that Buddhist practitioners ought not to engage in trades or occupations which, either directly or indirectly, result in harm to other living beings. Such occupations include "trading in arms and lethal weapons, intoxicating drinks, poisons, killing animals, [and] cheating", among others. "Business in human beings"-such as slave trading and prostitution-is also forbidden, as are several other dishonest means of gaining wealth, such as "scheming, persuading, hinting, belittling, [and] pursuing gain with gain".

Mental Development (Samadhi)

The "mental development" subdivision of the Noble Eightfold Path is constituted by those elements that deal with how a Buddhist practitioner can best go about shaping his or her outlook towards the world.

Right Effort

Right effort (samyag-vyayama, samma-vayama) can also be translated as "right endeavour" and involves the Buddhist practitioner's continuous effort to, essentially, keep his or her mind free of thoughts that might impair his or her ability to realize or put into practice the other elements of the Noble Eightfold Path; for example, wishing ill towards another living being would contradict the injunction-contained in the "Right thought" element-to have good will towards others and the "Right effort" element refers to the process of attempting to root out such an ill wish and replace it with a good wish. The Buddhist monk Ajahn Chah, of the Thai forest tradition of Theravada Buddhism, described right effort as follows:

> *Proper effort is not the effort to make something particular happen. It is the effort to be aware and awake in each moment, the effort to overcome laziness and defilement, the effort to make each activity of our day meditation.*

By making right effort, a Buddhist practitioner is considered to be engaging in an effort that is wholesome in terms of karma; that is, in terms of that effort's ultimate consequences to the practitioner.

Right Mindfulness

Right mindfulness, also translated as "right memory", together with right concentration, is concerned broadly with the practice of Buddhist meditation. Roughly speaking, "mindfulness" refers to the practice of keeping the mind alert to phenomena as they are affecting the body and mind. In the Magga-vibhanga Sutta, this aspect of the Noble Eightfold Path is explained as follows:

And what, monks, is right mindfulness?

(i) There is the case where a monk remains focused on (his/her) body in and of itself... ardent, aware and mindful... having already put aside worldly desire and aversion.

(ii) (He/she) remains focused on feelings in and of themselves... ardent, aware and mindful... having already put aside worldly desire and aversion.

(iii) (He/she) remains focused on the mind in and of itself... ardent, aware and mindful... having already put aside worldly desire and aversion.

(iv) (He/she) remains focused on mental qualities in and of themselves... ardent, aware and mindful... having already put aside worldly desire and aversion.

This, monks, is called right mindfulness.

Bhikkhu Bodhi, a monk of the Theravadin tradition, further glosses the concept of mindfulness as follows:

The mind is deliberately kept at the level of bare attention, a detached observation of what is happening within us and around us in the present moment. In the practice of right mindfulness the mind is trained to remain in the present, open, quiet and alert, contemplating the present event. All judgments and interpretations have to be suspended, or if they occur, just registered and dropped.

Right Concentration

Right concentration (samyak-samadhi, samma-samadhi), together with right mindfulness, is concerned broadly with the practice of Buddhist meditation.

And what, monks, is right concentration?

(i) Quite withdrawn from sensuality, withdrawn from unwholesome states, a monk enters in the first jhana: rapture and pleasure born from detachment, accompanied by movement of the mind onto the object and retention of the mind on the object.

(ii) With the stilling of directed thought and evaluation, (he/she) enters and remains in the second jhana: rapture and pleasure born of concentration; fixed single-pointed awareness free from movement of the mind onto the object and retention of the mind on the object; assurance.

(iii) With the fading of rapture, (he/she) remains in equanimity, mindful and fully aware and physically sensitive of pleasure. (He/She) enters and remains in the third jhana which the Noble Ones declare to be "Equanimous and mindful, (he/she) has a pleasurable abiding."

(iv) With the abandoning of pleasure and pain...as with the earlier disappearance of elation and distress...(he/she) enters and remains in the fourth jhana: purity of equanimity and mindfulness, neither in pleasure nor in pain.

This, monks, is called right concentration.

The Ninth and Tenth Elements

In the Great Forty Sutra (Mahacattarisaka Sutta), which appears in the Pali Canon, the Buddha explains that cultivation of the Eightfold Path leads to the development of two further stages once enlightenment has been reached.

These also fall under the category of panna and are Right Knowledge (sammanana) and Right Liberation (or Right Release; sammavimutti). Some consider Right Association as an implicit ninth aspect of the Path.

The Noble Eightfold Path and Cognitive Psychology

From the standpoint of modern cognitive psychology, the Noble Eightfold Path can be seen as rooted in what is called cognitive dissonance, which is the perception of incompatibility between two cognitions. In the essay "Buddhism Meets Western Science", Gay Watson explains this dissonance as it relates to Buddhist teaching:

> *Buddhism has always been concerned with feelings, emotions, sensations and cognition. The Buddha points both to cognitive and emotional causes of suffering. The emotional cause is desire and its negative opposite, aversion. The cognitive cause is ignorance of the way things truly occur, or of three marks of existence: that all things are unsatisfactory, impermanent and without essential self.*

The Noble Eightfold Path is, from this psychological viewpoint, an attempt to resolve this dissonance by changing patterns of thought and behaviour. It is for this reason that the first element of the path is right understanding, which is how one's mind views the world. Under the wisdom (panna) subdivision of the Noble Eightfold Path, this worldview is intimately connected with the second element, right thought, which concerns the patterns of thought and intention that controls one's actions. These elements can be seen at work, for example, in the opening verses of the Dhammapada:

> *Preceded by perception are mental states,*
> *For them is perception supreme,*
> *From perception have they sprung.*
> *If, with perception polluted, one speaks or acts,*
> *Thence suffering follows*
> *As a wheel the draught ox's foot.*
> *Preceded by perception are mental states,*
> *For them is perception supreme,*

From perception have they sprung.

If, with tranquil perception, one speaks or acts,

Thence ease follows

As a shadow that never departs.

Thus, by wilfully altering one's distorted worldview-as well as the behaviours stemming from that worldview-and bringing out "tranquil perception" in the place of "perception polluted", one is enabled to potentially escape from suffering and develop one's mind. Watson points this out from a psychological standpoint:

THE FIVE PRECEPTS

The five precepts constitute the basic Buddhist code of ethics, undertaken by lay followers of the Buddha Gautama in the Theravadin tradition.

The laity undertake to follow these training rules at the same time as they become Buddhists, taking refuge in the Triple Gem: In the Buddha (teacher), in the Dharma (teaching) and thirdly in the Sangha (community of monks and nuns). A lay practitioner who has undertaken the precepts is called an Upasaka.

The Buddha is said to have taught the five precepts out of compassion, not out of any desire to control his followers and so they are to be undertaken voluntarily rather than as commandments from a god. They are to be seen as guidelines to how one who is awakened lives, not as mere moral injunctions imposed from outside and to be obeyed literally at all times. The Buddha said that undertaking the precepts is a gift to oneself and others. He also described the rewards of following the precepts and the bad consequences of breaking the precepts.

The following are the five precepts rendered in English and then Pali.

1. I undertake the precept to refrain from taking the life (killing) of living beings.

   Panatipata veramani sikkhapadam samadiyami

2. I undertake the precept to refrain from stealing.

   Adinnadana veramani sikkhapadam samadiyami

3. I undertake the precept to refrain from sexual misconduct (adultery, rape, etc.).

   Kamesu micchacara veramani sikkhapadam samadiyami

4. I undertake the precept to refrain from false speech (lying).

   Musavada veramani sikkhapadam samadiyami

5. I undertake the precept to refrain from intoxicants which lead to heedlessness.

   Sura meraya majja pamadatthana veramani sikkhapadam samadiyami

Chinese Version of Five Precepts

The Chinese version as found in the Supplement to the Canon hardly differs:

1. As the Buddha refrained from killing until the end of his life, so I too will refrain from killing until the end of my life.
2. As the Buddha refrained from stealing until the end of his life, so I too will refrain from stealing until the end of my life.
3. As the Buddha refrained from sexual misconduct until the end of his life, so I too will refrain from sexual misconduct until the end of my life.
4. As the Buddha refrained from false speech until the end of his life, so I too will refrain from false speech until the end of my life.
5. As the Buddha refrained from alcohol until the end of his life, so I too will refrain from alcohol until the end of my life.

4

BUDDHIST MONASTERIES IN WORLD

MONASTERIES IN RUSSIA

Datsan

Datsan is the term used for Buddhist university monasteries in the Tibetan tradition of Gelukpa located throughout Russia, but concentrated in Eastern Siberia. As a rule, in a datsan there are two departments-philosophical and medical. Sometimes to them is added the department of the tantric practices where the monks studied only after the finishing education of the philosophical department. In pre-20th century Russia, datsans traditionally existed only in Buryatia and Transbaikalia.

Datsans were officially acknowledged in the Imperial Russia in 1734. By statute of 1853 were recognized 34 datsans: two in the Irkutsk governorate and others in Zabaykalsky Governorate. The first datsan in Europe was Gunzechoyney datsan. It was built in St. Petersburg between 1903 and 1913 and started to operate on February 21, 1913.

Between 1927 and 1938 all 47 datsans, existed in Buryatia and Transbaikalia were closed or destroyed. In 1945 Ivolginsky datsan was opened, several years later Aginsky datsan resume operations. The following ten datsans were not opend until 1991.

List of Datsans in Russia

- Khambyn Khure datsan in Ulan-Ude
- Aginsky datsan in Aginskoye
- Kurumkansky datsan in Kurumkan
- Sartuul Gegetuy datsan in Gegetuy
- Egituysky datsan in Egituy
- Sanaginsky datsan in Sanaga
- Ivolginsky datsan in Verkhnyaya Ivolga
- Kizhinginsky datsan in Kizhinga
- Baldan Breybun datsan in Murochi
- Tugnuysky datsan in Mukhorshibir
- Okinsky datsan in Orlik
- Tamchinsky datsan in Gusinoozyorsk
- Kyrensky datsan in Kyren
- Khoymorsky datsan in Arshan
- Ugdansky datsan
- Ust-Ordynsky datsan in Ust-Ordynsky
- Aninsky datsan in Ana
- Chesansky datsan in Chesan
- Tsugolsky datsan in Tsugol
- Gunzechoyney datsan in Saint Petersburg

Ivolginsky Datsan

Ivolginsky datsan is the Buddhist Temple located in Buryatia 23 km from Ulan Ude, near Verkhnyaya Ivolga village.

History: The datsan was opened in 1945 as the only Buddhist spiritual centre of USSR. In the course of time the little "Khambin's sume" changed into the Monastic centre with a residence of Pandido Khambo lama, the leader of all Russian Lamas.

Buddhist Centre: It was just here located the residence of the Central Spiritual Buddhist Board of the Soviet Union (Buddhist Traditional Sangkha of Russia since 1995) and

Pandido Khambo lama-head of Buddhist church. Spiritual activity of the datsan is manifested in temple rites, medical practice, Buddhist education traditional system. Buddhist university "Dashi Choinkhorling" was opened in 1991 attached to the datsan.

Treasures of Culture: Wonderful samples of old Buryat art-picturesque thangkas, sculptures, ritual subjects are gathered and preserved in the Ivolginsky datsan. One of the monastery's treasures is a rare collection of old Buddhist manuscripts written in Tibetan language on natural silk and a greenhouse with a holly Bodskhva tree. Being a cultural and religion monument the Datsan is protected by the State. The Datsan Centre consists of such temples as Sockshin-gugan, Maidrin-sume, Devazhin and Sackhjusan-sume. There are also a library, hotel, the philosophic faculty-Choyra, building of the Buddhistic University-Dashy Choinhorlin, museum of monuments of Buryat art, sacred tumbs-suburgans, some service buildings and houses for lamas there.

Itigelov: In 1927, the 12th Pandito Hambo Lama of the Ivolginsky Datsan, Dashi-Dorzho Itigelov, told his students and fellow monks to bury his body after his death and to check on it again in 30 years. According to the story, Itigelov then sat in the lotus position, began chanting the prayer of death and died, mid-meditation. The monks followed Itigilov's directions, but when they exhumed his body 30 years later, they were amazed to find none of the usual signs of decay and decomposition. On the contrary, Itigilov looked as if he had been dead only a few hours, rather than three decades. Fearful of the Soviet response to their "miracle", the monks reburied Itigilov's body in an unmarked grave.

Itigelov's story was not forgotten over the years and on 11 September of 2002 the body was finally exhumed and transferred to Ivolginsky Datsan where it was closely examined by monks and, which is now more important, by scientists and pathologists. The official statement was issued about the body-very well preserved, without any signs of decay, whole muscles and inner tissue, soft joints and skin. The interesting thing is that the body was never embalmed or mummified.

TIBETAN BUDDHIST MONASTERIES

Ani Tsankhung Nunnery

Ani Tsankhung Monastery is a Buddhist nunnery in Lhasa the administrative centre of Tibet. It was built in the 7th century by Songsten Gampo who used its meditation chamber.

The monastery is a yellow building which lies on the street parallel and north of Chingdol Dong Lu in Lhasa.

Since the 12th century the monastery has been used chiefly by Buddhist nuns.

The nunnery's main hall contains a beautiful image of Chenrezi, the multi-armed bodhisattva of Compassion. The sacred meditation chamber lies behind it.

An air of quiet serenity pervades the ancient place with its flower bushes and spotless compound and is one of the quieter tourist locations in the Tibetan capital.

Ani Tsankhung Nunnery

Ani Tsankhung Monastery is a Buddhist nunnery in Lhasa the administrative centre of Tibet. It was built in the 7th century by Songsten Gampo who used its meditation chamber.

The monastery is a yellow building which lies on the street parallel and north of Chingdol Dong Lu in Lhasa.

Since the 12th century the monastery has been used chiefly by Buddhist nuns.

The nunnery's main hall contains a beautiful image of Chenrezi, the multi-armed bodhisattva of Compassion. The sacred meditation chamber lies behind it.

An air of quiet serenity pervades the ancient place with its flower bushes and spotless compound and is one of the quieter tourist locations in the Tibetan capital.

Barkhor

The Barkhor is an area of narrow streets and a public square located around Jokhang Temple in the Lhasa, Tibet. Other nearby small monasteries include Muru Ningba Monastery.

Buchasergyi Lakang Monastery

Buchasergyi Lakang Monastery is a Buddhist temple that was built by King Songsten Gampo near the town of Nyingchi in eastern Tibet, China. The monastery was built in the eight century by the great Tibetan King to apparently subdue the great she-demon. Only ruins remain at the site.

Changzhu Temple

Changzhu Temple is an ancient Buddhist monastery located in Changzhu village 5km south of Tsedang on the road to Yumbi Lakang in Tibet. Very little remains of the temple which was thought to have been founded in the 7th century, during the reign of King Songtsen Gampo.

The original temple was made from wood and thatch but in the 14th century it was rebuilt and enlargened and turned into a monastery that supported 300 monks. Changzhu monastery contained numerous halls including a Great Hall which closely resembled that of the Jokhang Temple in Lhasa. The hall was famous for its grand bell and sublime statuary. In the forecourt of the temple the immense pillars and massive beams of the 14th century entrance can still be seen and one small temple still remains in the inner courtyard. Its centrepiece is a splendid old banner embroidered in almost 30,000 pearls representing Chenrezi in repose. Restored in the 1980s, Changzhu Temple is now a repository for ancient religious objects of value that have been found throughout Tibet.

Drepung Monastery

Drepung Monastery is one of the "great three" Gelukpa university monasteries of Tibet. The other two are Ganden and

Sera. Drepung is the largest of all Tibetan monasteries and indeed at its peak was the largest monastery of any religion in the world. It was founded in 1416 by Jamyang Chojey, a direct disciple of Je Tsongkhapa, the founder of the Gelukpa school. It is located on the Gambo Utse mountain, 5 kilometres from the western suburb of Lhasa. At its largest, before the Chinese invasion of Tibet in 1959, the monastery housed fifteen thousand celibate monks. It was known for the high standards of its academic study and was called the "Nalanda" of Tibet, a reference to the great Buddhist monastic university of Nalanda.

Drepung is divided into what are known as the seven great colleges-Gomang (sGo-mang), Loseling (Blo-gsal gling), Deyang (bDe-dbyangs), Shagkor (Shag-skor), Gyelwa (rGyal-ba) or Tosamling (Thos-bsam gling), Dulwa ('Dul-ba) and Ngagpa (sNgags-pa).

Today the population at the monastery located in Tibet is much smaller with merely a few hundred monks, due to population capping enforced by the Chinese government. However the institution has continued its tradition in exile within South India, relocated to land in Karnataka given to the Tibetan community in exile by Prime Minister Nehru. The monastery in India today houses over five thousand celibate monks, with around 3,000 at Drepung Loseling and some 2,000 at Drepung Gomang. Hundreds of new monks are admitted each year, many of them refugees from Tibet.

Drigung Monastery

Drigung Monastery is a notable monastery in Tibet, known for performing sky burials.

The monastery is named after its location in a valley about 150 km east from Lhasa, in Drigung district and is the mother monastery of the Drigung Kagyu (Drikung Kargyu) tradition.

It was founded in 1179 by the founder of that tradition, Drigung Kyobpa Jigten-gonpo-rinchenpel. The tradition emphasizes on its founders tantric meditation and Phowa practices.

After destructions by the Chinese, after 1959, reconstruction works began in 1980. Drigung Kagyu traditions are nowadays also kept at the Jangchubling Drikung Kargyu Institute at Dehra Dun, Uttar Pradesh, India, founded in 1985.

Dzogchen Monastery

Dzogchen Monastery is one of the six great monasteries of the Nyingma tradition, the original Buddhist tradition in Tibet. It is located in Eastern Tibet in the Chinese province of Sichuan.

It is the main monastery for over three hundred branch monasteries in the Kham, Amdo and Central regions of Tibet. Since the early eighties the monastery has been undergoing reconstruction and it is currently home to around two hundred and fifty monks. About one kilometre from Dzogchen Monastery is the prestigious Buddhist University of Dzogchen Shira Sing. It is one of the main centres of learning in Tibet and enjoys a reputation for scholarly excellence. The university is famous in Tibet and world-wide for the standard of education it provides and students come from all over Tibet to study at Shira Sing University. Pema Tung, or the Lotus Ground, is a newly built retreat centre and temple complex situated deep in the Dzogchen valley. The centre is dedicated to the teaching and practice of the Dzogchen tradition and is a natural haven for peaceful reflection and meditation.

Ganden Monastery

Ganden Monastery is one of the 'great three' Gelukpa university monasteries of Tibet, located on Wangbur Mountain, Tagtse County, 47 kilometres from Lhasa. The other two are Sera Monastery and Drepung Monastery. Being the furthest from Lhasa of the three university monasteries, Ganden traditionally had a smaller population with some 6,000 monks in the early 20th century. However, it was the original monastery of the Geluk order, founded by Tsongkhapa himself in 1409 and traditionally considered to be the seat of Geluk administrative and political power. The Ganden Tripa or 'throne-holder of Ganden' is the head of the Gelukpa school (and not the Dalai Lama as is widely misunderstood).

Ganden Monastery consisted of two colleges, Jangtse and Shartse, meaning North Peak and East Peak respectively. The monastery was completely destroyed following the Chinese invasion of Tibet and since the 1980s, a small part is being re-built and in use. Ganden has been re-established on a much larger scale in Karnataka, India by the Tibetan population in exile.

Jokhang

The Jokhang, also called the Jokhang Temple or the Jokhang Monastery, is a famous Buddhist temple located on Barkhor Square in Lhasa, Tibet. Along with the Potala Palace, it is probably the most popular tourist attraction in Lhasa. It is part of the UNESCO World Heritage Site "Historic Ensemble of the Potala Palace" and a spiritual centre of Lhasa.

Jokhang temple was constructed by King Songtsen Gampo starting in the year 639. This temple has remained a centre of Buddhist pilgrimage for centuries. In the past several centuries the temple complex was expanded and now covers an area of about 25,000 sq. metres. Jokhang temple is a four-story construction, with roofs covered with gilded bronze tiles. The architectural style is based on the Indian vihara design and was later extended resulting in a blend of Indian, Nepalese and Tang Dynasty styles. The rooftop statues of two golden deer flanking a Dharma wheel is iconic.

Jokhang temple complex has several decorated shrines and rooms. The main hall of the temple houses the Jowo Shakyamuni Buddha statue, perhaps the single most venerated object in Tibetan Buddhism. There are also statues of King Songtsan Gambo and his two famous foreign brides, Princess Wen Cheng (daughter of Emperor Taizong of Tang China) and Princess Bhrikuti of Nepal.

Menri Monastery

The Menri Monastery is a Buddhist monastery in Tibet. It was established in 1405 by Nyammey Sherab-gyeltsen (1356-1416) and became the main Bon monastery in Tibet.

Muru Ningba Monastery

Muru Ningba Monastery is a small Buddhist monastery located between the larger monasteries of Jokhang and Barkhor in the holy city of Lhasa, Tibet.

Namgyal Monastery

Namgyal Monastery is any of several Tibetan Buddhist institutions associated with the Dalai Lama(s).

(1) The monastery (dratsang) historically housed within the Potala Palace, to which the Dalai Lama traditionally belongs. It was founded by the Third Dalai Lama, Sonam Gyatso, in 1575 and has focused on ritual duties associated with the Dalai Lama in his religious role. Whether the Peoples Republic of China has maintained an institution with this name is unclear.

(2) The same institution in exile in Dharamsala. For several decades its monks have accompanied the fourteenth Dalai Lama overseas and demonstrated such things as lama dances and Tibetan sand painting or sand Mandalas at various venues.

(3) An American branch of the above, founded 1992 in Ithaca, New York. Its several monks (rotated in and out from Dharamsala) teach a several-year curriculum in "sutra and tantra," including Tibetan language, to a clientele consisting predominantly of Western dharma students. In addition it sponsors various lectures, short courses and retreats. Its full name is "Namgyal Monastery Institute of Buddhist Studies." Also one third of Nirvana lead singer Kurt Cobains ashes were scattered here.

Narthang Monastery

Narthang Monastery is a monastery 15km west of Shigatse in Tibet. Founded in 1153 by one of the disciples of Atisha, Nathang was the fourth great monastery of Tsang with Shalu Monastery, Sakya and Tashilhunpo. Narthang was first famous for its scriptual teaching and monastic discipline. After the fourteenth century it gained great eminence as the oldest of Tibet's three great printing centres (the other being the Potala and the Derge).

The Fifth Panchen Lama took control of the monastery and it continued printing the Buddhist scriptures the Kangyur and the Tengyur up until 1959. Narrthang's five main buildings and large chanting hall were razed to the ground by the Chinese in 1966. They had contained priceless 14th century murals possibly painted by the artist scholars of nearby Shalu Monastery. Today only the mud-brick foundations can be discerned although parts of the Mongolian styled high-fortress walls are still standing.

Palcho Monastery

The Palcho Monastery or Pelkor Chode Monastery is the main monastery in Gyantse, Tibet. It is most notable for its Kumbum, which has 108 chapels in its four floors. The monastery was founded in 1418 by the first Panchen Reldrup. In the early 20th century, the town and monastery were attacked by British soldiers and bullet holes remain in the monastery to this day.

Pyenzhangling Monastery

Pyenzhangling Monastery is a small Tibetan Buddhist monastery in a tiny village called Zhonggang, Tibet that is consecrated to the eleventh century Tibetan legend, Milarepa. It is built around the cave where he once lived.

Ralung Monastery

Ralung Monastery, located in the Tsang region of western Tibet, is the traditional seat of the Drukpa Kagyu order of

Tibetan Buddhism. It was founded in 1180 by Tsangpa Gyare who was the First Gyalwang Drukpa and the founder of the Drukpa order.

The monastery is located in present-day Gyantse county several kilometres south of the road connecting Nakartse and Lungmar, immediately north of the Gasa district of Bhutan. In previous times, trade could be conducted across the Yak La pass across the high Himalayas, extending the influence of Ralung to the south.

The monastery is surrounded by the towering peaks and glacier fields of Gyetong Soksum (6,244m), Jangzang Lhamo (6,324m) and Nojin Gangzang (7,191m). From the beginning the location was recognized as especially auspicious:

> *"The eight auspicious symbols adorned the surrounding: The mountain in front of the monastery appeared in the form of a white conch turning clock-wise; the peak of Rala pass appeared like a precious open parasol; the peak behind Pokya appeared like a brimming vase; the Tsenchu peak appeared like a victory banner hoisted high; the Yangon hill appeared like a pair of golden fish; the ground at Gormo appeared like a golden wheel; the hill in the direction of Penthang appeared like an open lotus stem with the twin streams appearing like two birds facing each other; and Gyamo meadow appeared like an auspicious knot."*

The founder of Bhutan, the first Shabdrung, Ngawang Namgyel, was the 18th abbott of Ralung monastery. In 1616 he fled Tibet when his recognition as the reincarnation of renowned scholar Pema Karpo was challenged by the governor of Tsang province. Ngawang Namgyel proved to be a worthy incarnation of Pema Karpo, as he far surpassed the accomplishments of his tormentors by unifying the warring valleys of Bhutan, fending off attacks from Tibet, forming a national identity and establishing a Drukpa theocracy that continues to this day in modified form as the Royal Government of Bhutan.

Other names for Ralung monastery include Shedrub Chokhar Ling Gompa (the original name), Druk Ralung and Ralung Gompa.

Ramoche Temple

Ramoche Temple is a Buddhist monastery situated in the northwest of the Tibetan capital of Lhasa, covering a total area of 4000 square metres (one acre). This temple is one of the key cultural relic protection sites of the Tibet Autonomous Region as well as a popular attraction in Lhasa.

The original building complex has a strong Tang architecture influence, for it was first built by Han Chinese architects in the middle of the 7th century (during the Tang Dynasty). Han Princess Wencheng took charge of this project and ordered the temple be erected facing east to show her homesickness.

Erroneously referred to as Little Jokhang it stands in the northern older part of the holy city and originally housed Wen Cheng's statue of Sakyamuni, now the Holy of Holies of Jokhang Monastery. In the 8th century an exchange was made and a Nepalese Chizun princess's small bronze statue of Sakyamuni aged eight was enshrined at Ramoche instead, brought by the Wencheng Princess from the capital Chang'an during the Tang Dynasty. As one of the precious cultural relics of Tibet, the statue is now placed in Jokhang Temple (Da Zhao Si), 500 metres (0.31mile) south of Ramoche Monastery.

The temple was gutted and partially destroyed in the 1960s and the bronze statue disappeared. Years later it was found and is now housed in the Ramoche Temple which was restored in the 1986.

Following the large restoration of 1986, the main building in the temple now has three stories. The first story includes an atrium, a scripture hall and a Buddha palace with winding corridors. The third story was the bedroom once reserved for Dalai Lama. Upon entering the main building, one can see the ten pillars holding some of the remaining Tibetan relics such as the encased lotus flowers, coiling cloud, jewellery and particular Tibetan Characters. The golden peak of the temple with the Han-style upturned eave can be seen from any direction in Lhasa city. Needless to say, the temple is a wonderful example of the combination of Han and Tibetan architectural styles.

Nowadays, the temple has become the very place for the Tibetan monks to study the Mi Zong (one of the sects of Buddhism).

Sakya Monastery

Sakya Monastery is an important old Buddhist monastery of the Sakya school 128 kilometres west of Shigatse in the Tibet Autonomous Region of China. Founded in 1071, by the powerful noble family of the Tsang its strong abbots governed Tibet during the whole of the 13th century after the downfall of the kings I.

Its medieval Mongolian architecture is quite different from that of temples in Lhasa and Yarlong. Originally built as a cave into the mountainside, it was funded in 1268 by Kublai Khan to be developed into a new magnificent monastery across the river, a site which remained a secular and religious centre in Tibet for almost a century.

Sera Monastery

Sera Monastery is one of the 'great three' Gelukpa university monasteries of Tibet. The other two are Ganden Monastery and Drepung Monastery

The original Sera monastery is in Lhasa, Tibet.

It was founded in 1414, by Jamchen Chojey (Sakya Yeshe), a disciple of Tsong Khapa.

Like the Drepung and Ganden monasteries, it had three colleges:

- Sera Mey Dratsang, built in 1419
- Sera Jey Dratsang, built in 1435
- Ngagpa Dratsang, built in 1559.

After the Chinese invasion of Tibet and the destruction of the majority of the monasteries in Tibet, Sera monastery was reformed in Bylakuppe, India, near Mysore. Because none of the monks of the Ngagpa Dratsang (Tantric College) survived the invasion, only the Sera Mey College and Sera Jey College were reformed in India. Sera Monastery is still standing in Tibet and once again houses some Tibetan Buddhist monks.

Graduates of Sera Jey College who are known in the west include:

- Lama Thubten Yeshe
- Geshe Kelsang Gyatso
- Lama Thubten Zopa Rinpoche

Graduates of Sera Mey college who are known in the west include:

- Pabongka Rinpoche-Author of Liberation in the Palm of Your Hands
- Kyabje Trijang Rinpoche-one of the current Dalai Lama's teachers
- Sermey Khensur Rinpoche Geshe Lobsang Tharchin-former abbot of Sera Mey university in Bylakuppe
- Geshe Michael Roach-founder of Asian Classics Institute, Asian Classics Input Project and Diamond Mountain University and retreat centre.

Shalu Monastery

Shalu Monastery is small monastery 22km south of Shigatse in Tibet. Founded in 1040 by Chetsun Sherab Jungnay, for centuries it was renowned as a centre of scholarly learning and psychic training and its mural paintings were considered to be the most ancient and beautiful in Tibet. Shalu was the first of the major monasteries to be built by noble families of the Tsang Dynasty during Tibet's great revival of Buddhism.

History: In 1329 a devastating earthquake demolished the temple of Shalu but was later rebuilt in 1333 by local lords under the command of the Mongol Emperor of China. The new architectural framework of the monastery was dominated by Mongolian styles with massive inward-sloping walls around a main courtyard and strong woodwork and glazed roof tiles from Qinghai.

At the time of the new establishment in the 1330s Shalu Temple was under the command of the 11th Abbot Buton Rinchen Drub who lived 1290-1364. Buton was not merely a capable administrator but he is still remembered to this very day as a prodigious scholar and writer and is Tibet's most celebrated historian. Buston catalogued all of the Buddhist scriptures at Shalah, some 4,569 religious and philosophical works and formatted them in a logical, coherent order. He wrote the famous book the History of Buddhism in India and Tibet at Shalu which many Tibetan scholars utilize into their study today.

Buton's activity inevitably attracted a great deal of attention to the monastery and brought in other Buddhist interllectuals around Tibet and India to study in the grounds amounting to some 3000 by 1360. After his death the monastery became an important epicentre of esoteric studies and psychic training for centuries.

The avowed purpose of lamas who cultivated paranormal abilities were not to become magicians or miracle workers but to attain philosophical enlightenment, a belief that all earthly phenomena are a state of the mind. Shalu Temple became known throughout the far east for its dedication to these philosophies and its enlightenment of the Buddhist faith.

However by the 1800s the monastery had become less influential and Tibetan scholars chose to study at the Samye monastery which had grown to be one of the most politically powerful in the Tibetan lands by this time. The monastery fell into ruin and little of the original 1330 structure remains, although the outer wall and the main building with damaged roofs still stands and a number of 14th century murals on the outer walls of the temple still follow an iconographic scheme developed by the great Buton himself.

One of the murals is an allegory in which an elephant representing a human soul evolves through many steps and earthly trials to Nirvana becoming progressively white and purer in the cleansing process.

Precise rules are still imbedded into the walls on what the monks should wear, place their robes and how to behave in the central courtyard Deyangshar. Remnants of former Mandala murals are concealed by over 100 Thanka most of which were emboidered in Hangzou in eastern China in the 1920s. Only two chapels of the Shalu temple are open to tourists although funds were allocated in 1995 for roof repair and the eventual restoration of the fine 14th century structure by 2005.

Inside Shalu Monastery: Shalu Lakhang temple is in the centre of the monastery. On the ground floor, in the Tshomchen, Sakyamuni and his disciples are enshrined. The chapels flanking it house the Tanjur and the Kanjur books respectively. Chapels on the roof floor are typical Chinese blue tiled structures, housing Sakyamuni, Buton and Arhats Buddhas. Massive delicate and old murals cover the walls of the monastery, mostly depicting stories from the life of the Buddha. Restoration and preservation are badly needed to protect those arts.

Inside Treasures: Shalu has four treasures which are of notable value. One is a sutra board, which is 700 years old and cannot be reassembled once broken apart, a piece of sutra printed against the board is regarded as good luck. Another is a brass urn, which is usually covered with a piece of red cloth and sealed; the holy water may clean 108 filths and is changed every 12 years. Another is a stone basin, which was the washbasin of the builder Chetsun Sherab Jungnay dating back to 1040; and another is a stone tablet, which was uncovered in the first construction of Shalu. The tablet displays a mantra which reads "om mani Padme Hum" and has four dagoba carved into it.

Shechen Monastery

The Shechen Monastery is one of the primary Nyingma monasteries in Tibet. It was founded in 1695. There are also now Shechen monasteries in Nepal and India.

Surmang Monastery

Surmang Monastery consists of a complex of nine Kagyupa monasteries founded about 600 years ago in Kham, eastern Tibet. It is the seat of the Trungpa tulkus, the line of incarnate lamas that heads Surmang. The present head of the Surmang monasteries is Choseng Trungpa Rinpoche, the XII Trungpa Tulku.

Tashilhunpo

Tashilhunpo Monastery, built in 1447, is a historic and culturally important monastery in Shigatse, Tibet. The monastery is the traditional seat of successive Panchen Lamas, the second highest ranking tulku lineage in the Gelukpa tradition.

Located on a hill in the centre of the city, the full name in Tibetan of the monastery means "all fortune and happiness gathered here" or "heap of glory".

History: This monastery was originally built by Gedun Drub the First Dalai Lama, financed by donations from local nobles. Later Lobsang Chokyi Gyalsten, the Fourth Panchen Lama and the first Panchen Lama to be recognized as such by the rulers of Mongolia, made major expansions to the monastery. Since then all Panchen Lamas have resided at Tashilhunpo and have managed to expand it gradually. Choekyi Gyalpo, the 11th Panchen Lama according to the government of the People's Republic of China, has been enthroned there, while Gedhun Choekyi Nyima, the 11th Panchen Lama recognised by the Dalai Lama, has been held under "protective custody" by the Chinese authorities since 1995.

In 1791 the monastery was attacked and looted by an army of Nepalese Gurkha warriors but were driven out by the Chinese who at the same time strengthened their control, over the temple and Tibet. Tashilhunpo in its prime had over 4,000 monks and had four Tantric colleges each with its own Abbot. After the death of a Panchen Lama, these four abbots led the search for his infant incarnation and one of them always acted as a Prime Minster of Tsang under the control of the Dalai Lama in Lhasa.

In 1960 however the monastery was disbanded by the Chinese army whilst the Panchen Lama was absent although less damage was inflicted on the monastery as on others around Tibet.

During the 1960s many senior lamas and monastics left Tibet and helped re-establish new monasteries in India, Nepal and Bhutan. The late Panchen Lama did not leave Tibet and consequently many of the senior lamas from Tashilhunpo Monastery remained inside Tibet. Therefore, while other monasteries-in-exile have expanded and developed under the guidance of senior lamas, Tashilhunpo has remained at a disadvantage, although in 1972 a new campus of Tashilhunpo Monastery was built by Tibetan exiles at a settlement in Bylakuppe, Karnataka in southern India. Since the early 1980s parts of the Tashilhunpo monastery have been open to the public and it is an important tourist attraction in Tibet today.

Halls of the Tashilhunpo Monastery

Jamba Chyenmu 'The Maitreya Temple': The Maitreya Temple known as (Jambu Chyenmu)) on the west side is the tallest building of the monastery. It was erected in 1914 by the Ninth Panchen Lama to house a gigantic statue of the Maitreya Buddha and is 26.2 metres (86 feet) in height. The staue sits on a splendid lotus throne in the 'European' posture with its hands in the symbolic teaching pose. A single finger of the giant figure is almost 4 feet in length. The statue contains 279kg (614lbs) of gold and 150,000kg (330,000lb) of copper and brass moulded on a solid wooden frame by Tibetan and Nepalese craftsmen. Small versions of the Maitreya are positioned in all four corners of the chamber and the murals on either side of the door show a more active, antic style than any to be seen in Lhasa.

Gudong: The Panchen Lama's Palace: On the east side of the monastery is the old living quarters of the Panchen lama, the Panchen Lama's Palace known as Gudong. Within, a narrow courtyard gives access to the temple containing the Fourth Panchen Lama's tomb. The temple vestibule has very large inscriptions at either end praising his holiness. Inside, the silver and gold stupa tomb rivals any in the Potala Palace in Lhasa for the splendour of its craftsmenship and jewels.

Measuring 11 metres (36ft) in height it contains 85kg (187lb) of gold and countless semi-precious stones. On the left is three statues representing Amitabha, the Buddha of Infinite Light, whom the Panchen Lams are thought to embody. An upper level has a number of long chapels embroidered in silk thangka's that relate the lives and events surrounded the Panchen Lamas. Most were made in Hangzou as indeed many throughout Tibet were during the 1920s. The old living quarters of the Panchen Lama are no longer open to the public but the rooms are more modest and human that any of the rooms at the Potala.

Main Chanting Hall: The main chanting hall contains the throne of the Panchen Lama and two connected chapels. The left-one is devoted to an elaborately ensconced Sakyamuni with eight Bodhisattva robed in bocade. The right hand one is dedicated to Tara the goddess who sanctifies the mountain above and whose image is depicted throughout the temple. A White Tara goddess occupies the centre of the altar with a Jade Green Tara on either side.

Sutra Hall: Sutra Hall is the repository chamber of the monastery containing some 10,000 hand-carved wooden blocks used for printing the Buddhist scriptures. These are all Tibetan translations of the original Sanskrit text. Visitors to the temple can buy coloured prayer flags and Tibetan lunar calendars as souvenirs which are printed in the chamber.

Gyeni Chanting Hall: The Gyeni Chanting Hall is a chanting chamber of the Tashilhunpo Monastery on the south-east side where Tibetan Buddhism is practised. It has a debating garden in its courtyard with many fine trees. The roof of the chanting hall has a chapel on the north side where two very tall guardians are formed from its structural columns by the use of masks and ancient armour. Outside it are some extraordinary colourful Buddha murals and animal murals which have emerged from folklore and animism It is situated near the smaller chanting hall of the Ngagang college on the west side.

Ngang College: Ngang College is a smaller chanting chamber of the monastery on the west side of the main path upstairs of the Deyangshar courtyard. A Ngang a morning chanting ceremony with musical instruments usually takes place between the few remaining monks of the temple. Pilgrims may circumambulate the hall but tourists, particularly photographers are asked to be extremely sensitive to the religious atmosphere.

Chuajing Duogang: The Great Courtyard: The great flagstoned courtyard of Tashilhunpo, known as (Chuajing Duogang) has walls which are covered by over 1000 repeated Sakyamuni, with their hands gesturing the five symbolic poses (mudras).

The Great Gallery: The gallery of the monastery surrounds the Deyangshar courtyard and leads to the chapels on the east side housing many hundreds of tiny Buddha statues.

The Roof Chapels: The roof of Tashilhunpo has several bronze-gated chapels located on two-tiered levels. On the north side, above the chapels of the chanting hall is the funerary stupa of the First Dalai Lama, the only one not entombed in Lhasa.

On the east side is a small 'chamber of horrors' chapel. Painted demons, considered now to be defenders of Buddhism betray their origins as the terrifying gods of the old animist Bon faith who only later were absorbed by Buddhism. On the south side is a charming Tara chapel with blue and gold murals on the walls depicting Tibetan history.

Tsurphu Monastery

Tsurphu is a Tibetan Buddhist monastery which served as the traditional seat of the Karmapa. It is located in the Tolung area of Central Tibet in the Dowo Lung valley, 70 km from Lhasa. It is 14000 feet above sea level and built in the middle of the valley facing south, with high mountains surrounding the monastery complex. Tsurphu is a 300m2 complex with walls up to 4 metres thick.

Tsurphu was founded by the first Karmapa, Dusum Khyenpa in 1159 after he visited the site and laid the foundation for an establishment of a seat there by making offerings to the local protectors. In 1189 he revisited the site and founded his main seat there. The monastery grew to hold 1000 monks. It was totally destroyed in 1966 during the Chinese Cultural Revolution and began to be rebuilt in 1980 by the 16th Karmapa, Rangjung Rikpai Dorje. Following the recognition of Urgyen Trinley Dorje by Tai Situpa and the Chinese government, Urgyen Trinley was enthroned at Tsurphu. He resided there until he escaped from Tibet to India in 2000.

Ka-Nying Shedrub Ling

Ka-Nying Shedrub Ling is a Tibetan Buddhist monastery near Boudhinath, on the outskirts of Kathmandu, Nepal. It has ties to both the Nyingma and Kagyu sects.

The Sixteenth Karmapa instructed Kyabje Tulku Urgyen Rinpoche to found a monastery in Nepal. Tulku Urgyen obeyed, taking his wife Kunsang Dechen and two sons, Chokyi Nyima and Chokling Rinpoche. Construction began in 1972 and the monastery was dedicated in 1976. HM King Birendra attended. Tulku Urgyen died that same year, whereupon his son Chokyi

Nyima succeeded him as abbot (his brother becoming "vajra master").

Today the monastery boasts about 180 monks and 108 nuns at an affiliated nunnery, Nagi Gompa (located some distance away).

In 1981 the monastery established the Ranjung Yeshe Institute (or Shedra Institute), a multi-year course in Tibetan language and Buddhist theology designed for Western dharma students. It has since entered into a cooperation agreement with Kathmandu University whereby its students can receive an honours degree (4-year Bachelors) from that institution, with a major in "Buddhist Studies with Himalayan Language." General Description

Ka-Nying Shedrub Ling Monastery

Ka-Nying Shedrub Ling Monastery is a Tibetan Buddhist monastery founded by Tulku Urgyen Rinpoche at the great stupa of Boudhanath in Nepal. The abbot and vajra master are Chokyi Nyima Rinpoche and Chokling Rinpoche, respectively.

Kagyu Samye Ling Monastery and Tibetan Centre

Kagyu Samye Ling Monastery and Tibetan Centre is a Tibetan Buddhist complex associated with the Kagyu school located at Eskdalemuir, near Langholm, Dumfries and Galloway, Scotland.

History: The building that now houses Samye Ling was originally a hunting lodge. The Johnstone House Contemplative Community was founded there by a Canadian Theravada monk named Anandabodhi. When the community declined, Anadabodhi returned to Canada; he was subsequently ordained in the Tibetan Mahayana tradition and enthroned as Namgyal Rinpoche by the 16th Gyalwa Karmapa.

In 1967, the Theravadins gave the centre to two Tibetan lamas and refugees named Chogyam Trungpa Rinpoche and Akong Rinpoche, who renamed it Samye Ling. Samye refers to the first Buddhist monastic university in Tibet, while Ling means a large house with grounds. Trungpa Rinpoche later left and founded further centres in the United States and elsewhere.

The centre flourished and developed under the guidance of Akong Rinpoche and his brother Lama Yeshe Losal, who served as Abbot and Retreat Master, respectively. The centre includes the first Tibetan temple to be constructed in Europe, a large stupa and accommodation for those taking a range of courses on Buddhism, meditation, spiritual development and art.

Preservation of Tibetan Art and Crafts: Under the guidance of the celebrated Tibetan artist Sherab Palden Beru, Samye Ling has also become a centre for the creation, repair and restoration of thangkas, principally in the Karma Gadri style. Since the 1970s Sherab has trained a number of western practitioners in the highly specialised techniques needed to create thangkas. The temple walls are decorated with many exquisite examples of the work of both Sherab Palden Beru and his western pupils.

Traditional deity and monumental sculpture and the creation of prayer-wheels are also carried out at the centre under the direction of resident and visiting Tibetan experts. The grounds of the centre feature many examples of their work, such as a statue of Nagarjuna.

Kopan Monastery

Kopan Monastery is a Tibetan Buddhist monastery near Boudhanath, on the outskirts of Kathmandu, Nepal. It was founded by Lamas Thubten Yeshe and Thubten Zopa Rinpoche, who bought the property from Nepal's royal astrologer in 1969. Its name comes from the name of the hill on which it was built. The name Kopan Monastery is generally used to refer to two separate institutions-the Monastery itself on top of Kopan hill and the Khachoe Ghakyi Ling Nunnery which is located nearby.

Though monastic life at Kopan resembles that of other Tibetan monasteries in many ways, it has become especially famous for teaching Buddhism to visiting Western foreigners.

The first of what would become annual month-long (November-December) meditation courses was held in 1971, although Lama Yeshe and Lama Zopa had been teaching Westerners since at least 1965. These courses generally combine traditional Lam Rim teachings with informal discussion, several periods of guided meditation and a vegetarian diet.

Over the decades Kopan Monastery has become somewhat less important in the Foundation for the Preservation of the Mahayana Tradition, the organization of which it now forms part (though predating it by several years), as the FPMT has grown to encompass centres in numerous other countries. For example, Kopan no longer serves as its administrative headquarters. At the same time, various building projects have transformed Kopan's appearance. The gold roofs of its central temple have come to be used as an orienting landmark by pilots landing at Kathmandu's airport.

Kopan Monastery is a Tibetan Buddhist monastery near Boudhanath, on the outskirts of Kathmandu, Nepal. It was founded by Lamas Thubten Yeshe and Thubten Zopa Rinpoche, who bought the property from Nepal's royal astrologer in 1969. Its name comes from the name of the hill on which it was built.

Labrang Monastery

Labrang Monastery is one of the six great monasteries of the Geluk (Yellow Hat) school of Tibetan Buddhism, of which the Dalai Lama is a member. Labrang is located in Xiahe County in Gansu province and also in the traditional Tibetan province of Amdo. Labrang Monastery is home to the largest number of monks outside of Tibet Autonomous Region. Xiahe is located about 8 hours from the city of Lanzhou, the capital of Gansu.

Labrang Monastery is located in the town of Xiahe, which belongs to the Gannan Tibetan Autonomous Prefecture. The town is reflection of the different minorities that can be found in China, such as Tibetans about 70% of the population), Hui Chinese (20%) and Han Chinese (10%).

Although the region is mostly rural and pastoral (including yak and other animal rearing), tourism is growing rapidly mainly due to the monastery. The monastery was founded in 1709 by the first Jamyang Zhaypa, Ngawang Tsondru. It is Tibetan Buddhism's most important monastery town outside the Tibetan Autonomous Region.

The monastery complex dominates the northern village. The white walls and golden roofs feature a blend of Tibetan and Han architectural styles. The monastery contains 18 halls, six institutes of learning, a golden stupa, a sutra debate and nearly 60,000 sutras. There are more than 2000 monks in residence. It has a Buddhist museum with a large collection of Buddha statues, sutras and murals. In addition, a large amount of Tibetan language books, including history is available for purchase, together with medicines, calendars, music and art objects.

The monastery today is an important place for Buddhist ceremonies and activities. From 4 to 17 January and 26 June to 15 July (these dates may change according to the lunar calendar), the great Buddhist ceremony will be held with Buddha-unfolding, sutra enchanting, praying, sutra debates, etc.

The monks are extremely friendly to foreigners and used every opportunity to practice their basic English which in most cases is self-taught. Accommodation is easy to find and a great variety of articles and souvenirs are available.

Lamayuru

Lamayuru is a Tibetan Buddhist Gompa in Kargil District, Western Laddakh, situated on the Srinagar-Kargil-Leh road 15km east of the Fatu La pass, at a height of 3510m.

Founded by the Indian scholar Mahasiddhacarya Naropa in the 11th century (alledgedly on the site of a dried-up lake) after spending many years meditating, Lamayuru is the largest and oldest gompa in Laddakh with a population of around 150 permanent monks resident. It has, in the past, housed up to

400 monks, many of which are now based in gompas in surrounding villages. Lamayuru is host to two yearly masked dance festivals, in the second and fifth months of the Tibetan lunar calendar, when all the monks from these surrounding gompas gather together to pray.

Namgyal Monastery

It has been suggested that this article be split into multiple articles accessible from a disambiguation page. (Discuss) Namgyal Monastery is any of several Tibetan Buddhist institutions associated with the Dalai Lama(s).

(1) The monastery (dratsang) historically housed within the Potala Palace, to which the Dalai Lama traditionally belongs. It was founded by the Third Dalai Lama, Sonam Gyatso, in 1575 and has focused on ritual duties associated with the Dalai Lama in his religious role. Whether the Peoples Republic of China has maintained an institution with this name is unclear.

(2) The same institution in exile in Dharamsala. For several decades its monks have accompanied the fourteenth Dalai Lama overseas and demonstrated such things as lama dances and Tibetan sand painting or sand Mandalas at various venues.

(3) An American branch of the above, founded 1992 in Ithaca, New York. Its several monks (rotated in and out from Dharamsala) teach a several-year curriculum in "sutra and tantra," including Tibetan language, to a clientele consisting predominantly of Western dharma students. In addition it sponsors various lectures, short courses and retreats. Its full name is "Namgyal Monastery Institute of Buddhist Studies." Also one third of Nirvana lead singer Kurt Cobains ashes were scattered here.

Rumtek Monastery

Rumtek, also called the Dharmachakra Centre, is a Tibetan Buddhist monastery located in the Indian state of Sikkim near the capital Gangtok. Originally built by the 9th Karmapa Wangchuk Dorje in 1740, Rumtek served as the main seat of the Karma Kagyu lineage in Sikkim for some time. But when the 16th Karmapa arrived in Sikkim in 1959, after fleeing before the Chinese occupation of Tibet, it was in ruins. Despite being offered other sites, the Karmapa decided to rebuild Rumtek. To him, the site possessed many auspicious qualities and was surrounded by the most favourable attributes. For example, flowing streams, mountains behind, a snow range in front and a river below. With the generosity and help of the Sikkim royal family and the Indian government, it has been built by the 16th Karmapa as his main seat in exile.

After four years, construction of the monastery was completed. The sacred items and relics brought out from Tsurphu, the Karmapa's seat in Tibet, were installed. On Tibetan New Year's day (Losar) in 1966 the 16th Karmapa officially inaugurated the new seat called, "The Dharmachakra Centre, a place of erudition and spiritual accomplishment, the seat of the glorious Karmapa."

The monastery is currently the largest in Sikkim. It is home to the community of monks and where they perform the rituals and practices of the Karma Kagyu lineage. A Golden Stupa contains the relics of the 16th Karmapa. Opposite that building is a college, Karma Shri Nalanda Institute for Higher Buddhist Studies.

Rumtek is located 24 km from Gangtok, the capital of the Sikkim, at an altitude of about 1500 m.

Rumtek is currently at the centre of the Karmapa controversy with a lengthy battle being played out in the Indian courts. Two rival organisations, both supporting different candidates for the 17th Karmapa claim stewardship of the monastery and its contents. The two organisations are the Karmapa Charitable Trust (supporting Thaye Dorje) and the Tsurpu Labrang (supporting Urgyen Trinley Dorje). Currently neither Karmapa candidate resides at Rumtek.

Shechen Monastery

The Shechen Monastery is one of the primary Nyingma monasteries in Tibet. It was founded in 1695. There are also now Shechen monasteries in Nepal and India.

Yonghe Temple

The Yonghe Temple, also known as the "Palace of Peace and Harmony Lama Temple", the "Yonghe Lamasery", or-popularly-the "Lama Temple" is a temple and monastery of the Geluk School of Tibetan Buddhism located in the northeastern part of Beijing, China. It is one of the largest and most important Tibetan Buddhist monasteries in the world. The building and the artworks of the temple combine Han Chinese and Tibetan styles.

History: Building work on the Yonghegong Temple started in 1694 during the Qing Dynasty. It originally served as an official residence for court eunuchs. It was then converted into the court of the Prince Yong (Yin Zhen), a son of the Kangxi Emperor and himself the future Yongzheng Emperor. After Yongzheng's ascension to the throne in 1722, half of the building was converted into a lamasery, a monastery for monks of Tibetan Buddhism. The other half remained an imperial palace.

After Yongzheng's death in 1735, his coffin was placed in the temple. The Qianlong Emperor, Yongzheng's successor, gave the temple imperial status signified by having its turquoise tiles replaced with yellow tiles which were reserved for the emperor. Subsequently, the monastery became a residence for large numbers of Tibetan Buddhist monks from Mongolia and Tibet and so the Yonghe Lamasery became the national centre of Lama administration. The temple is said to have survived the Cultural Revolution due to the intervention of Prime Minister Zhou Enlai. It was reopened to the public in 1981.

Architecture and Artworks: The Yonghe Temple is arranged along a north-south central axis, which has a length of 480m. The main gate is at the southern end of this axis.

Along the axis, there are five main halls which are separated by courtyards: the Hall of the Heavenly Kings (Tian Wang Dian or Devaraja Hall), the Hall of Harmony and Peace (Yonghegong), the Hall of Everlasting Protection (Yongyoudian), the Hall of the Wheel of the Law (Falundian) and the Pavilion of Ten Thousand Happinesses (Wanfuge).

The Hall of the Heavenly Kings is the southernmost of the main halls, it served originally as the main entrance to the monastery. In the centre of the hall stands a statue of the Maitreya Buddha, along the walls statues of the four Heavenly Kings are arranged.

The Hall of Harmony and Peace is the main building of the temple. It houses three bronze statues of the Buddhas of the Three Ages, the statue of the Gautama Buddha (Buddha of the Present) is in the centre, it is flanked by the statue of Kasyapa Matanga (Buddha of the Past, right) and the Maitreya Buddha (Buddha of the Future, left).

Along the sides of the hall, the statues of the 18 Arhats are placed. A mural in the hall shows the bodhisattva Avalokitesvara. The Hall of Everlasting Protection was Emperor Yongzheng's living quarters as a prince and the place where his coffin was placed after his death. Today, a statue of the Bhaisajya-guru (healing Buddha) stands in this hall.

The Hall of the Wheel of the Law functions as a place for reading scriptures and conducting religious ceremonies. It contains a large statue of Je Tsongkhapa, founder of the Geluk School.

The hall also contains the Five-Hundred-Arhat-Hill, a carving make of red sandalwood with statues of the arhats made from five different metals (gold, silver, copper, iron and tin). The Pavilion of Ten Thousand Happinesses contains an 18m tall statue of the Maitreya Buddha carved from a single piece of White Sandalwood. The statue is one of three artworks in the Temple which were included in the Guinness Book of Records in 1993.

MONASTERIES IN BHUTAN

Taktshang

Taktshang is the most famous of monasteries in Bhutan. It hangs on a cliff at 3,120 metres (10,200 feet), some 700 metres (2,300 feet) above the bottom of Paro valley. Famous visitors include Ngawang Namgyal in the 17th century and Milarepa. The name means "Tiger's nest", the legend being that Padmasambhava (Guru Rinpoche) flew there on the back of a tiger. The monastery includes seven temples which can all be visited. The monastery suffered several blazes and is a recent restoration. Climbing to the monastery is on foot or mule.

Kurjey Lhakhang

Kurjey Lhakang, also known as Kurjey Monastery, is located in the beautiful Bumthang valley in the Bumthang district of Bhutan. This is the final resting place of the remains of the first three kings of Bhutan. As well, a large tree behind one of the temple buildings is believed to be a terma (Buddhism) that was left there by Padmasambhava.

Tamshing Lhakhang

Tamshing Lhakang (temple) in the Bumthang District of central Bhutan is the most important Nyingmapa temple in Bhutan. The temple and monastery are remarkable for their direct connection to the Bhutanese saint Pema Lingpa. It is now a seat of Lama Sungtrul Rinpoche the current speech incarnation of Pema Lingpa. Tamshing consists of a deteriorating temple and cramped monks quarters. The monastery supports a body of over 95 monks.

History: From an interview of Lopen Kharma, teacher and administrator of Tamshing Lhakang, conducted by Friends of Tamshing in December 2005:

The temple was built by Pema Lingpa himself in 1501.

Before 1960 Tamshing was a privately owned temple (like many other temples in Bhutan). After Pema Lingpa died in the temple at the age of seventy-two in 1521, his descendants took over care of the temple. Gradually, over many years, Tamshing fell into a state of disrepair and neglect. The temple courtyard was used as a granary and local people came less and less, except for special days.

In 1959, when many Tibetans (including the present Dalai Lama) fled their country for fear of being killed quite a few came to the Bumthang region, which is the cradle of Buddhism in Bhutan. In his time, Pema Lingpa received a vision to travel to Tibet where he revealed a treasure hidden by Guru Rinpoche (Padmasambhava) many centuries before. He was given land in the Longti area of the Siti valley and built a temple there which is called Lhalung. This temple was later enlarged by his third (Tibetan) incarnation. Pema Lingpa travelled frequently to Tibet and most of his incarnations were Tibetan.

The 10th incarnation of Pema Lingpa died in Tibet shortly before the Tibetan diaspora. In 1960, a group of three monks from Lhalung monk body headed by Lhalung's second in command, Thinley Kuenchap (d. 1975) came to Tamshing to reestablish the Lhalung monk body at Tamshing.

Lopen Thinley Kuenchap was well known to the exiled Tibetan monks in Bhutan. Hearing of his arrival at Tamshing, many gathered there in late 1960 and established the current monk body. Over time, this group has grown from 10 or 15 monks to over 95.

When the Khudun, Lopen Kharma, came to Tamshing as a young boy in 1980, most of the senior monks from Tibet had passed on, however, Lopen Tseten who came from Tibet to Tamshing as a 10 year old monk in 1960 was still there. Today, Lopen Tseten is the head of the monastery organization and its senior teacher.

The present spiritual head of Tamshing is the 11th incarnation of Pema Lingpa, the Lama Sungtrul Rinpoche (speech incarnation) he was born in the Chumi Valley of Bumthang, Bhutan in 1967.

Tamshing Today: The core missions of Tamshing are teaching the Dharma, performing religious services for the community and educating the young monks under its care. Since Tamshing is not government supported it faces increasing challenges posed by supporting 95 monks while maintaining the ancient physical structures.

Mostly under the age of 15, the monks are either orphans or from very poor families who can't afford to send their children to a state school. As the economy of the country changes and as the culture becomes more outward looking, it is inevitable that some of the old ways of supporting the temples and monasteries, (which are the repositories of traditional wisdom), are being tested. Tamshing has no endowment; no mission to make money, its only mission is to meet the needs of the community. Currently, the monastery runs at a loss.

Tamshing and Bhutanese Dance: Tamshing is the original home of sacred dances that are celebrated at traditional Tsechus (festivals) throughout Bhutan. According to Joseph Houseal, director of Core of Culture Dance Preservation:

"Dance...is the living tradition of their founding identity and the means by which Pema Lingpa sought to teach the world Buddhism-and the treasure he specifically left the Tamshing monks. It is the life of the order, the Buddhist truth they maintain. That is one reason we have focused on Tamshing: their dances were revealed by the most famous Bhutanese saint and Tamshing alone performs the dances correctly..."

SANTACITTARAMA

Santacittarama is the name of the Italian Theravada Buddhist monastery of the Forest in the Ajahn Chah lineage located near Rome. It was established in the 90's by the former Italian Bhikku Ajahn Thannavaro, a disciple of Ajahn Sumedho's, near Latina in the south of Rome.

Later, with the important contribution of the Thai community, a location was found at Poggio Nativo in the beautiful countryside of Sabina and a larger monastery was established with separate buildings for visitors and Kuti's in the wood for resident and visiting Bhikkus. After the disvesting of the previous Abbot, Ven. Ajahn Chandapalo was invited to become the new abbot, a charge hold to the present day.

SHANKH MONASTERY

Shankh Monastery (Shank Khiid; West Monastery) is one of the oldest and most important monasteries in Mongolia, founded in 1647 by Zanabazar. It is located in the Ovorhangay Aimag, Western Mongolia.

SOMAPURA

Somapura Mahavihara was among the best known Buddhist viharas in India. The excavations at Paharpur has been identified with the Somapura Mahavihara, built by the Dharmapala (c 781-821 AD). The Pala rulers were devout Buddhists and they founded a number of viharas in their domain.

The monastery was renovated during the rule of Mahipala I (c 995-1043 AD). The Tibetan text Pag Sam Jon Zang mentions that the same king used to visit Somapura Vihara to offer his homage. Somapura Mahavihara gradually declined and was finally abandoned during the 13th century, when the region was conquered by the Muslims. Many Tibetan monks visited the Somapura during 9th and 12th century AD. Atisha Dipankar Srijnan stayed here for many years and translated the Madhyamaka Ratnapradipa into Tibetan. His spiritual preceptor, Ratnakara Shanti and several other famous scholars like Mahapanditacharya Bodhibhadra Kalamahapada, Viryendra and Karunashrimitra were associated with this vihara.

TAKTSHANG

Taktshang is the most famous of monasteries in Bhutan. It hangs on a cliff at 3,120 metres (10,200 feet), some 700 metres (2,300 feet) above the bottom of Paro valley. Famous visitors include Ngawang Namgyal in the 17th century and Milarepa. The name means "Tiger's nest", the legend being that Padmasambhava (Guru Rinpoche) flew there on the back of a tiger. The monastery includes seven temples which can all be visited. The monastery suffered several blazes and is a recent restoration. Climbing to the monastery is on foot or mule.

THARPA CHOLING MONASTERY

The Tharpa Choling Monastery is a Buddhist monastery near Kalimpong in West Bengal, India. Built atop Tirpai Hill in 1937, the monastery belongs to the Gelukpa sect (Yellow Hat) of Tibetan Buddhism. The monastery has a collection of rare Buddhist manuscripts and thangkas (images of deities on cloth). It also imparts religious training to young Buddhist monks.

UNIFIED BUDDHIST CHURCH

The Unified Buddhist Church (Eglise Bouddhique Unifiee) was founded by Thich Nhat Hanh in France in 1969, during the Vietnam War (not part of the Unified Buddhist Church of Vietnam). The Unified Buddhist Church established Sweet Potatoes Community in 1975 which became the Plum Village monastery, France in 1982, the Dharma Cloud Temple and the Dharma Nectar Temple in 1988 and the Adornment of Loving Kindness Temple in 1995. Thich Nhat Hanh's Sangha (community of practice) in France is usually referred to as the Plum Village Sangha. The Unified Buddhist Church also has a mindfulness practice centre called Intersein in Bavaria, Germany. A sangha of about 150 monks, nuns and resident lay-practitioners live permanently in Plum Village.

The Unified Buddhist Church is the legally recognized governance body for Plum Village in France; for Maple Forest Monastery and Green Mountain Dharma Centre in Vermont; and, since March, 1999, for the Community of Mindful Living, Parallax Press and Deer Park Monastery in California. The

Unified Buddhist Church, Inc. (UBC), a non-profit corporation, was founded in 1998 to officially represent Thich Nhat Hanh and his Sangha in the United States of America. It is a sister organization of Unified Buddhist Church (Eglise Bouddhique Unifiee) founded in France. The UBC in America is represented by Sr. Annabel Laity, Abbess of the Green Mountain Dharma Centre which acts as the headquarters of the Unified Buddhist Church in the U.S.

WA SAU TOI

Wa Sau Toi was a monastery on the sacred mountain Luofushan. It was destroyed in 1949. The Chan (Zen) teacher and Dragon Kung Fu master Tai Yuk was a monk at Wa Sau Toi. Lai Chi, the founder of the Wu Jo An nunnery in Guangzhou, was 35th generation in the Caodong (Japanese: Soto) school of Chan Buddhism from Wa Sau Toi.

WAT FLORIDA DHAMMARAM

Wat Florida Dhammaram is a Buddhist monastery in Kissimmee, Florida, established by Lung-po Chaokhun Phra Tepvaraporn (Im Arindhamo) in the mid-1990s. Over a decade ago, Lung-po visited lay-devotees in Florida and perceived the lack of a Buddhist monastery in the Central Florida area. With approval from the late abbot of Wat Sommanat Vihara, Chaokhun Somdej Phra Wannarat Chop Thitadhammamahathera, he began fund raising in Thailand. In 1993, three monks were sent with Prakrupalad Sunnan (now Chaokhun Phra Vijitrdhammapani, the present abbot) to establish and further the development of Wat Florida Dhammaram.

ZANG DHOK PALRI PHODANG

The Zang Dhok Palri Phodang is a Buddhist monastery in Kalimpong in West Bengal, India. The monastery is located atop Durpin Hill, one of the two hills of the town. It was consecrated in 1976 by the visiting Dalai Lama.

The monastery houses many rare scriptures that were brought into India after the invasion of Tibet in 1959. It also houses the 108 volumes of the Kangyur.

ABHAYAGIRI BUDDHIST MONASTERY

Abhayagiri is the name of a Theravadin Buddhist monastery in Redwood Valley, California. It is located approximately 13 miles north of Ukiah, California.

In Pali, the name means "Fearless Mountain".

The seeds for the monastery's existence were laid in the 1980s when the senior western disciple of Ajahn Chah, Ajahn Sumedho, developed a following through periodic visits to California. The Sanghapala Foundation was set up in 1988, for the purpose of creating a branch monastery of Ajahn Chah's lineage.

The monastery's grounds were deeded to the Sanghapala Foundation by the followers of Venerable Hsuan Hua as he approached his death, a Chinese Mahayana teacher and abbot of the City of Ten Thousand Buddhas located in Talmage, California. Followers of Venerable Hua offered 120 acres of land to the followers of Ajahn Chah, in the mountains of Redwood Valley. It is on this ground that the monastery now sits.

As of December 5, 2006 there are 12 monks in permanent residence: two abbots, two anagarikas (postulants), two samaneras (novices) and six fully ordained bhikkhus. In addition, teachers from locations as diverse as rural Thailand and urban Britain are hosted periodically. The daily schedule, in keeping with the tradition, is very rigorous. Most residents (temporary lay residents and permanent monastics alike) rise well before sunrise, usually no later than 4:30 in the morning. There is a morning puja at 5:00 that lasts an hour and a half, followed by a half hour chore period and a breakfast of oatmeal. Three hours of physical labour follow breakfast, ending at lunch. Following lunch is free time to be used for studying, meditating and/or walking the extensive network of handmade trails that wind about the mountainside. After time for personal practice, at approximately 5:00, evening tea is served, followed occasionally by a Dhamma reading and later by another puja. On Lunar Observance days (which mark the four moon quarters) evening puja lasts until 3:00 the following morning.

Male residents live in kutis, comparatively primitive shacks nestled in the forest, whereas female residents (currently, there are no nuns) live in a house that was donated to the monastery, increasing the property owned by the Sangha.

Currently, a number of large construction projects are underway at the monastery in order to provide more rooms for the laity, extra bathrooms and other necessities. The monastery offers a wide variety of books and audio CDs on Theravada Buddhism for free distribution, which can be obtained off the website, by mail (if the requester includes shipping costs) or in the Guest House of the monastery proper. It also publishes a newsletter, Fearless Mountain, also for free distribution. It can be obtained electronically from the monastery's website or in printed form via mail or again at the monastery itself.

AMARAVATI BUDDHIST MONASTERY

Amaravati Buddhist Monastery is a monastery in the Thai Forest Tradition of the Theravada lineage of Buddhism. Amaravati Buddhist Monastery is a centre of teaching and practice. It is located in Hemel Hempstead, Hertfordshire, England. Amaravati means "Deathless Realm" in Pali, one of the Buddhist scriptural languages. The temple was founded by the disciples of the noted Thai meditation master, Luang Por Chah. Its current abbot is Ajahn Sumedho.

Amaravati Buddhist Monastery also has a retreat centre, where meditation retreats of varying lengths are held for lay people and which is run on donations.

Amaravati was created in 1984 when the English Sangha Trust purchased a residential school (previously an army base) from Buckinghamshire County Council. The official opening was in 1985. Recently, in the late 1990s, a new temple was constructed at Amaravati which was officially opened by the Princess of Thailand.

AMARBAYASGALANT KHIID

The Amarbayasgalant Monastery or "monastery of tranquil felicity", once one of the three largest Buddhist centres in Mongolia is located near the Selenge River in the Iven Valley, at the foot of Mount Buren-Khaan. Built between 1727 and 1736, it is one of the very few monasteries to have partly escaped the destruction of 1937, after which only the buildings of the central section remained. The entire contents: the tankas, statues and manuscripts were looted by the Communists or hidden until more fortunate times. Restoration work began in 1988 and some of the new deities were commissioned in Delhi, India.

The monastery was originally built to house the remains of Zanabazar, the first Bogd Gegeen, the "August light". Unlike the monastery of Erdene Zuu, which is composed of an ensemble of temple halls of different styles, Amarbayasgalant shows great stylistic unity. The overall style is Chinese, despite some Mongol and Tibetan influence. The plan is symmetrical and the main buildings succeed one another along a North-South axis, while the secondary buildings are laid out on parallel side axes.

BHUTIA BUSTY MONASTERY

Bhutia Busty monastery or Karmaa Dorjee Chyoling monastery is a Buddhist monastery located in Darjeeling, India. It belongs to the Red Sect of Buddhist Lamas. Originally a branch of the Nygmapa sect's Phodang Monastery in Sikkim, it was transferred to Darjeeling in 1879. The original location was on the Obsevatory Hill.

It was destroyed by a nepaleese invasion in the 19th century. The monastery relocared to its present location. However, the monastery in new location was also destroyed in an earthquake in 1934. Chogyal of Sikkim helped rebuilding it. The monastery has a collection of old Buddhist scripts.

BODHIVANA MONASTERY

Bodhivana Monastery is a Buddhist monastery in Australia, from the Theravada tradition, more specifically the Forest Sangha tradition.

Abbot: The current abbot of Bodhivana Monastery is Ajahn Kalyano. He was born in London in 1962. Venerable Ajahn Kalyano received his ordination in North East Thailand in 1985 at Venerable Ajahn Chah's monastery.

Location: Bodhivana is located in East Warburton, Victoria, Australia. It is about 90 minutes drive away from the centre of Melbourne.

Activities: Bodhivana monastery is a branch monastery in the tradition of Venerable Ajahn Chah. It was established to provide a place where candidates can train for ordination as Buddhist monks.

Anyone is welcome to visit the monastery. There is an alms-giving ceremony from 10.30 a.m. to 12 p.m. everyday. Occasionally, there will be Dhamma talk on evenings.

Since Bodhivana is a new monastery, there is still a lot of building work to be done. Limited amounts of Laypeople can also stay at the monastery, to practise meditation and help out at the monastery. Food is provided by the alms-givers and there is no monetary charge whatsoever. Those who wish to stay there need to at least give a phone call to confirm their arrival and length of stay. Unfortunately, at present there are no facilities for women who wish to stay there.

CHUDAMANI VIHARA

Chudamani Vihara was a Buddhist vihara in Nagapattinam, Tamil Nadu, India. Chudamani Vihara was constructed in 1006 AD by the Indonesian king Sri Vijaya Soolamanivarman with the patronage of Rajaraja Chola. The vihara building survived in dilapidated condition till 1867, when Jesuit missionaries demolished it. Since 1856, about 350 Buddha bronzes have been found at Nagapattinam, dating from the 11th to the 16th century.

History: The heritage of Nagapattinam is mentioned in the Burmese historical text of 3rd century B.C. which mentions of a Budha Vihar built by the great Ashoka. The Chinese traveller Hiuen Tsang also mentioned the vihar. Nagappattinam is mentioned as Padarithitha in the ancient Buddhist literature. The Animangalam Copperplate of Kulothunga Chola mentions that Kasiba Thera (Buddhist Monk) renovated the Buddhist shrine in 6th century AD with the help of monks of "Naganadu" (Nagapattinam). The Pallava King Rajasimha (690-728) permitted a Chinese king to build Buddha Vihar in Nagappattinam. According to the copperplate record of Chola king Rajaraja, the Sailendra king, Sri Mara-vijayottunga-varman constructed the vihara with the support of Rajaraja.

One statue, now at John D. Rockefeller Collection of Asian Art in New York, has an inscription that mentions that this Buddha was created to be carried in a procession during the temple's sacred festival. The inscription has been translated by Vidya Dehejia as: Well-being [and] prosperity. The nayakar [Buddha], of all of the eighteen countries, of the metalworkers. The procession image, for the sacred festival of the alvar temple, which was caused to be taken in procession by the respected one (utaiyar) endowed of the four gunas from Cirutavur; [in] the perum-palli (great place of worship or great vihara) of the metalworkers, [in] the perum-palli of Rajendra Chola.

DEER PARK MONASTERY

Deer Park Monastery in California: Deer Park Monastery is a 400 acre Buddhist sanctuary in Escondido, California. It was founded in July 2000 by monastic and lay practitioners from Plum Village in France.

The monastery is under the direction of the Thich Nhat Hanh's Order of Interbeing in the Vietnamese Zen tradition. Deer Park follows the same practices and schedule as Plum Village and its sister monasteries Maple Forest Monastery and Green Mountain Dharma Centre in Vermont. Since its founding the monastery has grown to be very active. Deer Park hosts an annual retreat when Thich Nhat Hanh travels to North

America. Over the years several people have taken novice vows and members of the other monasteries have moved to Deer Park so the ordained sangha has been growing. Lay practitioners also live at the monastery. The monastery is now composed of two hamlets; Solidity Hamlet for monks and laymen and Clarity Hamlet for nuns and laywomen.

Deer Park Monastery in Wisconsin: The Deer Park Monastery in Oregon, WI whch pre-dates the founding of the Deer Park Monastery in Escondido, CA by 25 years, carries the same name and can be confusing to the casual inquisitor. The Wisconsin monastery is headed by Geshe Lhundub Sopa, the first Tibetan tenured professor in an American University who went on to teach Buddhist philosophy, language and culture at the University of Wisconsin-Madison for 30 years. During that time, Geshe Sopa trained many of this country's first generation of respected Buddhist scholars and translators, including Jeffrey Hopkins, Jose Cabezon and John Makransky.

The Deer Park Corp. is currently in the process of building a new $2.7M Temple Project to house an extensive collection of Tibetan art and artifacts, provide greater capacity for group meetings and educational sessions, continue the expansion of Tibetan Buddhism in the New World by training a successive string of new Monks and to continue the promotion of the cause of Tibetan freedom from China. Part of the project also includes restoration work that will be done on the current temple, which was originally an open-air pavilion erected to house the first Kalachakra Initiation performed by the Dalai Lama in the western world. That event, performed in 1981, is commemorated by the stupa that was erected the following year near the current temple.

Geshe Sopa founded Deer Park Buddhist Centre in 1975, after students began requesting instruction outside the formal academic setting. Deer Park today remains the only full-scale monastic and teaching centre upholding the Dalai Lama's tradition in the Midwest, attracting students from around the world to its annual programmes. Geshe Sopa has facilitated an ongoing relationship between His Holiness the Dalai Lama and the University of Wisconsin, Madison, which His Holiness has visited five times and from which he has received an honourary doctoral degree.

GHOOM MONASTERY

Ghoom Monastery is the popular name of the Yiga-Choling Monastery located at Ghoom near the town of Darjeeling in the state of West Bengal, India. The monastery belongs to the Yellow Sect of Buddhists. There is a famed statue of "Coming Buddha" (Maitreya Buddha) in the monastery. It was built in 1875 by Lama Sherab Gyatso. Rare scripts on Buddhism have been kept in the monastery for decades.

Green Mountain Dharma Centre

Green Mountain Dharma Centre (GMDC) was founded in April 1998 and is located in Hartland-Four-Corners, VT. As of 2006, 6 nuns and 3 monks are in residence there. Recently, the GMDC has been developing in a new direction by becoming a Fourfold (monks, nuns, laymen, laywomen) Retreat and Practice Centre for the teachings of Thich Nhat Hanh. They are closely in touch with Plum Village and share the same practice. During a stay at the GMDC, retreatants are encouraged to practice and observe the monastic way of life. Retreatants are invited to help in communal activities such as preparing meals, general cleaning, washing dishes, etc. as a way of continuing mindfulness practice while performing everyday tasks.

The Abbess of the centre is Annabel Laity, Sister True Virtue (Vietnamese: Chan Duc) a senior Dharma Teacher of the Order of Interbeing. She has been a disciple of Thich Nhat Hanh since 1986, became a Dharma Teacher in 1990 and was Director of Practice at Plum Village. Since 1997, she has been Director of the Maple Forest Monastery and was installed as Abbess at the Green Mountain Dharma Centre in 1998. She has travelled widely, leading meditation retreats and giving talks in many different countries of the world. She has translated many of Thich Nhat Hanh's books into English.

JETAVANA

Jetavana was one of the most famous of the Buddhist monasteries in India. It was the second monastery donated to Buddha, after the Veluvana in Rajagaha. Jetavana is located just outside the old city of Savatthi. Jetavana was the place where Buddha gave many teachings and discourses, more than in any other place. Mainly, this is because Buddha spent 19 (out of 45) rainy-seasons (also pansah or vassa) at Jetavana, more than in any other monastery. The remains of Jetavana and Savatthi were locally known as Sahet-Mahet. Alexander Cunningham used the ancient (6th century AD) accounts of Chinese pilgrim-monks to determine that Sahet-Mahet actually referred to Jetavana and Savatthi.

The site of Jetavana was donated by Anathapindaka to Buddha himself. Originally it was owned by Prince Jeta, a son of King Pasenadi. Anathapindaka covered the ground by gold coins in order to buy the land. This event is frequently portrayed in Buddhist art, such as the art of Sanchi. Jetavana is currently a historical park, with remains of many ancient buildings such as monasteries, huts (such as the Gandhakuti and the Kosambakuti) and stupas. In Jetavana is also located the second-holiest tree of Buddhism: the Anandabodhi Tree. A visit to Savatthi and Jetavana is part of the Buddhist pilgrim route in North-India. The most revered place in Jetavana is the Gandhakuti, where Buddha used to stay.

KURJEY LHAKHANG

Kurjey Lhakang, also known as Kurjey Monastery, is located in the beautiful Bumthang valley in the Bumthang district of Bhutan. This is the final resting place of the remains of the first three kings of Bhutan. As well, a large tree behind one of the temple buildings is believed to be a terma (Buddhism) that was left there by Padmasambhava.

LONGXING MONASTERY

The Longxing Monastery is an ancient Buddhist monastery located near the town of Zhengding in Hebei Province, China, approximately 15 kilometres north of the provincial capital of Shijiazhuang. It has been referred to as the "First Temple south of Beijing". The monastery was first built in 586 AD, during the Sui Dynasty.

Some of the oldest stelas still standing on the monastery grounds date back to this period. Following a common pattern, the monastery complex features a central axis along which a sequence of buildings and focal points is arranged. The first building is the Hall of the Heavenly Kings.

At the opposite end of the axis is the Main Hall (Da Bei Ge), a 33-metre-high wooden structure, which houses a bronze statue of Guan Yin. This bronze was built during the early years of the Song Dynasty; its height exceeds 20 metres. Inside the hall, a staircase leads around the statue which allows it to be seen from top to bottom. Other notable artworks of the monastery are a colourful wooden carving of Guanyin sitting in a grotto and statues of Buddha sitting on a lotus throne.

A unique piece of wood architecture from the Song Dynasty in the Longxing Monastery is the Pavilion of the Rotating Library, which was restored in the 20th century. The pavilion houses a rotating bookshelf which was formerly used to store holy texts. The Longxing Monastery is today open to the public as a museum.

MAG-DHOG YOLMOWA MONASTERY

Mag-Dhog Yolmowa Monastery is a Buddhist monastery in the town of Darjeeling in the Indian state of West Bengal. The monastery is also known as "Aloobari" monastery after the locality it is located in. The monastery was built under the supervision of Sri Sangay Lama, a highly revered religious head of the Yolmowas-a small ethnic group hailing from north-east of Nepal and later settled in Darjeeling. The construction of the monastery started in 1914, the year World War I started.

The name Mag-Dhog means warding off the war and the monastery was dedicated for world peace. The monastery contains several idols of Lord Buddha and Padmasambhava and varied paintings on the wall which are said to be done with grass and herbs. The monastery also preserves several ancient Buddhist manuscripts. The monastery was built under the supervision of Sri Sangay Lama, a highly revered religious head of the Yolmo or Yolmowas-a small ethnic group hailing from Nepal and later settled in Darjeeling.

MAGNOLIA VILLAGE PRACTICE CENTRE

Magnolia Village Mindfulness Practice Centre is a retreat and practice centre located in Batesville, Mississippi. The 120 acre grounds are located near Memphis, Tennessee. The centre is part of the Order of Interbeing and practices in the tradition of Thich Nhat Hanh, who visited Magnolia Village in October of 2005 and officially accepted Magnolia Village. They are closely in touch with Plum Village for resources and support.

MAHAMEVNAWA BUDDHIST MONASTERY

Mahamevnawa is an organization of monasteries established for the sake of spiritual development of human beings through the teachings of the Sakyamuni Buddha. It has 18 more monastries for meditation through out the Sri Lanka's rural and some in urban areas. The chief Buddhist monk incharge of these monasteries is Venerable Kiribathgoda Gnananada thero is born to a Roman Catholic family converted to be a Buddhist monk. Venerable Kiribathgoda Gnananada Thero learnt buddhism from India and came to Sri Lanka and teaching buddhism to local and international community.

Practice of Meditation: According to Lord Buddha's teachings that birth as a human being is, indeed, a very rare opportunity. Fortunate people who achieve that rare opportunity should develop their minds to reach the ultimate goal of Nibbana. So the Mahamevnawa monastery is teaching the people how to practice meditation to reach the Nibbana.

Four Noble Truths: The meditation is based on the Lord Buddha's doctrine of the Four Noble Truths and this world to make known and explain the four Noble Truths.

1. Suffering (Dukkha Arya Satya)-It incorporates suffering, both mental and physical, dissatisfaction, unpleasant, unsatisfactory and many others.
2. Origin of Suffering (Dukkha Samudaya Arya Satya)
3. Cessation of Suffering (Dukkha Nirodha Arya Satya)
4. Noble Eightfold Path (Marga Arya Satya)

MAPLE FOREST MONASTERY

Maple Forest Monastery is part of Thich Nhat Hanh's Order of Interbeing and a men's monastery. Established in 1997, after the donation of a 120-acre property in Woodstock, Vermont. The governing body for the monastery is the Unified Buddhist Church. They are closely in touch with Plum Village for resources and support.

NAVA VIHARA

Nava Vihara was a Buddhist temple or monastery near the ancient city of Balkh, in the Khorasan province of Persia (now in present-day Afghanistan). The temple may have been an old Zoroastrian fire-temple, or it may have been converted to a Zoroastrian temple. From the Memoirs of Xuanzang, we learn that, at the time of his visit in the 7th century, there were in Balkh, or its vicinity, about a hundred Buddhist convents, with 3,000 devotees and that there was a large number of stupas and other religious monuments.

Nau Behar was he most remarkable and it possessed a very costly statue of the Buddha. The temple was led by Kashmiri Brahmins called Pramukh (who, under the arabized name of Barmak, came to be known as the Barmakids). A curious notice of this building is found in the writings of Arabian geographer Ibn Hawqal, an Arabian traveller of the 10th century.

The word Navbehar (or it's variants) appears in several locations of present-day Iran, a sign of the extend of Buddhism in ancient times. The Arch of Nawbahar can still be seen today near Balkh.

ODANTAPURI

Odantapuri, also called Uddandapura, was a Buddhist vihara in what is now Bihar, India.

REWALSAR

Rawalsar (also spelled Rewalsar) is a town and a nagar panchayat in Mandi district in the Indian state of Himachal Pradesh.

Demographics: As of 2001 India census GR India, Rawalsar had a population of 1369. Males constitute 54% of the population and females 46%. Rawalsar has an average literacy rate of 76%, higher than the national average of 59.5%: male literacy is 78% and female literacy is 73%. In Rawalsar, 12% of the population is under 6 years of age.

Geography: Rawalsar is located at an altitude of 1360 m above sea level. It is connected to Mandi by a motorable road and is about 25 km from Mandi. Lying in the Southern Himalayan belt, winters in Rawalsar can be freezing, while summers are generally pleasant.

Religion: Rawalsar is sacred to adherents of three major religions-Hinduism, Buddhism and Sikhism.

Hinduism: Seven mythological lakes associated with the Pandavas of Mahabharata are located above Rawalsar. Also associated with Rawalsar are the legends of Lord Shiva and Lomas Rishi. There is also a famous Krishna temple in the town.

Sikhism: The tenth Guru of Sikhs, Guru Gobind Singh visited Rawalsar to consult with kings of the Hill states seeking support against Aurangzeb. He stayed at Rawalsar for a month. Raja Joginder Sen of Mandi built a gurudwara at Rawalsar in 1930 to commemorate the Guru's visit. The place is particularly sacred to Namdhari Sikhs due to its mention in Sau Sakhi as a sanctuary.

Buddhism: The famous Rawalsar lake is associated with Padmasambhava (also known as Guru Rinpoche), a Buddhist monk. One version of a legend has it that the king of Mandi had Padmasambhava burnt alive after rumours that the monk had flirted with the king's daughter. The lake appeared at the spot where the monk was burnt and Padmasambhava manifested himself from within a lotus in the middle of the lake.

The king, repenting his actions, married his daughter with Padmasambhava. It was from Rawalsar that Padmasambhava went to Tibet to spread Mahayana Buddhism. The Tsechu fair was held in Rawalsar in 2004 to commemorate the birthday of Padmasambhava.

The fair was inaugurated by the Dalai Lama and was attended by Urgyen Trinley Dorje Karmapa along with 50,000 other Buddhist pilgrims. The fair was held after a gap of 12 years. There are other versions that mention that the lake associated with Padmasambhava's birth was located in Pakistan or Afghanistan. However, Rawalsar came to be known as a sacred place for Buddhists and two monasteries-the Drikung Kadyud Gompa and Tso-Pema Ogyen Heru-kai Nyingmapa Gompa are located here.

Rawalsar Lake: The lake around which the town of Rawalsar is established has a maximum depth of 6.5 metres. The lake is oligotrophic in nature. It is rectangular in shape, with the catchment area situated to its north and west.

5

BUDDHIST TEMPLES IN WORLD

TEMPLES IN INDIA

Kanheri Caves

The Kanheri Caves are a number of rock-cut Buddhist caves located in Mumbai, India. The caves date back to the 1st century BC when the area was under the rule of the Maurayan and Kushan empires. The caves lie deep inside the Sanjay Gandhi National Park, a National Park in northern Mumbai at 19.205° N 72.907° E. The caves are at a height of about 450 metres (1,500 feet) above sea level and command a panoramic view of the surroundings. The Arabian Sea and the Vasai Creek can be seen in the distance.

These caves, which used to be a settlement for travellers number around 109 and were in use from the 1st century BC to the 9th century AD. Inscriptions found in the caves refer to the area as Krishnagiri; Krishnasila; Kanhasila or Kanhagiri, which means "Black Mountain" or "Black Rock". "Kanheri" appears to have been derived from the Sanskrit word Krishnagiri, which means "Black Mountain".

Initially the caves were spartan, with basic amenities such as stone beds and cisterns to store water. In due course of time, as it began to have permanent residents halls began to be carved out of the rock.

Ornate statues and images of Buddha and the Bodhisattvas were also carved on the walls. By the third century, Kanheri had risen to being the most prominent Buddhist settlement on the Konkan coast. Its increase in stature meant that funds from nearby cities were easy to obtain.

Mahabodhi Temple

The Mahabodhi Temple is a Buddhist temple in Bodh Gaya, the location where Siddhartha Gautama, the Buddha, attained enlightenment. Bodh Gaya is located about 96 km (60 miles) from Patna, Bihar state, India. Next to the temple, to its western side, is the holy Bodhi tree.

History

Rise of Buddhism: Traditional accounts say that, around 530 BC, Gautama Buddha, wandering as a monk, reached the sylvan banks of Falgu River, near the city of Gaya, India. There he sat in meditation under a peepul tree (Ficus religiosa or Sacred Fig), which later became known as the Bodhi tree. According to Buddhist scriptures, after three days and three nights, Siddharta attained enlightenment and the answers that he had sought. Mahabodhi Temple was built to mark that location.

The Buddha then spent the succeeding seven weeks at seven different spots in the vicinity meditating and considering his experience. Several specific places at the current Mahabodhi Temple relate to the traditions surrounding these seven weeks:

- The first week was spent under the Bodhi tree.
- During the second week, the Buddha remained standing and stared, uninterrupted, at the Bodhi tree. This spot is marked by the Animeshlocha Stupa, that is, the unblinking stupa or shrine, which is located on the north-east of the Mahabodhi Temple complex. There stands a statute of Buddha with his eyes fixed towards the Bodhi tree.
- The Buddha is said to have walked back and forth between the location of the Animeshlocha Stupa and

the Bodhi tree. According to legend, lotus flowers sprung up along this route, it is now called Ratnachakarma or the jewel walk.

Construction: In approximately 250 BC, about 250 years after the Buddha attained Enlightenment, Buddhist Emperor Ashoka visited Bodh Gaya with the intention of establishing a monastery and shrine. As part of the temple he built, the diamond throne (called the Vajrasana), attempting to mark the exact spot of the Buddha's enlightenment, was established. Ashoka is considered the founder of the Mahabodhi Temple.

Decline: Buddhism declined when the dynasties patronizing it declined, following White Hun and the early Islamic invasions such as that of Muhammad bin Qasim. A strong revival occurred under the Pala Empire in the northeast of the subcontinent (where the temple is situated). Mahayana Buddhism flourished under the Palas between the 8th and the 12th century. However, after the defeat of the Palas by the Hindu Sena dynasty, Buddhism's position again began to erode and became nearly extinct in India.

During the 12th century AD, Bodh Gaya and the nearby regions were invaded by Muslim armies. During this period, the Mahabodhi Temple fell into disrepair and was largely abandoned. During the 16th century, a Hindu monastery was established near Bodh Gaya. Over the following centuries, the monastery's abbot or mahant became the area's primary landholder and claimed ownership of the Mahabodhi Temple grounds.

Restoration: In the 1880s, the-then British government of India began to restore Mahabodhi Temple under the direction of Sir Alexander Cunningham. A short time later, in 1891, the Sri Lankan Buddhist leader Anagarika Dharmapala started a campaign to return control of the temple to Buddhists, over the objections of the mahant. The campaign was partially successful in 1949, when control passed from the Hindu mahant to the state government of Bihar, which established a temple management committee. The committee has nine members, a majority of whom, including the chairman, must by law be Hindus. Mahabodhi's first head monk under the management committee was Anagarika Munindra, a Bengali man who had been an active member of the Maha Bodhi Society.

Architectural Style: Mahabodhi Temple is constructed of brick and is one of the oldest brick structures to have survived in eastern India. It considered to a fine example of Indian brickwork and was highly influential in the development of later architectural traditions. According UNESCO, "the present temple is one of the earliest and most imposing structures built entirely in brick from the late Gupta period".

Mahabodhi Temple's central towers rise to 55 metres and were heavily renovated in the 19th century. The central tower is surrounded by four smaller towers, constructed in the same style.

The Mahabodhi Temple is surrounded on all four sides by stone railings, about two metres high. The railings reveal two distinct types, both in style as well as the materials used. The older ones, made of sandstone, date to about 150 BC and the others, constructed from unpolished coarse granite, are believed to be of the Gupta period (300 AD-600 AD).

The older railings have scenes such as Lakshmi, the Hindu goddess of wealth, being bathed by elephants; and Surya, the Hindu sun god, riding a chariot drawn by four horses. The newer railings have figures of stupas (reliquary shrines) and garudas (eagles). Images of lotus flowers also appear commonly.

Current Status and Management: Mahabodhi Temple is claimed as property of state government of Bihar, part of India. Under the terms of the Bodh Gaya Temple Act of 1949, the state government makes itself responsible for the protection, management and monitoring of temple and its properties. The Act also has provisions for a Temple Management Committee, along with an advisory Board, which consists of the governor of Bihar state and twenty to twenty-five other members, half of them from foreign Buddhist countries.

The Temple Management Committee is the executive body for management of the Mahabodhi Temple and certain adjoining areas. The TMC functions under the supervision, direction and control of the state government of Bihar.

In June 2002, the Mahabodhi Temple became a UNESCO World Heritage Site, specifically nominated for the International World Heritage Programme.

All finds of religious artifacts in the area are legally protected under the Treasure Trove Act of 1878.

Rumtek Monastery

Rumtek, also called the Dharmachakra Centre, is a Tibetan Buddhist monastery located in the Indian state of Sikkim near the capital Gangtok. Originally built by the 9th Karmapa Wangchuk Dorje in 1740, Rumtek served as the main seat of the Karma Kagyu lineage in Sikkim for some time. But when the 16th Karmapa arrived in Sikkim in 1959, after fleeing before the Chinese occupation of Tibet, it was in ruins. Despite being offered other sites, the Karmapa decided to rebuild Rumtek. To him, the site possessed many auspicious qualities and was surrounded by the most favorable attributes. For example, flowing streams, mountains behind, a snow range in front and a river below. With the generosity and help of the Sikkim royal family and the Indian government, it has been built by the 16th Karmapa as his main seat in exile.

After four years, construction of the monastery was completed. The sacred items and relics brought out from Tsurphu, the Karmapa's seat in Tibet, were installed. On Tibetan New Year's day (Losar) in 1966 the 16th Karmapa officially inaugurated the new seat called, "The Dharmachakra Centre, a place of erudition and spiritual accomplishment, the seat of the glorious Karmapa."

The monastery is currently the largest in Sikkim. It is home to the community of monks and where they perform the rituals and practices of the Karma Kagyu lineage. A Golden Stupa contains the relics of the 16th Karmapa. Opposite that building is a college, Karma Shri Nalanda Institute for Higher Buddhist Studies.

Rumtek is located 24 km from Gangtok, the capital of the Sikkim, at an altitude of about 1500 m.

Rumtek is currently at the centre of the Karmapa controversy with a lengthy battle being played out in the Indian courts. Two rival organisations, both supporting different candidates for the 17th Karmapa claim stewardship of the monastery and its contents. The two organisations are the Karmapa Charitable Trust (supporting Thaye Dorje) and the Tsurpu Labrang (supporting Urgyen Trinley Dorje). Currently neither Karmapa candidate resides at Rumtek.

Chaukhandi Stupa

Chaukhandi Stupa is an important Buddhist stupa in Sarnath, located 13 kilometres from Varanasi, Uttar Pradesh, India. Stupas are decendents of burial mounds and serve as a shrine for a relic of the Buddha.

History: The Chaukhandi Stupa is thought originally to have been built as a terraced temple during the Gupta period between the 4th to 6th Century to mark the site where Lord Buddha and his first disciples met traveling from Bodh Gaya to Sarnath. Later Govardhan, the son of a Raja, modified the stupa to its the present shape by building the octagonal tower to commemorate the visit of Humayun, the powerful Mughal ruler.

Today the stupa is a high earthen mound covered with a brickwork edifice topped by an octagonal tower. It is maintained by the Archaeological Survey of India.

Dambal: Dambal is a village near Dharwar in the Gadag district of the state of Karnataka, India. It was an ancient centre of Buddhism and remained so as late as the 12th century.

History: Under the rule of the Mauryas and Satvahanas, the teachings of Buddha flourished in Karnataka. On a temple of the Buddhist deity Tara in Dambal, there is an inscription of 1095 AD. However, as time passed Buddhism was assimilated by the increasing popularity of Hinduism.

Temples: There are three Hindu temples here. The Dodda Basappa temple is of the Western Chalukya architectural style and has a star-shaped plan for the vimana with so many star points that it almost becomes circular in appearance. Each right angle is divided into four 22.5 degrees angles. Then each angle is again divided and covered with intricate carvings.

Dhamek Stupa

Dhamek Stupa (also spelled Dhamekh) is located at Sarnath, 13 km away from Varanasi in the state of Uttar Pradesh. It was built by the great Mauryan king Ashoka in 249 B.C.E., along with several other monuments, to commemorate his pilgrimage there. It is said to mark the spot where the Buddha gave his first historic sermon and set in motion the Wheel of Dhamma. Stupas are low circular funeral mounds encircle by large stones. King Ashoka built stupas to enshrine body relics in the form of small pieces of calcinated bone of Buddhist monks and holy men.

Design: The Dhamekh Stupa is cylindrical in form, a 43.6 metres high and 28 metre in diameter tower solidly built of bricks and stone. It is the most massive structure in Sarnath. The stone facing the lower part is chiseled with delicate floral carvings of Gupta origin. The borders are covered with exquisitely carved figures of humans and birds.

Toran

Toran is the name in Hindustani of a sacred or honourific gateway in Buddhist architecture. Its typical form is a projecting cross-piece resting on two uprights or posts. It is made of wood or stone and the cross-piece is generally of three bars placed one on the top of the other; both cross-piece and posts are usually sculptured.

Borobudur

Borobudur is a ninth century Buddhist Mahayana monument in Central Java, Indonesia. It is built on top of a hill with 55,000 m^3 of stones. It features 2,672 relief panels and 504 Buddha statues. Six square platforms form the lower portion with three circular platforms on top. The top platforms are filled with 72 perforated stupas surrounding the main dome. Each stupa has one sitting Buddha statue inside.

The whole monument is considered both a shrine for the Lord Buddha and a place for Buddhist pilgrimage. The journey for pilgrims starts from the base of the monument, in the world of desires (or Kamadhatu), where men are still bounded with greed, hate and ignorance. Starting from the eastern stairway, the journey enters the world of forms (or Rupadhatu) in which men bound with forms and names are searching for the light of the Highest Perfect Wisdom.

The monument guides this journey by the system of stairways and corridors with 1,460 narrative relief panels on the wall and the balustrades. The story starts from the birth of Buddha, descended from the Tushita heaven. It continues with the story of Prince Siddharta and other legendary persons. The final relief story is about Sudhana's ultimate search for perfect knowledge. The journey ends in the circular platforms, the world of formless (or Arupadhatu) in which men are released all their desires from the phenomenal world. This is the complete Buddhist cosmology in a single monument.

Borobudur was evidently abandoned after the decline of Buddhist and Hindu kingdoms in Java around the fourteenth century and the Javanese conversion to Islam. It was re-discovered in 1814 by Sir Thomas Raffles, the British ruler of Java. Since then, Borobudur has been preserved through several restorations. The biggest restoration project was performed between 1975-1982 by the Indonesian government and UNESCO. Since 1991, Borobudur has been listed as one of the UNESCO World Heritage Sites. Borobudur is still used for pilgrimage and is also a major attraction for tourism in Indonesia.

Etymology: In Indonesian, temples are known as candi, or formerly chandi. The term is also used more loosely to describe any ancient structure, for example, gates and bathing strucutures. In the case of most candis, the original name is unknown. Furthermore, often even the local people did not know of the existence of a candi. As a result, the origins of the name Borobudur is unclear. The name of Borobudur was first written in the Sir Thomas Raffles book on Java history. Raffles wrote about the existence of a monument called borobudur in the village of Bumisegoro. There is, however, no ancient documents mentioning this name. In an old Javanese manuscript, Nagarakertagama, written by Mpu Prapanca in AD 1365, there is mention of Budur as a Buddhist sanctuary. It is likely that it is associated with Borobudur, but the manuscript lacks any further information to make a definite identification.

Most candis are simply named after the nearby village and in the vicinity of Borobudur, is a village called Bore. The name of 'Bore-Budur' and thus 'BoroBudur', was thus suspected as written by Raffles in English grammar. If it followed Javanese language, the monument should have been named as BudurBoro. Raffles also suggested that Budur might correspond to the modern Javanese word Buda ('ancient')-*i.e.*, 'ancient Boro'. Another hypothesis is that 'Boro' was taken from an old Javanese term bhara ('honourable'), describing the monument as "The Honourable Buddha . A more plausible interpretation comes from Javanese word of biara ('monastery'). Thus the name simply points to the 'monastery of Budur', where Budur is mentioned in the Nagarakertagama manuscript.

Location: Borobudur is situated in the province of Central Java, 40 km (25 miles) from Yogyakarta on the Kedu Plain. Buddhist and Hindu temple compounds are located within a radius of the confluence of the Progo and Elo Rivers. From west to east the main Buddhist temples are Borobudur, Pawon,

Mendhut and Ngawe. Two twin volcanoes surround the plain: Merapi and Merbabu to the east and Sundoro and Sumbing to the west. This unique location, according to Soekmono (1976) is extremely fertile, has an industrious population and is known as the 'garden of Java'. 15 kilometers from Borobudur, on the outskirts of the city of Magelang is the hill of Tidar. One of the sacred places in Java, the hill is the geographical centre of Java and Javanese legend refers to it as the Nail of Java, preventing it from floating around the ocean..

Borobudur itself is built on a hill. In 1931, Nieuwenkamp, a Dutch artist, theorised that the Kedu Plain was once a lake and Borobudur originally represented a lotus flower floating on the lake. According to the theory, the two other Buddhist temples, Mendhut and Pawon, were said to be located on the edge of the lake. The lotus flôwer is a mythical Buddhism in which the future Buddha will be born. Nieuwenkamp idea was based on his discovery that the ground plan of Borobudur shows a lotus rosette. The location of the Borobudur on a hill suggested him that the monument represents a floating lotus.

In 1949, geologists found clay sediments near the site that supports the old lake idea. The lake may have been created by the eruption of a nearby volcanoes. It may have existed in the area as recently as between the 12th and 14th centuries. However, it was not at all clear whether the lake dried up before the stupa was built, or the site pre-dated a lake. The final conclusion still awaits further extensive research.

History

Usage: There is no written documents to the authority who had built Borobudur, nor the purposes of which it was intended for. The construction time is estimated by the similarity of the carved reliefs on the hidden foot with the inscriptions commonly used in royal charters between eight and ninth century. Borobudur was likely founded around AD 800. This conforms with the period between AD 750-850 where it was the Golden Age of the Sailendra dynasty.

There has been some confusion between Hindu and Buddhist rulers in Java around that time. The Sailendras are known as ardent followers of Lord Buddha, but he was said as Hindu according to a stone inscription found at Sojomerto, Central Java. It was during that time that many Hindu and Buddhist monuments were built in plains and slopes of mountains around Central Java. The plains of Kedu (Buddhist) and Prambanan (Hindu Shiva) temples were erected close together.

In AD 732, king Sanjaya, the founder of the dynasty, commissioned a Hindu Shiva lingga sanctuary to be built on the hill Ukir, only 10 km east of Borobudur. Sanjaya's immediate successor, Rakai Panangkaran, was associated with a Buddhist temple, Kalasan, as shown in the Kalasan charter dated AD 778. Anthropologists believe that religion in Java has never been a serious conflict. It was possible for a Hindu king to patronize the establishment of a Buddhist monument; or for a Buddhist king to act likewise. The official religion could take place without affecting the continuity of a dynasty and of cultural life.

Apostasy: For centuries, Borobudur laid hidden under layers of volcanic ash and jungle growth. The facts behind the desertion of this magnificent monument still remain a mystery. It is unknown when the monument was still in active use and when it ceased to function as the pilgrimage centre of Buddhism. A general assumption is that the temples were disbanded when the population were converted to Islam in the fifteenth century. Another theory is that a famine caused by an eruption had forced local inhabitants to leave their lands and the monument in search for a new location. The eruption is estimated in circa AD 1006. The event was said to trigger the movement of Javanese power from the Borobudur area to the east of Java nearby the Brantas valley as early as AD 928.

However, the great monument was never completely removed from the local inhabitants memory. Instead of glorifying story about the monument, the memory was then gradually shifted into a more superstitious beliefs associated with bad luck and misery. Two old Javanese manuscripts of the eighteenth century mention a case of bad luck associated with the monument. According to the Babad Tanah Jawi (or the History of Java), the monument was a fatal factor for a rebel who revolted against the king of Mataram in AD 1709. The hill was besieged and the resurgents were defeated who were then sentenced to death by the king.

In the Babad Mataram (or the History of the Mataram Kingdom), the monument was associated with the bad luck of the crown prince of Yogyakarta Sultanate in AD 1757. In spite of a restriction to visit the monument, he took what is written as the knight who was captured in a cage (a statue in one of the perforated stupas). As soon as he arrived to his palace, he died unexpectedly after a one-day illness.

Rediscovery: After the Anglo-Dutch Java War, Java fell under the British administration between 1811-1816. The appointed ruler was Lieutenant Governor-General Thomas Stamford Raffles, who was extremely interested in the history of Java. He collected Java antiquities and made notes through contacts with local inhabitants during his tour throughout the island. On an inspection tour to Semarang in 1814, he was informed with a big monument called Chandi Borobodur deep in a jungle near a village called Bumisegoro. He was not able to make the discovery himself and he sent H.C. Cornellius, a Dutch engineer, to investigate the information.

In two months, Cornellius and his 200 men had to cut trees, burn down bushes and dig down the earth to reveal the monument. Due to the danger of being collapse, he couldn't unearth all of the galleries. He made reports to Raffles, supplemented with various drawings. However, this hard labour work was not much appreciated in Raffles two volumes of the History of Java publication. Although the discovery is only mentioned by a few sentences, Raffles has been credited to have rescued the monument and brought it to the notice to the world.

Hartmann, a Dutch administrator of the Kedu region, continued Cornellius work. In 1835, the site was freed that the whole monument was finally unearthed. His interest to Borobudur was rather personally rather than as a government official. However, it was such a pity that Hartmann did not write any reports of his activities. Particularly, the alleged story that he discovered the large statue of Buddha in the main stupa. The main stupa is empty. In 1842, Hartmann made an investigation to the main dome. What he discovered remains unknown. The Dutch East Indies government then commissioned a Dutch engineer official, F.C. Wilsen. In 1853, Wilsen made a report of a large Buddha statue of the size of one hundred other Borobudur statues.

Besides making hundreds of relief sketches, Wilsen made the study of the monument itself. He had prepared three articles about it. The Dutch East Indies government, meanwhile, had appointed Brumund to make a detail study of the monument that was completed in 1859. Brumundi thought that he would published an article supplemented by Wilsen's drawings. However, the government decided otherwise. Brumundi then refused to cooperate. The government then asked another scholar, C. Leemans, who compiled a monograph based on Brumundi's and Wilsen's sources. In 1873, the first monograph of the detailed study of Borobudur was published to the public. The French translation was then appeared in 1874. In 1873, Isidore van Kinsbergen took the first photographs of the monument.

Appreciations to the site developed slowly. Some reliefs and ornaments were routinely removed by thieves and souvenir hunters. In 1882, the chief inspector of cultural artefacts recommended that Borobudur be entirely disassembled with the reliefs placed in museums due to the unstable condition of the monument complex.

The government then appointed an archeologist, Groenveldt, to make a thorough investigation of the site and assess the actual condition of the monument. The report said that the fear of its condition could not be justified and the monument was left intact for years.

Contemporary Events: Since the major 1973 renovation, Borobudur has been reused its function for a place of worship and pilgrimage. Once a year, during the full moon in May or June, Buddhists in Indonesia observe Vesak (Indonesian: Waisak) day to commemorate the birth, the death and the time when Boddhisatva attained the highest wisdom to become Buddha. Vesak is an official national holiday and the ceremony is centred at the three Buddhist temples by walking from Candi Mendut to Candi Pawon and finally ended at Borobodur.

Daily purpose of the monument is a major tourist attraction in Indonesia. According to local folklore, touching the finger and toe of a particular Buddha through the holes in the stupa wall brings good luck. The creation of facilities for domestic and international tourism around the monument, however, has been controversial.

On 21 January 1985, nine stupas were badly damaged by nine bombs attack. In 1991, a blind Muslim evangelist, Husein Ali Al Habsyie, was sentenced to life imprisonment for masterminding a series of bombings in the mid 1980s including the temple attack. Two other members of a right-wing extremist group that carried out the bombings had each been sentenced to 20 years in 1986 and another man received a 13-year prison term.

On 27 May 2006, an earthquake of 6.2 magnitude on Richter scale struck the south coast of Central Java. It caused severe damage and casualties to the nearby city of Yogyakarta. Fortunately, Borobudur was left intact from the event.

Architecture: Borobudur is built as a single large stupa and when viewed from above takes the form of a giant Mandala. The foundation is a square, 118 metres (387 ft) on each side. It has nine platforms, of which the lower six are square and the upper three are circular. The upper platform features seventy-two small stupas surrounding one large central stupa.

Each stupa is bell-shaped and pierced by numerous decorative openings. Statues of the Buddha sit inside the pierced enclosures.

Design: Borobodur is completely different from the general design of such a structure. Instead of building on a flat surface, Borobudur is built on a natural hill. There is no inner space as in other temples, but a large statue in a similar shape of a pyramid. The building technique is, however, similar to other temples in Java. One school of thought considers Borobudur a stupa, rather than a temple (or candi in Indonesian).

A stupa is originally intended as a shrine for the Lord Buddha. Sometimes stupas were built only as a devotional symbol of Buddhism. A temple, on the other hand, is used as a house of deity and have inner spaces for the people to pray. Given, however, the complexity of the monument with such a meticulous design suggests it is in fact a temple. With no inner space in Borobudur, for congregational worship, the monument is a place for pilgrimage. Pilgrims were guided by the system of staircases and corridors ascending to the top platform. Each platform represents one stage of enlightment. The path that guides pilgrims was designed with the symbolism of sacred knowledge according to the Buddhism cosmology.

Construction: The monument was built from approximately 55,000 m^3 (almost 2 million cubic feet) of stone taken from neighbouring rivers. The stone was cut to size, transported to the site and laid without mortar. Knobs, indentations and dovetails were used to form joints between stones. Reliefs were created in-situ after the building had been completed.

The main vertical structure can be divided into three groups: base (or foot), body and top. The base is a 123x123 m^2 square in size and 4 metres (13 ft) high of walls. The body is composed of five square platforms each with diminishing heights. The first terrace is set back 7 metres (23 ft) from the edge of the base. The other terraces are set back by 2 metres (6.5 ft), leaving a narrow corridor at each stage. The top consists of 3 circular platforms, with each stage supporting a row of perforated stupas, arranged in concentric circles. In the centre, there is one giant stupa, the dome of which is 35 metres (115 ft) above ground level.

Access to the upper part is through stairways at each middle side. The main entrance is at the eastern side, which is the beginning of the narrative reliefs. On the slopes of the hill, there are also stairways linking the monument to the low-lying plain. Gates are watched by a total of 32 lion statues.

The original designer provided a drainage system to cater for the area's high stormwater run-off. To avoid being flooded by rain water, 100 spouts are provided at each corner with a unique carved gargoyles (makaras).

Structure: Buddhism emphasises stages of mental preparation towards the ultimate goal. This is represented by dividing the monument into three worlds: Kamadhatu (world of desires), Rupadhatu (world of forms) and finally Arupadhatu (the formless world). Kamadhatu is represented by the base, Rupadhatu by the five square platforms (the body) and Arupadhatu by the three circular platforms and the large topmost stupa.

The architectural features of Arupadhatu differ completely with Rupadhatu. Square platforms become circular and detailed decorations in the Rupadhatu disappear in Arupadhatu. It represents how the world of forms-where men are still attached with forms and names-changes into the world of the formless, with plainless circular platforms. Man is said to have released all his desires and bond to the phenomenal world.

The base did not originally represent the Kamadhatu. It is not the original support of the monument, rather it serves as an encasement that hides the real base. The real base is known as the hidden foot because it was not initially visible to the visitor. In 1885, it was discovered that the base has its own reliefs. 160 of them are narrative panels with short inscriptions that apparently describe instructions for the sculptors, illustrating the scene to be carved.

It is thought that the real base had to be covered to prevent a disastrous subsidence of the monument through the hill. There is another theory that the encasement base was added because the original hidden foot was incorrectly designed, according to Vastu Shastra, the Indian ancient book about architecture and town planning. The encasement of the base, however, was built with detailed and meticulous design with aesthetics and religious compensation. The base serves as a place for pilgrims to perform a preliminary round at their leisure before entering the 'narrow path of Buddhism'.

Reliefs: Borobudur contains approximately 2,670 individual bas reliefs, which cover the facades and balustrades. 1,460 are narrative panels and 1,212 are decorative. The most important are the narrative panels and they tell the story of Sudhana and Manohara. The total relief surface is 2,500 m^2. The reliefs are located at the hidden foot (Kamadhatu) and the five square platforms (Rupadhatu). The 1,460 narrative panels are grouped into 11 series that go around the monument with the total length of 3,000 metres (1.86 mi). The hidden foot contains the first series with 160 narrative panels. The remaining 10 series are distributed throughout walls and balustrades in four galleries.

Narrative panels on the wall read from right to left and from left to right on the balustrades. This conforms with pradaksina, the ritual of circumambulation performed by pilgrims who move in a clockwise direction while keeping the sanctuary to their right. The story starts from the eastern entrance stairway and continues to the left.

The hidden foot depicts the story about the law of karma, according to the Mahakarmavibhangga text. The wall of the first galleries (over 3,5 metres or 11.5 ft high) has two superimposed series of reliefs; each consists of 120 panels. The upper part depicts the biography of Buddha, according to Lalitavistara text. The lower part of the wall in the first gallery, ballustrades in the first and the second galleries tell the story of Buddha's former lives as told in the jatakas and avadanas.

The main wall of the second gallery and the whole third and fourth galleries are devoted to Sudhana's further wandering about his search; terminated by his attainment of the Perfect Wisdom, according to Gandavyuha text.

The Law of Karma (Karmavibhangga): The 160 hidden panels do not form a continuous story, but each panel provides one complete illustration of cause and effect. There are depictions of blameworthy activities, from gossip to murder, with their corresponding punishments. There are also praiseworthy activities, that include charity and pilgrimage to sanctuaries and their subsequent rewards. The pains of hell and the pleasure of heaven are also illustrated. There are scenes of daily life, complete with the full panorama of samsara (the endless cycle of birth and death).

The Birth of Buddha (Lalitavistara): The story starts from the glorious descent of the Lord Buddha from the Tushita heaven and ends with his first sermon in the Deer Park near Benares. The relief shows the birth of Buddha as Prince Siddharta, son of King Suddhodana and Queen Maya of Kapilavastu (in present-day Nepal).

The story is preceded by 27 panels showing various preparations, in heavens and on earth, to welcome the final incarnation of Bodhisattva. Before descending from Tushita heaven, Bodhisattva entrusted his crown to his successor, the future Buddha Maitreya. He descended on earth in the shape of white elephants with six tusks, penetrated to Queen Maya's right womb. Queen Maya had a dream of this event, which was interpreted that his son would become either a sovereign or a Buddha.

While Queen Maya felt that it was the time to give the birth, she went to the Lumbini park outside the Kapilavastu city. She stood under a plaksa tree, holding one branch with her right hand and she gave birth to a son, Prince Siddharta. The story on the panels continues until the prince became Buddha.

Prince Siddharta Story (Jataka) and Other Legendary Persons (Avadana): Jatakas are stories about the Buddha before he was born as Prince Siddharta. Avadanas are similar with jatakas, but the main figure is not Bodhisattva himself. The saintly deeds in avadanas are attributed to other legendary persons. Jatakas and avadanas are treated in one and the same series in the reliefs of Borobudur.

The first 20 lower panels in the first gallery on the wall depict the Sudhanakumara-vadana or the saintly deeds of Prince Sudhanakumara. The first 135 upper panels in the same gallery on the balustrades are devoted to the 34 legends of the Jatakamala. The remaining 237 panels depict stories from other sources, as do for the lower series and panels in the second gallery. Some jatakas stories are depicted twice, for example the story of King Sibhi.

Sudhana Search of the Ultimate Truth (Gandavyuha): Gandavyuha is a story about Sudhana's tireless wandering in search of the Highest Perfect Wisdom. It covers two galleries (third and fourth) and also half of the second gallery; comprising in total of 460 panels. The principal figure of the story, the youth Sudhana, son of an extremely rich merchant, appears on the 16th panel. The preceding 15 panels form a prologue to the story of the miracles during Buddha's samadhi in the Garden of Jeta at Sravasti.

During his search, Sudhana visited no less than 30 teachers but none of them had satisfied him completely. He was then instructed by Manjusri to meet the monk Megasri, where he was given the first doctrine. Sudhana journey continues to meet in the following order Supratisthita, the physician Megha (Spirit of Knowledge), the banker Muktaka, the monk Saradhvaja, the upasika Asa (Spirit of Supreme Enlightment), Bhismottaranirghosa, the Brahmin Jayosmayatna, Princess Maitrayani, the monk Sudarsana, a boy called Indriyesvara, the upasika Prabhuta, the banker Ratnachuda, King Anala, the god Siva Mahadeva, Queen Maya, Bodhisattva Maitreya and then back to Manjusri. Each meeting has given Sudhana a specific doctrine, knowledge and wisdom. These meetings are shown in the third gallery.

After the last meeting with Manjusri, Sudhana went to the residence of Bodhisattva Samantabhadra; depicted in the fourth gallery. The entire series of the fourth gallery is devoted to the teaching of Samantabhadra. The narrative panels finally end with the Sudhana's achievement of the Supreme Knowledge and the Ultimate Truth.

Buddha Statues: Apart from the story of Buddhist cosmology carved in stones, Borobudur has many Buddha statues. The cross-legged Buddha statues are seated with lotus position. They are distributed on the five square platforms (the Rupadhatu level) and on the top platform (the Arupadhatu level).

The Buddha statues are in niches at the Rupadhatu level, arranged in rows on the outer sides of the balustrades. As platforms progressively diminish to the upper level, the number of Buddha statues are decreasing. The first balustrades have 104 niches, the second 104, the third 88, the fourth 72 and the fifth 64. In total, there are 432 Buddha status at the Rupadhatu level. At the Arupadhatu level (or the three circular platforms), Buddha statues are placed inside perforated stupas. The first circular platform has 32 stupas, the second 24 and the third 16, that sum up to 72 stupas. Of the total 504 Buddha statues, over 300 are mutilated (mostly headless) and 43 are completely missing.

At glance, all Buddha statues are equal, but there is subtle difference between them in the mudras or the position of the hands. There are 5 groups of mudra: North, East, South, West and Zenith, which represent the five cardinal compass according to Mahayana. The first four balustrades have the first four mudras: North, East, South and West, of which Buddha statues that face one compass direction has the corresponding mudra. Buddha statues at the fifth balustrades and inside the 72 stupas on the top platform have the same mudra: Zenith. Each mudra represent one of the Five Dhyani Buddhas; each has its own symbolism. They are Abhaya mudra for Amogashiddi (north), Vara mudra for Ratnasambhava (south), Dhyana mudra for Amitabha (west), Bhumisparsa mudra for Aksobhya (east) and Dharmachakra mudra for Vairochana (zenith).

Restoration: Borobudur attracted attention in 1885, when Yzerman, the Chairman of the Archaeological Society in Yogyakarta, made a discovery about the hidden foot. Photographs that reveal reliefs on the hidden foot was made in 1890-1891. The discovery has led the Dutch East Indies government to take a necessary step to safeguard the monument. In 1900, the government set up a commission consisted of three officials to assess the monument: Brandes, an art historian, Theodoor van Erp, a Dutch army engineer officer and Van de Kamer, a construction engineer from the Department of Public Works. In 1902, the commission submitted a threefold plan of proposal to the government. First, the immediate dangers should be avoided by resetting the corners, removing stones that endangers the adjacent parts, strengthening the first balustrades and restoring several niches, archways, stupas and the main dome. Second, fencing off the courtyards, providing proper maintenance and improving drainage by restoring floors and spouts. Third, all loose stones should be removed, cleared up the monument up to the first balustrades, removed disfigured stones and restored the main dome. The total cost was estimated at that time around 48,800 Dutch guilders.

The restoration then was carried out between 1907-1911, led by Theodor van Erp. The first seven months of his restoration was excavating the grounds around the monument to find missing Buddha heads and panel stones. Van Erp dismantled and rebuilt the upper three circular platforms and stupas. Along the way, Van Erp discovered more things to improve the monument that he submitted another proposal that was agreed with the additional cost of 34,600 guilders. At first glance Borobudur had been restored to its old glory.

Due to the limited budget, the restoration had been primarily focused on cleaning the sculptures, but Van Erp did not solve the drainage problem. Within fifteen years, the gallery walls were sagging and the reliefs showed signs of new cracks and deterioration. Van Erp used concrete from which alkali salts and calcium hydroxide are leached and transported into the rest of the construction. This has caused some problems that a further thorough renovation is urgently needed.

Small restorations have been performed since then, but not for a complete protection. In the late 1960s, the Indonesian government had requested a major renovation to protect the monument to the international community. In 1973, a master plan to restore Borobudur was created. The Indonesian government and UNESCO then undertook the complete overhaul of the monument in a big restoration project between 1975-1982. The foundation was stabilized and all 1,460 panels were cleaned. The restoration involved the dismantling of the five square platforms and improved the drainage by embedding water channels into the monument. Both impermeable and filter layers were added. This colossal project involved around 600 people to restore the monument and cost in total of US$ 6,901,243. After the renovation was finished, UNESCO listed Borobudur as a World Heritage Site in 1991.

Candi Kalasan

Candi Kalasan is an eight sided thousand year old temple just south of the Yogyakarta to Prambanan road 'Jalan Solo' in Central Java, Indonesia Renovated and partially rebuilt during the Dutch colonial era.

The Kala Face above the southern door has been photographed and used by a number of foreign academics in their books to give an idea of the artistry in stone by Central Javanese artists of a millennia ago. Niches where statues would have been located are found inside and outside the temple. It is located south west of Candi Sari and west of the Prambanan complex. The eight sided aspect of the structure has led to speculation of non-Buddhist elements in the temple, similar to some interpretations of the early Borobudur structure.

Ratu Boko's Palace

Ratu Boko's Palace is a remaining of monastery and King Boko's palace that was built around 8th century in Yogyakarta, Indonesia under the reign of Rakai Panangkaran, descendant of Syailendra dynasty. This palace is one of many Buddha temples in Indonesia. The King, Rakai Panangkaran, embraced Buddhism while the majority of his people embraced Hinduism. The original name of this palace is Abhayagiri Vihara (means a temple on a peaceful hill). This palace is located 196 m above the sea level, from which one will be able to see city of Yogyakarta and Prambanan temple with Mount Merapi as the background.

It is believed that this temple was built for seclusion purpose. The total area of this palace is about 250,000 m^2 wide. This palace consists of monastery, temples, square terrace and ponds. Those ponds are used by the royal family of King Boko for bathing purpose.

Main Gate: It is read on the main gate Panabwara that was written by Rakai Panabwara, descendant of Rakai Panangkaran. He carved his name there in order to legitimate his authority of this palace.

Candi Batu Putih: Literally, Batu Putih means white stone. There is a temple of white stone about 50 m from the main gate. Near to this temple, tourists will be able to find a square area (about 26x26 m) with two terraces. The function of that building is to burn corpses.

The Amerta Mantana: Amerta Mantana is a name of the well located inside Ratu Boko's Palace. It is believed that the water of Amerta brings luck for anyone who uses it. Hindu people use it in Tawur Agung ceremony, one day before the Nyepi day, to support the achievement of self purify and to return the earth into her initial harmony.

Buddhism Hinduism: At the eastern part of the palace, lies two caves that were formed of sediment stones. The upper cave is called Gua Lanang (Male Cave) and the lower cave is called Gua Wadon (Female Cave). In front of Gua Lanang, there is a pond and three effigies. Based on the research, the effigy is known as Aksobya, one of Buddha Pantheons.

Even though it was built by a Buddhist, there are Hindu elements in it. This can be seen from the presence of Lingga and Yoni, Ganesha statue and golden plate with the writing "Om Rudra ya namah swaha" on it as form of worship to Rudra as the other name of Shiva. This proved that the Hindus and Buddhist live together with tolerance.

TEMPLES AND SHRINES IN HIROSHIMA

Hiroshima Gokoku Shrine

Hiroshima Gokoku Jinja is a Japanese Shinto Shrine in Hiroshima, Japan.

Overview: The original shrine was founded in 1868, the first year of the Meiji period, in Futabanosato Hiroshima. The shrine was established to mourn the Hiroshima-Han victims of the Boshin War. In 1934 it was dismantled and moved to where the Hiroshima Municipal Stadium now stands and in 1939 its name was changed to the Hiroshima Gokoku Shrine. In 1945 it was destroyed by the atomic bombing and was rebuilt within the Hiroshima Castle in 1965 with the aid of donations from the citizens of Hiroshima. The Hiroshima Gokoku Shrine is one of the most popular places for celebrating Hatsumode and Shichi-Go-San in Hiroshima.

Mitaki-dera

Mitaki-dera is a historic Japanese temple in the city of Hiroshima, Japan.

Overview: Mitaki-dera was founded in the year 809 during the Daido era.

Mitaki-dera is familiar with the name of "Mitaki-Kannon".

There are three falls and the water will be used as an offering of water to the victims of the atomic bomb during the Hiroshima Peace Memorial Ceremony. The Taho-to was dismantled from Hiro-Hachiman-jinja in Hirogawa, Wakayama in 1951, to hold a memorial service for the victims of the atomic bomb.

There is the wooden seated statue of Amida Nyorai in the Taho-to.

Mitaki-dera is famous for sakura, autumn leaves and maples.

Mitaki-dera is the 13th of Chugoku 33 Kannon Pilgrimage.

BUDDHIST TEMPLES IN LAOS

Wat Manorom

Wat Manorom is a major Buddhist temple and monastery in Luang Prabang, Laos. There are several theories as to the date of its founding; it may have been founded in 1372 or 1375 by Samsenthai, but it may also date from the reign of Laasaenthai Bouvanaat around 1492. The great bronze Buddha, 6 metres high, in the nave dates from the 1370s.

Pha That Luang

Pha That Luang (T-had Lu-uang) (Great Stupa in Laos) is a Buddhist temple in Vientiane, Laos. It was built in the 16th century on the ruins of an earlier 13th century Khmer temple, which the Lao believe was in turn built on a 3rd century Indian temple built by Buddhist missionaries from the Mauryan Empire who were sent by the Emperor Ashoka. Relics of The Buddha are said to be contained here. Pha That Luang was destroyed by the Thai invasion in the 19th century, then later restored to its original design. The architecture of the temple includes many references to Lao culture and identity and so has become a symbol of Lao nationalism.

Vat Yotkeo

Vat Yotkeo was a temple in Laos which was built between during the rule of King Sai Setthathirat. It was discovered in April 2006 during the construction of a major road and was destroyed in 1828 by the Thais, who burned and pillaged Vientiane following the defeat of the last king of the Vientiane dynasty of Lan Xang, Chao Anouvong. The remains included a ceremonial hall, pottery, roof tiles and various Buddha images.

Wat Phou

Wat Phou (Vat Phu) is a ruined Khmer temple complex in southern Laos. It is located at the base of mount Phu Kao, some 6 km from the Mekong river in Champassak province. There was a temple on the site as early as the 5th century, but the surviving structures date from the 11th to 13th centuries. The temple has a unique structure, in which the elements lead to a shrine where a linga was bathed in water from a mountain spring. The site later became a centre of Theravada Buddhist worship, which it remains today.

History: Wat Phou was initially associated with the city of Shrestapura, which lay on the bank of the Mekong directly east of mount Lingaparvata (now called Phu Kao). By the latter part of the 5th century the city was already the capital of a kingdom which texts and inscriptions connect with both Chenla and Champa and the first structure on the mountain was constructed around this time. The mountain gained spiritual importance from the linga-shaped protuberance on its summit; the mountain itself was therefore considered the home of Shiva and the river as representing the ocean or the Ganges River. The temple was naturally dedicated to Shiva, while the water from the spring which emerges directly behind the temple was considered sacred.

Wat Phou was a part of the Khmer empire, centred on Angkor to the southwest, at least as early as the reign of Yashovarman I in the early 10th century. Shrestapura was superseded by a new city in the Angkorian period, located directly south of the temple. In the later period, the original buildings were replaced, re-using some of the stone blocks; the temple now seen was built primarily during the Koh Ker and Baphuon periods of the 11th century. Minor changes were made during the following two centuries, before the temple, like most in the empire, was converted to Theravada Buddhist use. This continued after the area came under control of the Lao and a festival is held on the site each February. Little restoration work has been done, other than the restoration of boundary posts along the path. Wat Phou was designated a World Heritage Site in 2001.

The Site: Like most Khmer temples, Wat Phou is orientated towards the east, although the axis actually faces eight degrees south of due east, being determined primarily by the orientation of the mountain and the river. Including the barays it stretches 1.4 km east from the source of the spring, at the base of a cliff 100 m up the hill. 6 km east of the temple, on the west bank of the Mekong, lay the city, while a road south from the temple itself led to other temples and ultimately to the city of Angkor.

Approached from the city (of which little remains), the first part of the temple reached is a series of barays. Only one now contains water, the 600 by 200 m middle baray which lies directly along the temples's axis; there were further reservoirs north and south of this and a further pair on each side of the causeway between the middle baray and the palaces.

The two palaces stand on a terrace on either side of the axis. They are known as the north and south palaces or, without any evidence, the men's and women's palaces (the term "palace" is also a mere convention-their purpose is unknown). Each consisted of a rectangular courtyard with a corridor and entrance on the side towards the axis and false doors at the east and west ends. The courtyards of both buildings have laterite walls; the walls of the northern palace's corridor are also laterite, while those of the southern palace are sandstone. The northern building is now in better condition. The palaces are notable chiefly for their pediments and lintels, which are in the early Angkor Wat style.

The next terrace has a small shrine to Nandin (Shiva's mount) to the south, in poor condition. The road connecting Wat Phou to Angkor ran south from this temple. Continuing west, successive staircases lead up further terraces; between them stands a dvarapala which has come to be worshipped as king Kammatha, mythical builder of the temple. On the narrow next terrace are the remains of six small shrines destroyed by treasure-hunters.

The path culminates in seven sandstone tiers which rise to the upper terrace and central sanctuary. The sanctuary is in two parts. The front section, of sandstone, is now occupied by four Buddha images, while the brick rear part, which formerly contained the central linga, is empty. The entire roof is missing, although a makeshift covering has been added to the front. Water from the spring which emerges from the cliff about 60 m southwest of the sanctuary was channeled along stone aquaducts into the rear chamber, continuously bathing the linga. The sanctuary is later than the north and south palaces, belonging to the Baphuon period of the later 11th century. The east side has three doorways: from south to north, their pediments show Krishna defeating the naga Kaliya; Indra riding Airavata; and Vishnu riding Garuda. The east wall bears dvarapalas and devatas. Entrances to the south and north bear have inner and outer lintels, including one to the south of Krishna ripping Kamsa apart.

Other features of the area are a library, in poor condition, south of the sanctuary and a relief of the Hindu trinity to the northwest. There are other carvings further north: a Buddha's footprint on the cliff-face and boulders shaped to resemble elephants and a crocodile. The crocodile stone has acquired some notoriety as being possibly the site of an annual human sacrifice described in a 6th century Chinese text the identification is lent some plausibility by the similarity of the crocodile's dimensions to those of a human.

Wat Xieng Thong

Wat Xieng Thong is a Buddhist temple in Luang Phrabang, Laos. It was built in 1560 by King Setthathirath. It was under royal patronage during the Kingdom of Laos. Today it is a popular tourist attraction.

BUDDHIST TEMPLES IN MALAYSIA

Wat Chaiya Mangkalaram

Wat Chaiya Mangkalaram is a Thai Buddhist temple in George Town, Penang, Malaysia, most notable for its Reclining Buddha statue. The statue is the 3rd largest of its kind, being 33 metres in length. In the main shrine in front of the Reclining Buddha there are smaller shrines of different Buddhas and popular Thai deities. Also on the temple grounds many coloured statues of Devas and other mythical creatures are on display.

The temple was built in 1845 on a piece of land given by Queen Victoria to four women trustees as a gesture of goodwill to boost trading relations with Thailand. The first monk was a Theravada Buddhist monk from Thailand, Phorthan Kuat, also known as the "Powerful Monk". Legend has it that he was very fond of laksa, a local specialty and even today devotees bring a bowl of laksa as an offering to his shrine.

Cheng Hoon Teng

The Cheng Hoon Teng temple is a Buddhist temple in Jalan Tokong, Malacca, Malaysia. It is the oldest functioning temple in Malaysia.

Overview: The richly decorated Cheng Hoon Teng temple covers an area of 4,600 square metres. Featuring a magnificent main gate along Jalan Tokong, the Cheng Hoon Teng temple consists of a complex of several prayer halls, with a large main prayer hall dedicated to the goddess of mercy, Kuan Yin. Additional smaller prayer quarters were added later. One of these is dedicated to the Taoist gods of wealth, longevity and propagation, while another houses ancestral tablets.

One of the most dramatic features of Cheng Hoon Teng temple is the seven-metre red flag-pole facing the left wing of the main prayer hall, which houses the remains of two of the three Kapitans who contributed to the construction of the temple. Across the road is a traditional opera theatre, which forms a part of the Cheng Hoon Teng temple complex. The building conforms to the principles of feng shui. The complex is laid out to ensure a view of the river and high ground on either side.

History: Built in 1645 by Kapitan Lee Wei King with building materials imported from China, Cheng Hoon Teng served as the main place of worship for the local Hokkien community. The main hall was built by Kapitan Chan Ki Lock in 1704 and was rebuilt in 1801 by Kapitan China Chua Su Cheong, who contributed to the aesthetic and magnificent structural additions of the building. In 2003, Cheng Hoon Teng was listed as a UNESCO World Heritage Site, following restoration work carried out by the Malaysian government.

Kek Lok Si

The Kek Lok Si Temple is a Buddhist temple situated in Air Itam in Penang and is one of the best known temples on the island.

The construction of the temple begun in 1893 and was inspired by the chief monk of the Goddess of Mercy Temple at Pitt Street. With the support of the consular representative of China in Penang, the project received the sanction of the Manchu Emperor Guangxu, who bestowed a tablet and gift of 70,000 volumes of the Imperial Edition of the Buddhist Sutras.

In 1930, the seven storey main pagoda of the temple or the Pagoda of 10,000 Buddhas, was completed. This pagoda combines a Chinese octagonal base with a middle tier of Thai design and a Burmese crown; reflecting the temple's embrace of both Mahayana and Theravada Buddhism.

In 2002, a 30.2m bronze statue of the Kuan Yin was completed and opened to public. The statue is located on the hillside above the pagoda.

Snake Temple

The Snake Temple is situated in the small town of Bayan Lepas in Penang and is perhaps the only temple of its kind in the world. The temple is filled with the smoke of burning incense and a variety of pit vipers. The vipers are believed to be rendered harmless by the sacred smoke; but just for good measure, the snakes have also been de-venomed. Local devotees believe that the temple's snake population has come there of its own accord. The temple was built in about 1850 in memory of Chor Soo Kong-a Buddhist monk who moved to Penang. The statue of the deified healer was brought to Penang by a monk from China. The legend is that this pious monk gave shelter to the snakes of the jungle; when the temple was completed, the snakes moved in. The Snake Temple was originally named the "Temple of the Azure Cloud" in honour of the beauty of Penang's sky.

Believers from as far away as Singapore and Taiwan come to pray in the temple on Chor Soo Kong's birthday (the sixth day of the first lunar month).

Thean Hou Temple

The Thean Hou Temple is a striking six-tiered Chinese temple. It is located on a 1.67 acres (6,760 m^2) of land atop Robson Heights along Lorong Bellamy, overlooking Jalan Syed Putra (Federal Highway). It was completed in 1987 and officially opened in 1989. The property belongs to the Persatuan Hainan Selangor and Wilayah Persekutuan (Hainanese Association of Selangor and Federal Territory). This temple, built by the Hainanese community living in Kuala Lumpur is dedicated to Goddess Tian Hou (The Heavenly Mother).

This syncretic temple with elements of Buddhism, Taoism and Confucianism is a grandiose structure and represents a successful combination of modern architectural techniques and authentic traditional design featuring imposing pillars, spectacular roofs, ornate carvings and intricate embellishments. Its grand architecture has made it a popular tourist destination. The front entrance of the temple features a multi-arched gateway with red pillars, the colour symbolic of prosperity and good fortune. Souvenir stalls and a canteen are found on the 1st level. The 2nd level houses the multi-purpose hall while offices are located on the 3rd level. The 4th level has 3 tiers and the prayer hall is located here.

The prayer hall houses 3 altars, each with a sculpture of one deity or goddess. As one enters the prayer hall, the altar on the right is dedicated to Guan Yin, the Goddess of Mercy. Tian Hou is in the centre while Shui Wei Sheng Niang (the Goddess of the Waterfront) is at the left.

Despite the dedication to Tian Hou, worship of Guan Yin (or "Guan Shi-Yin") is a recurrent theme at the Thean Hou Temple. In addition to her altar in the prayer hall, there is also a smaller statue of Guan Yin to the right of the hall, set amongst rocks and falling water. Here one can kneel and receive a blessing of water from the statue. Outside the temple at the entrance to the grounds, there is a larger statue, similarly set amongst rocks and falling water. Finally there is a large statue of the goddess opposite the temple, along with a collection of other large statues that include representations of the twelve animals of Chinese astrology.

KOREAN BUDDHIST TEMPLES

Buddhist temples are an important part of the Korean landscape. This article gives a brief overview of Korean Buddhism, then describes some of the more important temples in Korea.

Introduction to Korean Buddhism

A distinctive form of Buddhism evolved in Korea. This was facilitated by the geographical location and cultural conditions. Buddhism first arrived in Korea in 372 in the Goguryeo Kingdom. In 374 the influential Chinese monk Ado arrived in the kingdom and inspired the King Sosurim in the following year. The first two temples Seongmunsa and Ilbullansa were built in 375 on the order of the king. Buddhism soon became the national religion of the Goguryeo.

With the advent of Taoism in 624 the rulers began to suppress Buddhism and its importance quickly declined. The Baekje Kingdom, on the other hand, flourished under the influence of Buddhism. In 552 Buddhist scriptures were sent to Japan. This eventually led to the establishment of Buddhism in Japan.

In Silla Buddhism was important, too. It flourished during the reign of the King Jinheung (540 to 576). The Heungnyunsa temple was completed where any commoner could become a monk. The study of scriptures was greatly highlighted. For about 250 years Buddhism thrived in Unified Silla.

Buddhism was admired by Wang Geon, the founder of the Goryeo Dynasty. Throughout the country pagodas and other Buddhist structures were built. In the late Goryeo period Buddhism became linked with the corruption of the regime. A great number of monks were involved in politics. Bit by bit anti-Buddhist sentiments grew, leading to chaos which was ended by the establishment of the Joseon Dynasty. The king Taejo himself was a devout Buddhist, but the influence of monks was reduced. At times monks were treated as outcasts, but generally there was no hindrance to their practising. Buddhist heritage can be found all over the country in the form of temples, pagodas, sculptures, paintings, handicrafts and buildings.

BUDDHIST TEMPLES IN NORTH KOREA

Pohyonsa

Pohyonsa is a Buddhist temple in North Pyongan Province, North Korea. It is located on Myohyang-san and was founded in 1024, during the Goryeo dynasty. The temple houses a copy of the Tripitaka Koreana and is maintained today as a historical museum. There are several other temples by the same name, including ones in Anbyong-gun, Kangwon, North Korea, in Gangneung-si, Gangwon, South Korea and in Cheongju, North Chungcheong, South Korea.

BUDDHIST TEMPLES IN SOUTH KOREA

Baekryeon Temple

Baekryeon Temple is a Buddhist temple located in Doam-myeon, Gangjin county, South Jeolla province, South Korea.

Its name means "White Lotus" temple and its physical form dates to the late Chosun Dynasty. Some records date the idea of a White Lotus temple to the 8th century AD. It was designated a Local Tangible Cultural Property in 1986.

Baekyangsa

Baekyangsa, also spelled Baegyangsa, is a head temple of the Jogye Order of Korean Buddhism. It is situated in Bukha-myeon, Jangseong County, in South Jeolla province, South Korea. Built in 632 under the Baekje kingdom, it lies on the slopes of Baegam-san in Naejangsan National Park. The name of the temple means "white sheep," and refers to a legend from the Goryeo period in which a white sheep came down from the mountain to listen to a sermon and was sufficiently enlightened that it was able to ascend into Paradise.

Beomeosa

Beomeosa is a Buddhist temple in Cheongnyong-dong, Geumjeong-gu, Busan, South Korea. Built on the slopes of Geumjeongsan, it is one of the country's leading urban temples. It was constructed in 678 during the reign of Silla king Munmu, by the monk Uisang. It became known as one of the ten great temples of the Hwaeom sect, although like most Korean temples it was later assimilated into the Jogye Order. At its largest, during the Koryo dynasty, it was much larger than it is today-with over 360 rooms and more than a thousand monks in residence. The temple was burned to the ground in 1592 during the Japanese Imjin Invasion. It was reconstructed in 1602, but was burned again by an accidental fire. In 1613 it was rebuilt again. The Main Hall (Taeungjon) and the front gate (Iljumun) date to this reconstruction.

The temple complex has several buildings and other objects which are designated as official treasures:

National Treasure 250-Three Story Stone Pagoda
National Treasure 434-Taeungjon

Tangible Cultural Asset 2-Iljumun
Tangible Cultural Asset 11-Wonhyoam Eastern Pagoda
Tangible Cultural Asset 12-Wonhyoam Western Pagoda
Tangible Cultural Asset 15-Flag Pole Holder
Tangible Cultural Asset 16-Stone Lamp

In addition to the main temple compound, there are eleven hermitages or smaller temples (am) nearby and administratively attached to Pomosa.

Chongnyong-am (Blue Lotus Hermitage)
Naewon-am (Buddha's Celestial Teaching Hall Hermitage)
Kyemyong-am (Rooster's Crow Hermitage)
Taesong-am (Great Saint Hermitage)
Kumgang-am (Diamond Hermitage)
Anyang-am (Peace Nurturing Hermitage)
Miruk-am (Maitreya Hermitage)
Wonhyo-am (Former hermitage residence of the famous monk, Wonhyo)
Saja-am (Lion Hermitage)
Mansong-am (Great Teacher Hermitage)
Chijang-am (Ksitigarbha Hermitage)

Beomeosa is located in the north part of Pusan, Korea. It is accessible from the subway (line 1-Beomeosa station). From the station walk east up the road to the #90 bus stop (about 200 metres) the bus runs every 30 minutes. Or hire a taxi; the trip should not exceed the standard fare by too much.

Beopjusa

Beopjusa is a head temple of the Jogye Order of Korean Buddhism. It is situated on the slopes of Songnisan in Naesongni-myeon, Boeun County, in the province of Chungcheongbuk-do, South Korea. It was initially constructed in 653 by the Silla monk Uisin. It has been historically associated with Beopsang thought and the worship of the Maitreya Buddha. In the Goryeo dynasty, this temple is said to have been home to as many as 3,000 monks. A few facilities from this period still remain on the temple grounds, including a cistern and iron pot for serving food and water to thousands of monks. It continued to play an important role in subsequent centuries, but shrank as the state's support for Buddhism disappeared under the Joseon Dynasty.

The temple is particularly known for Palsangjeon, a wooden pagoda. Like most of the other buildings, this burned to the ground in the Seven Year War. The pagoda was reconstructed in 1624. Joseon Dynasty founder Taejo is said to have retired to a spot near Beopjusa after tiring of his sons' fighting.

Bongseonsa

Bongseonsa is a head temple of the Jogye Order of Korean Buddhism. It stands in Jinjeop-eup, Namyangju, a short distance east of Seoul in Gyeonggi province, South Korea. It was built by National Preceptor Beobin in 969, under the Goryeo dynasty. At that time it bore the name "Unaksa." The current name dates to 1469, when Queen Jeonghui of the Joseon Dynasty changed the temple's name at the time that her husband King Sejo was buried nearby. The name can be interpreted as "temple of revering the sage." Thereafter, the temple continued to have a close relationship with the queens of Joseon.

Bongseonsa has been burned down and rebuilt several times, due to the 16th-century Seven Year War, 17th-century Manchu invasions of Korea and 20th-century Korean War.

Bongwonsa

Bongwon Temple (or Bongwonsa) is a Buddhist temple near Yonsei University in Seodaemun-gu, Seoul, South Korea.

Situated to the northeast on the university on the hillside, this is the head temple of the Taego Order of Korean Buddhism. Originally founded in 889 by Master Doseon and located on the current site of Yonsei University, it moved to its present location in 1748. Part of the temple was destroyed in 1950 during the Korean War. In 1966 a new hall was built but this was later moved to another part of the city. In 1991 while a new Hall of 3000 Buddhas was being built, a fire destroyed the Main Buddha Hall, which was rebuilt in 1994. Currently more than 50 monks live at the temple and are engaged in education and social welfare work.

Bulguksa

Bulguksa is a Buddhist temple in the North Gyeongsang province in South Korea. It is home to seven National treasures of Korea, including Dabotap and Seokgatap stone pagodas, Cheongun-gyo (Blue Cloud Bridge) and two gilt-bronze statutes of Buddha. The temple is classified as Historic and Scenic Site No. 1 by the South Korean government.. In 1995, Bulguksa was added to the UNESCO World Heritage List together with the Seokguram Grotto, which lies four kilometres to the east.

The temple is considered as a masterpiece of the golden age of Buddhist art in the Silla kingdom. It is currently the head temple of the 11th district of the Jogye Order of Korean Buddhism.

History: The temple's records state that a small temple was built on this site under King Beopheung in 528. The Samguk Yusa records that the current temple was constructed under King Gyeongdeok in 751, begun by Prime Minister Gim Daeseong to pacify the spirits of his parents. The building was completed in 774 by the Silla royal court, after Gim's death and given its current name Bulguksa (Temple of the Buddha Land).

The temple was renovated during the Goryeo Dynasty and the early Joseon Dynasty. During the Japanese invasions between 1592 and 1598, the wooden buildings were burned to the ground. After 1604, reconstruction and expansion of Bulguksa started, followed by about 40 renovations until 1805. During the Japanese occupation of 1910-1945, the Japanese conducted a restoration, but there are no records of the work done and known treasures disappeared during this time.

After World War II and the Korean War, a partial restoration was conducted in 1966. Upon an extensive archeological investigation, major restoration was conducted between 1969 and 1973 by the order of President Park Chung Hee, bringing Bulguksa to its current form. The famous stone structures are preserved from the original Silla construction.

Structure: The temple is located on the slopes of Tohamsan, in Jinheon-dong, Gyeongju. The entrance to the temple, Sokgyemun, has a double-sectioned staircase and bridge (National Treasure No. 23) that leads to the inside of the temple compound. The stairway is 33 steps high, corresponding to the 33 steps to enlightenment. The lower portion, Cheongungyo (Blue Cloud Bridge) is 6.3 metres long and has 17 steps. The upper portion, Baegungyo (White Cloud Bridge) is 5.4 metres and has 16 steps. The stairway leads to Jahamun (Mauve Mist Gate).

There are two pagodas on the temple site, which is unusual. The three-story Seokgatap (Sakyamuni Pagoda) which stands at 8.2 metres is a traditional Korean-style stone pagoda with simple lines and minimal detailing. Seokgatap is over 13 centuries old. Dabotap (Many Treasure Pagoda) is 10.4 metres tall and dedicated to the Many Treasures Buddha mentioned in the Lotus Sutra. In contrast to Seokgatap, Dabotap is known for its highly ornate structure. Its image is reproduced on the South Korean 10 won coin. Dabotap and Seokgatap are Korean National Treasures nos. 20 and 21, respectively.

The terrestrial and the two celestial abodes are manifested in Bulguksa: the terrestrial with a Shakyamuni Buddha Lotus Sutra, the celestial with Amitabha Buddha Avatamska Sutra. The large temple site is centred around two courts. One of the courts is centred on Daeungjeon, the hall which houses the Shakyamuni Buddha. The other is centred on Geungnakjeon, the hall of paradise where the Seven Treasure Bridge Chilbogyo is housed.

Daeung Jeon (The Hall of Great Enlightenment) is the main hall. Dabotap and Seokgatap stand before this hall. The hall enshrines the Sakyamuni Buddha and was built in 681 AD.. Behind the main hall stands Munseol Jeon, the Hall of No Words.. This hall gets its name from the belief that Buddha's teachings could not be taught by mere words alone. It is one of the oldest buildings in the complex and was probably built in 670 AD. The Kwaneum Jeon (Avalokitesvara's Shrine) houses an image of the Avalokitesvara, the Bodhisattva of Perfect Compassion and stands at the highest point of the complex.. The Biro Jeon, which sits below the Kwaneum Jeon, (Vairocana Buddha Hall) houses national treasure No.26 while the Geuknak Jeon (Hall of Supreme Bliss), standing near the main compound, houses the gilt-bronze buddha that is the national treasure No.27.

Official Treasures at Bulguksa

National Treasures No.20 and 21: The two famous stone pagodas, Dabotap and Seokgatap reside in the main courtyard of the Bulguksa Temple complex. They are, respectively, the twentieth and twenty-first national treasures of Korea and were designated on December 20, 1962.

National Treasure No.22: The Yeonhwagyo (Lotus Flower Bridge) and Chilbogyo (Seven Treasures Bridge) are a pair of bridges at Bulguksa.. This bridge was designated as the 22nd national treasure on December 20, 1962. The bridge lead to Anyangmun Gate (Peace Enhancing Gate) leading to Geungnakjeon (the Hall of the Pure Land). This pair were built at the same time as their brother bridges, National Treasure No.23.

These pair of bridges share the 45 degree incline, arch underneath and the combination bridge/staircase design of their brother bridges. However, one noticeable difference is that this bridge is smaller. The lower Lotus Flower Bridge has ten steps while the upper Seven Treasures Bridge contains eight. This bridge is on the west in relation to the Blue Cloud and White Cloud Bridges.

The Lotus Flower Bridge is known for its delicate carvings of Lotus Flowers on each step but these have faded with the weight of many pilgrims. Today, visitors are restricted from walking on the bridge.

National Treasure No.23: The Cheongungyo (Blue Cloud Bridge) and Baegungyo (White Cloud Bridge) Bridges of Bulguksa Temple are two bridges that are a part of a stairway that leads to the temple.. The bridges were probably built in 750 AD during the reign of King Gyeongdeok. Although built separately, they are designated together as one single national treasure. They were designated as the 23rd national treasure on December 20, 1962.

The Blue Cloud Bridge makes up the lower span of the stair while the White Cloud Bridge is the upper part. The bridges lead to the Jahamun Gate (Golden Purple Gate) which leads to Sakyamuni Hall. There are 33 steps on the stairway, which slopes at a 45 degree angle and each step corresponds to one of the 33 heavens of Buddhism. The lower Blue Cloud Bridge has seventeen steps while the upper White Cloud Bridge has sixteen. The large arch underneath the stairwell testifies to the use of arches in Silla-style bridges and the remains of a pond and once flowed underneath the bridge.

National Treasure No. 26: Natioanl Treasure No.26 (Bulguksa geumdong birojana buljwasang), designated on December 20, 1962, is a seated gilt-bronze Vairocana Buddha statue at Bulguksa Temple.

The Buddha of Enlightenment is enshrined in the Viro Hall. It is 1.77 metres in height and made from gilt-bronze. The head of the Buddha has an usnisa, a symbol of supreme wisdom. The head of the Buddha was made by fusing two shells to each other and the face is elongated and soft.

The robes of the Buddha are highly detailed and the simulation of folded cloth rippling down from the shoulder to the lap is done with high skill. The hands of the Buddha are in a position, the right index finger covered by the left hand, that often is used to symbolize the Buddha of Enlightenment. The figure is estimated to be from the 9th century AD due to stylistic evidence, including the overly wide lap and the lack of tension in the depiction of the robes and face of the Buddha.

National Treasure No.27: The seated gilt-bronze Amitabha Buddha statue of Bulguksa Temple is National Treasure No.27. (Bulguksa geumdong amita yeoraejwasang) and was designated on December 20, 1962.

The Amitabha Buddha statute is 1.66 metres in height and enshrined in Geumgnakjeon (the Hall of Heaven) in the temple complex. This gilt-bronze statue was probably cast in the late eighth or early part of the ninth century and it shares the style of National Treasure No.26. The head of the statue is made by fixing two shell-like pieces together. The face has a distinctively aquiline nose. The Buddha has broad shoulders and strong chest while the large lap gives the figure a sense of proportional harmony and stability. The style of the robe seems to be more stylized and haphazard. The position of the left hand raised at shoulder-level palm forward and the right hand is placed at the lap. The style of the Buddha seems to follow an abstract and stylized tradition rather than a representation of realism.

Treasure No.61: This sarira pagoda, or stupa, looks like a stone lantern. The artifact was at one point taken to Japan in 1906 but was eventually returned. It is from the Goryeo Dynasty and shows the influence of Silla Dynasty art.

A sarira is a container for the relics or remains of famous priests or royalty. It is said that this sarira contained the remains of eight priests or a queen. The three main features of the piece are the foundation stone, the main body and the ornamental top. The foundation is an octagonal stone decorated with carvings. Atop this foundation is a circular stone incised with louts motifs. The pillar supports of the main pody are carved with a cloud motif while the main pody is cylindrical and has four bas-reliefs of Buddha and bodhisattvas and are accompanied by flower motifs. The top of the pagoda has twelve sides which meet into a hexagonal shape.

Bunhwangsa

Bunhwangsa (literally "Famous Emperor Temple") is a temple complex from the Old Silla era.. The temple is recorded to have been built in 634 under the auspices of Queen Seondeok.. Today the temple is still used by a small group of worshippers but in its heyday, the temple covered several acres and was one of the four main temples of the Silla Kingdom used by the state to ask the Buddha to bless the kingdom.. The ruins of Hwangnyongsa Temple lay near by.

National Treasure No. 30: A notable ruin at the temple is the Bunhwangsa Pagoda (Kr. Bunhwangsa Seoktap, literally "Stone Pagoda of Bunhwangsa"), the oldest dated pagoda from the Silla Kingdom.. The pagoda is National Treasure of Korea No. 30 and was designated by the South Korean government on December 20th, 1962.. The pagoda is based on prototypes from the Tang Dynasty in China. However, unlike Tang pagodas which were made from brick, Silla architects used stones of black andesite cut like brick... Each story of the pagoda is progressively smaller in size and each story's roof is made by placing bricks in a staircase-like fashion.

Today, only three tiers of the pagoda remain. However, it is believed to have once stood seven or nine stories in height, though ancient records state the pagoda stood nine stories tall.. Although once hollow, the collapsed stories of the pagoda have filled the centre of pagoda with debris.

An excavation and partial restoration in 1915 by the Japanese uncovered a sarira, or relic box, of the cremated remains of a priest hidden in between the second and third stories... Precious artifacts such as gold and stone ornaments, coins, scissors and a needle were also found in the pagoda which indicated that a woman of royal blood, perhaps even Queen Seondeok herself, had once owned the objects.. Each side of the pagoda has what may have once been doors into the interior of the pagoda.

Two figures guard each doorway and are known as Geumgan-yeoksa (literally "Mighty Diamond Men") or Inwangsang, guardians of the Buddhist canon... Each corner of the one-step platform upon which the pagoda rests holds a guardian lion statue. Granite lotus blossoms also adorn the pagoda.. A contemporaneous pair of stone pagodas were built at the Baekje Mireuksa Temple and the Bunhwangsa Pagoda is oftentimes compared with them although those stone pagodas more closely imitated wood architectural styles.. Also of note is the flagpole holder which survives from the Silla era as well.

Daeheungsa

Daeheungsa, sometimes called Daedunsa, is a head temple of the Jogye Order of Korean Buddhism. It is located on the slopes of Duryun-san in Samsan-myeon, Haenam County, in the province of Jeollanam-do near the southern limit of South Korea. It is believed to date to the Three Kingdoms period, although no exact record of its founding has survived. The temple is known as a historical centre of Korean tea culture.

Donghwasa

Donghwasa, also Donghwa Temple, is a Buddhist temple of the Jogye Order in northern Daegu, South Korea. The temple is located on the slopes of Palgongsan, within the boundaries of Dohak-dong, Dong-gu, near Daegu's northern border. It is the seat of the 9th region of the Jogye Order. The name means "temple of paulownia blossoms."

The first temple on the site was built in 493. The name Donghwasa was applied during the Unified Silla period in 832. From this time to the present, it has remained one of the country's most powerful temples. During the Goryeo Dynasty, it was one of only four temples which administered the civil service examinations for monks. Buddhists were out of power during the Joseon Dynasty, but the temple retained a great deal of influence and continued building new structures.

Eunhaesa

Eunhaesa is a head temple of the Jogye Order of Korean Buddhism. It is located in Cheongtong-myeon, Yeongcheon, in the province of Gyeongsangbuk-do, South Korea. It stands on the eastern slopes of Palgongsan, not far from another major temple, Donghwasa. The temple was founded by National Preceptor Hyecheol in 809. The name means "temple of the silver sea." The original name was "temple of the tranquil sea," Haeansa. After the original temple burned to the ground following the Seven Year War in the 1590s, it was moved to its current location and named Eunhaesa.

Gamsansa

Gamsansa or Gamsan Temple, is the name of a Korean Buddhist temple established during the country's Unified Silla dynasty. Save for a partially reconstructed pagoda none of the original temple structures survive. Gamsansa was located approximately 20 kilometres south of the city of Gyeongju, at the time the capital of Silla, not far from the more famous Silla temple of Bulguksa.

According to engravings preserved on extant artifacts excavated from the temple site as well as the 13th century Korean work Samguk Yusa, Gamsan ('sweet mountain') Temple was established in 719 by the Silla aristocrat Kim Jiseong on the site of his own estate, apparently to prayer for the souls of his deceased parents and siblings as well as the future prosperity of the Silla kingdom. Two granite statues, of the Maitreya Buddha and Amithaba Buddha, were discovered during the Japanese colonial period in the early 20th century and later designated Korean National Treasures no. 81 and 82 respectively. The carving of the Maitreya Buddha had been commissioned by Kim and dedicated to the spirit of his father while the Amithaba was dedicated to the spirit of his mother. They are both currently held at the National Museum of Korea in Seoul. At the Gyeongju National Museum can be found 12 dancing zodiac figures carved in stone that once decorated the base of the temple's stone pagoda.

Geumgoksa

Geumgok Temple is a Buddhist temple in Gangjin county, South Jeolla province, South Korea. Its name means "Golden

Valley Temple." Three temples and numerous smaller shrines and burial mounds comprise the site. It is noted for its scenic beauty as well as a 3-tiered stone pagoda that dates to the Goryo Dynasty.

Geumsansa

Geumsansa is a head temple of the Jogye Order of Korean Buddhism. It stands on the slopes of Moak-san in Gimje City, Jeollabuk-do, South Korea. The temple was first constructed in 599. Several National treasures of South Korea are located on the temple grounds. These include a detailed lotus-shaped stone pedestal from the 10th century.

Golgulsa Temple

Golgulsa (Stone Buddha Temple) is located 20 km east of the ancient Silla Dynasty capital city of Gyeongju in Southeastern Korea. In the Golgulsa temple area can be found the oldest historical Buddhist ruins on Mt. Hamwol and the only cave temple in Korea. The original temple was built out of solid rock during the 6th century by Saint Kwang Yoo and his companions, Buddhist monks from India. This temple contains a sculptured Maya Tathagata Buddha (Buddha was known as the "Tathagata"; his mother was "Maya Devi") and twelve rock caves. Recently ex-Master Monk of Kirimsa (Kirim Temple), Seol Jeog-un constructed a road while simultaneously renovating the Golgulsa Temple.

Sunmudo Martial Art: The formal name of Sunmudo is Bulgyo Geumgang Yeong Gwon. It is a training method taught at Golgulsa Temple designed to extinguish worldly pains and attain enlightenment. The goal of this training is harmonization of mind and body united with breathing.

Golgulsa temple has run Sunmudo training programmes since 1992 for those who would like to experience the traditions of Korean Seon (Zen) Buddhism including Sonmudo.

The Breath of Seon: Sunmudo training is composed of: "still training," which includes "chwason," or sitting mediation, yoga-like exercises and Chinese Gi-gong/Qigong, as well as "active training," which includes gymnastics and martial arts. There is usually "still training" in the morning and "active training" in the evening.

Golgulsa Temple occupies half a mountain and actually contains several temples, administrative building, training hall, several dormitories, dining hall and so on.

Gounsa

Gounsa is a head temple of the Jogye Order of Korean Buddhism. It stands in Danchon-myeon, Uiseong County, in the province of Gyeongsangbuk-do, South Korea. The temple was built in 681 by Uisang, a leading Buddhist monk of Silla. The name means "lonely cloud"; these characters were chosen after the temple was visited by scholar Choe Chi-won. The temple had previously been known by the same name, but with the meaning of "high cloud." Gounsa served as a centre of uibyeong resistance in the Seven Year War, when it was one of few temples to escape being burned by the Japanese forces. The temple did burn in a catastrophic fire in 1835; thus, all current buildings date from the 19th or 20th century.

Guinsa

Guinsa, located near Danyang in Chungcheongbuk-do, South Korea, is the headquarters of the Korean Cheontae sect of Buddhism. Although the architecture of Guinsa follows that of many other Buddhist temples in Korea, it is also markedly different in that the structures are several stories tall, instead of the typical one or two stories that structures in many other Korean temples have. This may be due to the restraints of the valley in which it is located and to modern construction techniques, but it creates a visual experience that is both beautiful and unique from what one sees at other temples.

History: Unlike many of Korea's temples, Guinsa is fairly new, dating only back to 1945. The temple is strikingly located, squeezed into a narrow valley surrounded on all sides by mountains and its location was decreed by head monk Sangwol Wongak's interpretation of the Lotus Sutra. The original was burned down during the Korean War, but the reconstruction of the first building was completed in 1966 and the complex, which now incorporates over 50 buildings, is still expanding.

Structures

Notable structures include:

- The Four Heavenly Kings Gate, containing statues of the Four Heavenly Kings, which marks the start of the temple proper.
- The 5-Story Law Hall, reputedly one of the largest temple buildings in Korea, containing a large gilded main altar of the Buddha Shakyamuni flanked by his attendants.
- The Great Teacher Hall, a shrine erected in the memory of Sangwol Wongak, a large statue of whom can be found inside.

Haeinsa

Haeinsa (Temple of Reflection on a Smooth Sea) is one of the foremost Buddhist temples in South Korea. It is most notable for being the home of the Tripitaka Koreana, the whole of the Buddhist Scriptures carved onto 81,258 wooden printing blocks, which it has housed since 1398..

Haeinsa is one of the Three Jewel Temples of Korea and represents Dharma or the Buddha's teachings. It is located on Gaya Mountain in South Gyeongsang Province. It is still an active Seon practice centre in modern times and was the home temple of the influential Rev. Seongcheol, who died in 1993.

The temple was first built in 802. Legend says that two Korean monks returned from China, Suneung and Ijeong and healed King Aejang wife's of her illness. In gratitude of the Buddha's mercy, the king ordered the construction of the temple.. Another account, by Choe Chi-Won in 900 states that Suneung and his disciple Ijeong, gained the support of a queen dowager who converted to Buddhism and then helped to finance the construction of the temple. The temple complex was renovated in the 900s, 1488, 1622 and 1644. Hirang, the temple abbot enjoyed the patronage of Taejo of Goryeo during that king's reign. Haiensa was burned down in a fire in 1817 and the main hall was rebuilt in 1818.. Another renovation in 1964 uncovered a royal robe of King Gwanghaegun, who was responsible for the 1622 renovation and an inscription on a ridge beam.

The main hall, Daejeokkwangjeon (Hall of Great Silence and Light), is unusual because it is dedicated to Vairocana where most other Korean temples house Seokgamoni in their main halls.

The Temple of Haeinsa, the Depositories for the "Tripitaka Koreana" Woodblocks, was added to the UNESCO World Heritage List in 1995. The UNESCO committee noted that the buildings housing the Tripitaka Koreana are unique because no other historical structure was specifically dedicated to the preservation of artifacts and the techniques used were particularly ingenuous. The temple also holds several official treasures including a realistic wooden carving of a monk and interesting Buddhist paintings, stone pagodas and lanterns.

Janggyeong Panjeon (National Treasure No.52): The storage halls, known as the Janggyeong Panjeon complex, is the depository for the Tripitaka Koreana woodblocks at Haeinsa Temple are also designated by the Korean government as a national treasure of Korea. They are some of the largest storage facilities made of wood.. The halls were designated on December 20, 1962. Remarkably, the halls were untouched during the Japanese invasion during the Seven-Year War and the halls were spared from the fire that burnt most of the temple complex down in 1818. All told, the storage halls have survived seven serious temple fires and even a near bombing during the Korean War when a pilot disobeyed orders because he remembered that the temple held a priceless treasure.

Janggyeong Panjeon complex is the oldest part of the temple and houses the 81,258 wooden printing blocks from the

Tripitaka. Although when the hall which houses the Tripitaka Koreana was first built is uncertain, it is believed that King Sejo expanded and renovated the hall in 1457. The storage complex is made up of four halls arranged in a rectangle and the style is very plain because of its use as a storage facility. The northern hall is called Beopbojeon (Hall of Dharma) and the southern hall is called Sudarajang (Hall of Sutras). These two main halls are 60.44 metres in length, 8.73 metres in width and 7.8 metres in height. They both have fifteen rooms with the two adjoining rooms. Additionally, there are two small halls in the east and west which are two small libraries.

Several ingeniuous preservation techniques are utilized to preserve the wooden printing blocks. The architects also utilized nature to help preserve the Tripitaka. The storage complex was built at the highest point of the temple and is 655 metres above sea level. Janggyeong Panjeon faces the southwest to avoid damp southeasternly winds of the valley below and uses the mountain peaks to block the cold north wind. Different sized windows in the north and south of both main halls are used to ventilate the halls and the they utilize principles of hydrodynamics.

The windows were installed in every hall to maximize ventilation and moderate temperature. The clay floors were filled with charcoal, calcium oxide, salt, lime and sand which reduces humidity when it rained by absorbing excess moisture while retaining moisture during the dry winter months. The roof is also made with clay and the bracketing and wood rafters prevent sudden changes in temperature. Additionally, no part of the complex is exposed to shade. Apparently, animals, insects and birds avoid the complex but the reason for this is unknown. These sophisticated preservation measures are widely credited as the reason the woodblocks have survived in such fantastic condition to this day.

In 1970, a modern storage complex was built utilizing modern preservation techniques but when test woodblocks were found to have mildew, the intended move was canceled and the woodblocks are still stored at Haeinsa.

Hwaeomsa

Hwaeomsa is a head temple of the Jogye Order of Korean Buddhism. It is located on the slopes of Jiri-san, in Masan-myeon, Gurye County, in the province of Jeollanam-do, South Korea. It was constructed under the Silla dynasty in 544, burned down during the Seven Year War in the 1590s and rebuilt thereafter.

Four national treasures of South Korea are located within the temple. These include an ancient stone lantern and a three-storied stone pagoda supported by four stone lions.

Hwangnyongsa

Hwangnyongsa is the name of a former Buddhist temple in the city of Gyeongju, South Korea. Built in the 6th century, it was the centre of state-sponsored Buddhism during the Silla and Unified Silla eras. Its name means "Golden/Yellow Dragon Temple" or "Emperor/Imperial Dragon Temple." Archaeological excavations and other scientific studies of the temple began in April 1976 (OCPRI 1984) and continue today.

History: Hwangnyongsa was built during the Silla period, under the patronage of the Silla royal family, on a plain encircled by mountains near the royal palace compound of Banwolseong (Half-Moon Palace). Construction began in 553 under the reign of King Jinheung and was not fully completed until 644. King Jinheung originally intended for the temple to be the site of a new palace but when a dragon was seen on the proposed site, a temple was commissioned instead. Hwangnyongsa was designed to be a place where monks prayed for the welfare of the nation by asking for the divine protection of the Buddha and a means to impress foreign dignitaries.

Following the defeat of Baekje in the 660s, the Baekje architect, Abiji, was commissioned to build a nine-story wooden pagoda at the site. This fact indicates that the Baekje had superior knowledge or wooden architecture. The nine stories supposedly represented the nine nations of East Asia and Silla's future conquest of those states.. The pagoda stood until it was burned by Mongol forces in 1238. No wooden architecture from the Silla people survives today but the ruins of Hwangnyongsa suggest a Goguryeo influence.

The temple site in a valley within Gyeongju National Park near Toham Mountain and about 150 yards from Bunhwangsa Temple, was excavated in 1972, revealing the temple layout and covering 40,000 artifacts.

Legends Surrounding the Temple: Buddhism was strongly resisted by the nobles of Silla while the king personally supported the new religion. The king's Grand Secretary, Ichadon, suggested that he forge the king's royal seal and create an order that the people adopt the new religion. When the forgery was discovered by the nobles, Ichadon suggested that he be made the scapegoat and that through his death the power of Buddha made manifest. The king agreed to the plan. The nobles were predictably outraged when they discovered Ichadon's forgery and the king ordered his execution. When Ichadon was executed, a series of miracles occurred which proved the power and reality of the Buddhist faith and the nobles converted to the new state religion. Ichadon's sacrifice was the impetus to the building of Hwangnyongsa Temple.

Another legend concerns the giant golden Buddha statue that the temple possessed. It was cast in the reign of King Jinheung as the temple centerpiece. The legend states that the gold for the statue came from King Ashoka of India. Ashoka had apparently attempted to cast a golden triad but failed. He then put the gold in a boat along with scale models of Bodhisattvas. Each country that received the boat was equally unable to cast the statues and not until the boat had arrived in Silla could a statue be cast.

Dimensions of the Temple: Only the massive foundation stones of the temple remain in current times. The original complex took seventeen years to complete.

- The main hall was 155 feet in length and 55 metres in width.

- The longest outer wall of the temple was 288 metres in length and the area enclosed by the outer walls covered approxiamately 80,000 square metres.
- The temple ruins also contain pedestle stones which were for monumental Buddhist statues. One statue of the Sakyamuni Buddha was five metres tall.
- The temple was originally arranged in the "three Halls-one Pagoda" style which meant that the pagoda was in the centre of the complex and flanked by three main halls on the left, right and behind the central pagoda.
- The famous nine-story pagoda, which was commissioned by Queen Seondeok after the main temple was finished, was the largest Korean pagoda ever built. It was reported to be 224 feet tall and the body was made entirely of wood..

  Only its foundation stones remain today but they attest to the mammoth proportions of the original structure. The pagoda had a foundation area of 6084 square feet, was supported by eight pillars on each side and had sixty foundation stones.

Jikjisa

Jikjisa is a head temple of the Jogye Order of Korean Buddhism. It is located on the slopes of Hwangaksan in Daehang-myeon, Gimcheon, in the province of Gyeongsangbuk-do. It may be one of the oldest temples in South Korea. Jikjisa is relatively well-connected to train and bus service. Jikjisa Station is located at the foot of the mountain, along the Gyeongbu Line railroad.

It is served only by the local commuter trains, which run twice daily in each direction. Jikjisa is believed to have been first constructed by the Goguryeo monk Ado in the year 418, long before Buddhism gained general acceptance in Silla. Jikjisa was largely destroyed during the Seven Year War in the 1590s. The rebuilding lasted from 1610 to about 1670.

Jogyesa

Jogyesa is the chief temple of the Jogye Order of Korean Buddhism. It thus plays a leading role in the current state of Seon Buddhism in South Korea. The temple was first established in 1395, at the dawn of the Joseon Dynasty; the modern temple was founded in 1910 and initially called "Hwanggaksa."

The name was changed to "Taegosa" during the period of Japanese rule and then to the present name in 1954.

Jogyesa is located in Gyeonji-dong, Jongno-gu, in central Seoul. Natural monument 9, an ancient white pine tree, is located within the temple grounds. Jogyesa came to the attention of the international news media in December, 1998 due to several monks occupying the temple in a power struggle between factions of the Jogye Order.

In the end, riot police were called in to take control of the temple and oust the protestors after they had occupied the building for more than 40 days.

Korean Buddhist Temples

Buddhist temples are an important part of the Korean landscape. This article gives a brief overview of Korean Buddhism, then describes some of the more important temples in Korea. Most Korean temples have names ending in-sa, which means "temple".

Introduction to Korean Buddhism: A distinctive form of Buddhism evolved in Korea. This was facilitated by the geographical location and cultural conditions. Buddhism first arrived in Korea in 372 in the Goguryeo Kingdom. In 374 the influential Chinese monk Ado arrived in the kingdom and inspired the King Sosurim in the following year. The first two temples Seongmunsa and Ilbullansa were built in 375 on the order of the king. Buddhism soon became the national religion of the Goguryeo.

With the advent of Taoism in 624 the rulers began to suppress Buddhism and its importance quickly declined. The

Baekje Kingdom, on the other hand, flourished under the influence of Buddhism. In 552 Buddhist scriptures were sent to Japan. This eventually led to the establishment of Buddhism in Japan.

In Silla Buddhism was important, too. It flourished during the reign of the King Jinheung (540 to 576). The Heungnyunsa temple was completed where any commoner could become a monk. The study of scriptures was greatly highlighted. For about 250 years Buddhism thrived in Unified Silla.

Buddhism was admired by Wang Geon, the founder of the Goryeo Dynasty. Throughout the country pagodas and other Buddhist structures were built. In the late Goryeo period Buddhism became linked with the corruption of the regime. A great number of monks were involved in politics. Bit by bit anti-Buddhist sentiments grew, leading to chaos which was ended by the establishment of the Joseon Dynasty.

The king Taejo himself was a devout Buddhist, but the influence of monks was reduced. At times monks were treated as outcasts, but generally there was no hindrance to their practising. Buddhist heritage can be found all over the country in the form of temples, pagodas, sculptures, paintings, handicrafts and buildings.

Magoksa

Magoksa is a head temple of the Jogye Order of Korean Buddhism. It is located on the eastern slope of Taehwasan, in Sangok-myeon, Gongju, in the province of Chungcheongnam-do, South Korea. The temple is said to have been established in 640 by the monk Jajang, although this account is disputed by some since Gongju would have lain within Baekje territory at that time.

It was used as a place of refuge during the early Joseon Dynasty and was left largely untouched by the Seven Year War of the 1590s. It continued to play this role in the 20th century, when it was used as a hideout by Korean independence leader Kim Ku.

Mireuksa

Mireuksa was the largest Buddhist temple in the ancient Korean kingdom of Baekje, which fell in the 7th century. Its site was excavated in 1980 in Iksan City, North Jeolla Province. The excavation disclosed many hitherto unknown facts about Baekje architecture. The stone pagoda at Mireuksa is one of two extant Baekje pagodas. It is also the largest as well as being among the oldest of all Korean pagodas.

The legend of the creation of Miruke-sa is told in the Samguk Yusa. King Mu and his queen were said to have seen a vision of the Maitreya Buddha at a pond on Mount Yonghwasan. The King promptly had the pond drained to establish the Mireuksa temple complex. The nine-storey wooden pagoda that once stood in the centre of the complex is said to have been the work of Baekje master craftsman Abiji. Designated South Korean Historic Site No. 150, Mireuksa has been partially restored and now includes a museum.

Layout: The complex included a central wooden pagoda flanked by two stone pagodas. A causeway seems to have led to the outer entrance of the walled complex. Miruksa temple had a unique arrangement of three pagodas erected in a straight line going from east to west, each with a hall to its north. Each pagoda and hall appear to have been surrounded by covered corridors, giving the appearance of three separate temples of a style known as "one Hall-one Pagoda."

The pagoda at the centre was found to have been made of wood, while the other two were made of stone. The sites of a large main hall and a middle gate were unearthed to the north and south of the wooden pagoda.

National Treasure No.11: The stone pagoda at Mireuksa (Mireuksa jiseoktap) was designated as a national treasure of Korea on December 20, 1962 and is the oldest and largest stone pagoda that has survived till modern times. This pagoda was the western pagoda. It is believed to have been built during the reign of King Mu who ruled from 600 to 640 AD.

The pagoda is architecturally significant because it shows how the Baekje adopted their knowledge of wood working to stone. An examble of wood pagoda building techniques being adapted to stone is the fact that the base of the pagoda is low and only one story, like a wood pagoda. From this stone pagoda, scholars can glean wood working techniques which is especially useful because many Korean wood pagodas have not survived the ravages of time and war.

Currently, the pagoda has six floors. However, scholars are uncertain of how many stories the pagoda would have actually reached. Each side of the first story is divided into three sections and the middle section contains a door which lead into the pagoda. Walking into the centre of pagoda, one can observe a massive pillar. There are also corner pillars and stone supports which mimicked wood supports of a wood pagoda. The corners of the roof of the pagoda were slightly raised up and each progressive storey was smaller than the one that preceded it.

Treasure No.236: Also surviving at Mireuksa are flagpole supports of the temple site (Mireuksa Jidang Ganjiju). These two massive stones are set 90 centimeters apart. During special celebrations, a flagpole would sit and be supported by the two stone pillars. There were three holes for flags per pillar. The first pair of holes were square while the other two pairs were round. The base of the flagpoles has not survived. The undecorated nature of the pole, save for horizontal stripes carved on the exterior of the two poles suggests that the poles were created during the Unified Silla period.

Preservation and Restoration: In 1910 only a part of the west pagoda (South Korean National Treasure No. 11) was still standing. In 1914, the Japanese government supported it with a concrete backing. In the late twentieth century, Korean archaeologists conducted extensive excavations, laying the foundation for a partial reconstruction and the interpretive centre. The west stone pagoda's concrete support has been removed beginning in 1999 and the entire structure was dismantled. It is undergoing restoration, expected to be completed in 2009.

Archaeological Importance: Among the many finds at the temple complex have been stone lanterns and the foundation stones for the columns and terraces on which the temple structure stood. Private houses were simple structures with wooden floors. One record indicates that these houses were reached by ladders. Archaeologists excavating the Mireuksa and Imgangsa temple sites have exhumed tall foundation stones on which wooden floors would have rested. It would appear that this feature was adapted from private houses. The raised floor and heating system later became a characteristic structure of the Korean house.

Muwisa

Muwisa is a Buddhist temple in Gangjin County, South Jeolla province, South Korea. Though it was first constructed in the 7th century, much of the area was destroyed during the Seven Year War in the 16th century. Geungnakjeon Hall, National Treasure No. 13, is on the site.

Palsangjeon

Palsangjeon (Hall of Eight Pictures) is located at Beopjusa Temple and is the only wooden pagoda left in Korea. The pagoda gets its name from paintings depicting the eight merciful acts of the Buddha to save lay people. It is believed to have originally been built in 553 but like many other wooden buildings was destroyed by the Japanese during the Seven-Year War and was subsequently rebuilt beginning in 1605 and completed in 1626..

The dates of the rebuilding come from inscriptions on a sarira casket and roof that were discovered when the building was renovated in 1968. Because pagoda architecture was brought from Korea to Japan, some hypothesize that the original Palsangjeon may have inspired and resembled the five story pagoda at Horyu-ji.

The pagoda is the 55th national treasure of Korea and was designated on December 20, 1962. The pagoda is 22.7 metres in height and its base covers an area of eight metres square. Four walls of the interior depict eight panels of paintings of Buddha saving the lay people of the word through his merciful acts. A sarira containing relics of the Buddha or a holy person, a shrine for the Buddha and an area to pray also occupy space inside the pagoda.

The pagoda rests on a low platform with stairs on each side. The first and second floors contain five rooms while the third and fourth floors contain three. The fifth floor holds two rooms. Although generally acknowledged to be a pagoda, some scholars suggest that this is a hybrid of pagoda and worship hall architecture..

Pyochungsa

Pyochungsa, originally Jungnimsa, is a Korean Buddhist temple of the Jogye Order of Korean Buddhism. It stands on the slopes of Jaeyaksan mountain near Cheonhwangsan in the Yeongnam Alps in Danjang-myeon, northern Miryang, South Korea.

Pyochungsa was first established by Wonhyo in 654 under the name "Jungnimsa." It was rebuilt at its present location by Hwangmyeon in 857, in the reign of the Silla king Heungdeok. In the Goryeo period, the National Preceptor Iryeon gathered more than a thousand monks there.

After Hideyoshi's invasions of Korea in the late 16th century, the temple was renamed "Pyochungsa" (temple of fidelity displayed) in honour of Songun Yu Jeong, the monk who led various righteous armies against the Japanese. The Pyochung Seowon, the only seowon located within the grounds of a Buddhist temple, was also constructed there in Songun's memory.

Due to its rich history and location in the Yeongnam Alps, Pyochungsa is a leading tourist attraction of Miryang. The temple is home to an incense burner which is designated

National treasure of South Korea no. 75. In addition, the entire temple has been designated as Gyeongsangnam-do Provincial Monument 17.

Seonunsa

Seonunsa is a head temple of the Jogye Order of Korean Buddhism. It stands on the slopes of Dosolsan in Asan-myeon, Gochang County, near the Yellow Sea coast in western Jeollabuk-do province. It was first built by Seon master Geomdan in the 6th century, when the area was ruled by the Baekje kingdom. The temple was burned down by Japanese forces in 1597, during the Seven Year War and subsequently rebuilt. There is a camellia forest behind the main hall (daeungjeon) of the temple. The trees are roughly 500 years old and are designated by South Korea as a natural monument. The temple is known for its worship of the Ksitigarbha Bodhisattva and for its annual camellia festival

Silleuksa

Silleuksa (also written as Shilleuksa) is a Korean Buddhist temple situated against a low hill on the north side of the river Namhan, two miles east of Yeoju in Gyeonggi Province, approximately one-hour southeast of Seoul. The only riverside temple in Korea, Silleuksa is a sacred pilgrimage site and a repository of seven Treasures. A 500-year-old aromatic juniper tree and a 600-year-old ginkgo tree stand on the temple grounds.

Founded in circa 580 by Silla Dynasty monk Wonhyo, Silleuksa was enlarged, burned and rededicated several times. Silleuksa was made a prayer sanctuary to the royal mausoleum of King Sejong the Great in 1469 (himself moved from Seoul that year), during the reign of King Seongjong. Often referred to as the "wall temple" because of an impressive brick pagoda towering high above, Silleuksa is but small by standard measure.

Treasures: A six-tier brick pagoda overlooks the river, one of a handful of brick pagodas in the country (T. #226). Nearby is a Silla Dynasty memorial stone stela (T. #230) whose inscription concerns a library that once stood on the premises of the preservation of wood printing blocks of the sutras. In the centre courtyard is a seven-tier marble pagoda (T. #225) from the early Joseon Dynasty.

Relief carvings of dragons, lotus and wave patterns around its base are all done delicately, with consummate skill. To the side of the main hall is Chosa-dang, a small, rather undistinguished building (T. #180). This hall enshrines the portraits of important monks of the Goryeo Dynasty. To the rear of the building and up a hill is an octagonal gray marble lantern (T. #231) indicative of the Goryeo period, a bell shaped sari budo of monk Naong (T. #228) and a stone stela (T. #229)

Sinheungsa

Sinheungsa, sometimes spelled Shinheungsa, is a head temple of the Jogye Order of Korean Buddhism. It is situated on the slopes of Seoraksan in Sokcho, Gangwon, South Korea. Historical accounts vary as to whether the temple was first constructed by Jajang in 653, or in 637 following his return from Tang China. It burned to the ground in 699 and was rebuilt in its present location by Uisang. It burned again in 1645. The temple is located in Seoraksan National Park and many tourists pass by on their way to the high rocks of Ulsanbawi. Other temples named Sinheungsa are located in Seoul, Samcheok and Icheon.

Songgwangsa

Songgwangsa is one of the most important Seon Buddhist monasteries in Korea and is considered one of the Three Jewel Temples of Korea. It serves as the head temple for the 21st district of the Jogye Order. Songgwangsa is located on Jogye Mountain in Songgwang-myeon, Suncheon, Jeollanam-do, South Korea. Founded by Jinul during the Unified Silla period, this monastery is still very active today as a practice centre. The practices engaged in at this monastery have been reported on in Robert Buswell's The Zen Monastic Experience (1992).

Ssanggyesa

Ssanggyesa is a head temple of the Jogye Order of Korean Buddhism. It is located on the southern slopes of Jirisan in Hwagae-myeon, Hadong County, in the province of Gyeongsangnam-do, South Korea. The temple was founded in 722 by two disciples of Uisang named Sambeop and Daebi, who were guided to the location by a tiger. In the 9th century the temple was renamed "Ssanggyesa" by Jingam. A stele dedicated to Jingam still stands in the temple; it is designated South Korean national treasure 47. Most of the rest of the temple dates to the 17th century of thereafter; the temple was burned to the ground by Japanese invaders during the Seven Year War.

Sudeoksa

Sudeoksa is a head temple of the Jogye Order of Korean Buddhism. It is located on the southern slopes of Deoksung-san in Deoksan-myeon, Yesan County, in the province of Chungcheongnam-do, South Korea.

Sudeoksa was one of very few temples not destroyed during the Seven Year War in the 1590s. Its main hall is South Korea's oldest wooden building, having been constructed during the Goryeo dynasty in 1308. This hall, or daeungjeon, is South Korean National treasure 49.

Three Jewel Temples of Korea

The Three Jewel Temples of Korea are the three principal Buddhist temples in Korea, each representing one of the Three Jewels of Buddhism and all located in South Korea.

Tongdosa in South Gyeongsang Province represents the Buddha; Haeinsa, also in South Gyeongsang Province, represents the dharma or Buddhist teachings; and Songgwangsa in South Jeolla Province represents the sangha or Buddhist community. In most Korean Buddhist temples, the highest, most important and often largest building is the daeungjeon--the central hall containing statues of the historical Buddha and other important figures. In the Three Jewel Temples, however, the most important buildings are ones that emphasize each temple's particular jewel.

Thus, the main hall in Tongdosa opens out onto a stupa which the faithful claim contains relics of the Buddha; Haeinsa has two large buildings holding the Tripitaka Koreana; and Songgwangsa has several prominent buildings dedicated to its monastic community (including the numerous Seon (Zen) masters the temple has produced).

Tongdosa

Tongdosa is a major Buddhist temple and is one of the Three Jewel Temples of Korea. It represents the Buddha and is located on Yeonchuk-san in Yangsan City, Gyeongsangnam-do, South Korea. It was founded in 646 AD by the monk Jajang, during the reign of Queen Seondeok of Silla. It thrived throughout the Unified Silla and Goryeo periods, when Buddhism was the state religion and remained strong even in the Joseon Dynasty. Only one building, the daeungjeon hall, survived the Seven Year War in the late 16th century; the other buildings were rebuilt after that time. Tongdosa is often called "The temple without a Buddha" because it contains no outdoor statues of the Buddha, rather it is arranged around several stupas which contain Jajang's precious gifts and reputedly, relics of the historical Buddha, including his robe, begging bowl and a bone from his skull.

Unjusa

Unjusa is a Buddhist temple in Hwasun County, South Jeolla province, South Korea. It reportedly dates to the Silla Dynasty period. The temple is most notable for its numerous carvings and pagodas, especially National Treasure No. 796, a nine-story pagoda.

Woljeongsa

Woljeongsa is a head temple of the Jogye Order of Korean Buddhism. It is located on the eastern slopes of Odaesan in

Pyeongchang County, Gangwon (South Korea), South Korea. It was founded in 643 by the Silla monk Jajang.

Yongjusa

Yongjusa is a head temple of the Jogye Order of Korean Buddhism. It is located in on the slopes of Hwasan in Taean-eup, Hwaseong, in the province of Gyeonggi, South Korea. The temple's name means "dragon jewel temple." Two large bells in the temple are believed to date to the Unified Silla period. One of them is designated national treasure 120.

The temple was initially established in 854, under the name Garyangsa. It was expanded in the 10th century. It was rebuilt in the late 18th century under the orders of Jeongjo in honour of his deceased father, Prince Sado. This is one of few cases where the Joseon royal house supported Buddhism directly. At this time the temple changed to its current name. The temple is located near Seoul Subway Line 1 and is also connected to Suwon by intercity bus.

BUDDHIST TEMPLES IN AUSTRALIA

Nan Tien Temple

Nan Tien Temple is a Buddhist temple complex located in the industrial suburb of Berkeley, on the southern outskirts of the Australian city of Wollongong, approximately 80 km south of Sydney, Australia. Nan Tien is a Chinese term, which means "southern paradise".

It is one of the branch temples of Fo Guang Shan, founded in 1965 by Venerable Master Hsing Yun, which has over 120 branches worldwide. This is the biggest Buddhist temple in the southern hemisphere.

History: Fo Guang Shan Buddhism is rooted in the Mahayana tradition which emphasises that Buddhahood is within everyone's potential reach. Fo Guang Shan followers strive to bring Buddhism into daily life and describe their philosophy as "Humanistic Buddhism."

It was funded by and constructed under the auspices of the Mahayana Buddhist sect known as Fo Guang Shan and completed in 1995. The sect itself was founded in Taiwan in 1965 by Venerable Master Hsing Yun and has 120 branches throughout the world. The site of the Australian branch's temple was reputedly chosen by Hsing Yun due to its proximity to Mount Kembla, which is said to have an auspicious resemblance to a recumbent lion. It overlooks both Mount Keira and Mount Kembla. The land was bought from the Australian government for the symbolic sum of $1.

Temple Complex: The Nan Tien complex was built using traditional techniques and materials by Chinese craftsmen, but with numerous modern features. Occupying a semi-rural hillside site several square kilometres in size and set amidst landscaped gardens, it is the largest Buddhist temple in the southern hemisphere. It also has the largest terracotta tile roof of any building in the southern hemisphere.

In addition to various meeting rooms, a museum, cultural, conference and accommodation facilities and a restaurant, the Nan Tien temple complex includes two massive prayer halls (known as the Great Mercy Shrine and the Great Hero Hall) within which are located multiple monumental Buddha and Bodhisattva statues, as well as a 7 level pagoda intended to house the cremated remains of 7000 people. The front hall houses the Thousand Handed Avalokitesvara (known as Kuan Yin in Chinese culture) and the main hall in the back houses the Five Dhyani Buddhas, Amogasiddhi, Ratnasambhava, Vairocana, Amitabha and Akshobhya. Both halls have thousands of tiny statues of Buddha on the walls. The complex also has amenities for monks, nuns and visitors and a large garden with a pagoda.

The architecture of the complex is notable because it incorporates the features of several styles of Buddhism. The pagoda is distinctly Chinese, with flying eaves and an angular profile. The main temples incorporates features of Tibetan monastic architecture, with multi-storey painted temple buildings set atop high stone platforms. The courtyards feature Japanese-style gardens, while the statues and shrines often incorporate bright, South-East Asian colour schemes, in contrast to the more sombre and austere styles favoured in China. The halls are carpeted and pilgrims and visitors are required to remove shoes before entering, a practice more common in India, Korea and Japan than China.

Tourism: The temple has become a new venue for tourists wishing to know more about Buddhism and Chinese culture. It is regarded as an "orthodox" Buddhist temple by local Chinese Buddhists, in contrast with some other shrines which worship Buddhist, Taoist and mystical heroes in the same building. It frequently hosts festivals and retreats for the laity.

Phap Hoa Temple

Phap Hoa Temple, is a Vietnamese Buddhist temple located at 20 Butler Avenue, Pennington, South Australia, 5013. It was established in 1978 and moved to its current location in December 1989. It is a member of the United Vietnamese Buddhist Congregation and the head is the Most Venerable Thich Nhu Hue and the abbot is the Reverend Thich Vien Tri.

History: Phap Hoa Temple was established in 1978 at a small house located at 83, Addison Road, Rosewater, South Australia by a group of Vietnamese immigrants, led by Nguyen Van Tuoi for the purpose of attending to the spiritual needs of immigrant Vietnamese Buddhists. The Most Venerable Thich Nhu Hue was invited to come from Japan to direct the temple. Due to the small size, a search for a plot of larger land to construct a temple was undertaken and building of the temple in its current location began on a 5000 m² plot on 19 March 1984. The main hall of the temple was opened on 23 December 1989.

On 26 June 2003 the main hall suffered extensive damage, when an intruder irreperably vandalized the majority of the statues and decorations. This required the replacement of a large number of statues. Along with a new statue of Avalokitesvara Bodhisattva located in the courtyard of the Temple and a Three Entrance Fence, the refurbished hall was unveiled in a ceremony on 27 June 2004 in the presence of South Australian Premier Mike Rann and the Opposition leader Rob Kerin.

BUDDHIST TEMPLES IN BHUTAN

Tamshing Lhakhang

Tamshing Lhakang (temple) in the Bumthang District of central Bhutan is the most important Nyingmapa temple in Bhutan. The temple and monastery are remarkable for their direct connection to the Bhutanese saint Pema Lingpa. It is now a seat of Lama Sungtrul Rinpoche the current speech incarnation of Pema Lingpa. Tamshing consists of a deteriorating temple and cramped monks quarters. The monastery supports a body of over 95 monks.

History: From an interview of Lopen Kharma, teacher and administrator of Tamshing Lhakang, conducted by Friends of Tamshing in December 2005:

The temple was built by Pema Lingpa himself in 1501.

Before 1960 Tamshing was a privately owned temple (like many other temples in Bhutan). After Pema Lingpa died in the temple at the age of seventy-two in 1521, his descendants took over care of the temple. Gradually, over many years, Tamshing fell into a state of disrepair and neglect. The temple courtyard was used as a granary and local people came less and less, except for special days.

In 1959, when many Tibetans (including the present Dalai Lama) fled their country for fear of being killed quite a few came to the Bumthang region, which is the cradle of Buddhism in Bhutan. In his time, Pema Lingpa received a vision to travel to Tibet where he revealed a treasure hidden by Guru Rinpoche (Padmasambhava) many centuries before. He was given land in the Longti area of the Siti valley and built a temple there which is called Lhalung. This temple was later enlarged by his third (Tibetan) incarnation. Pema Lingpa travelled frequently to Tibet and most of his incarnations were Tibetan.

The 10th incarnation of Pema Lingpa died in Tibet shortly before the Tibetan diaspora. In 1960, a group of three monks from Lhalung monk body headed by Lhalung's second in command, Thinley Kuenchap (d. 1975) came to Tamshing to reestablish the Lhalung monk body at Tamshing.

Lopen Thinley Kuenchap was well known to the exiled Tibetan monks in Bhutan. Hearing of his arrival at Tamshing, many gathered there in late 1960 and established the current monk body. Over time, this group has grown from 10 or 15 monks to over 95.

When the Khudun, Lopen Kharma, came to Tamshing as a young boy in 1980, most of the senior monks from Tibet had passed on, however, Lopen Tseten who came from Tibet to Tamshing as a 10 year old monk in 1960 was still there. Today, Lopen Tseten is the head of the monastery organization and its senior teacher.

The present spiritual head of Tamshing is the 11th incarnation of Pema Lingpa, the Lama Sungtrul Rinpoche (speech incarnation) he was born in the Chumi Valley of Bumthang, Bhutan in 1967.

Tamshing Today: The core missions of Tamshing are teaching the Dharma, performing religious services for the community and educating the young monks under its care. Since Tamshing is not government supported it faces increasing challenges posed by supporting 95 monks while maintaining the ancient physical structures.

Mostly under the age of 15, the monks are either orphans or from very poor families who can't afford to send their children to a state school. As the economy of the country changes and as the culture becomes more outward looking, it is inevitable that some of the old ways of supporting the temples and monasteries, (which are the repositories of traditional wisdom), are being tested. Tamshing has no endowment; no mission to make money, its only mission is to meet the needs of the community. Currently, the monastery runs at a loss.

Tamshing and Bhutanese Dance: Tamshing is the original home of sacred dances that are celebrated at traditional Tsechus (festivals) throughout Bhutan. According to Joseph Houseal, director of Core of Culture Dance Preservation:

> *"Dance...is the living tradition of their founding identity and the means by which Pema Lingpa sought to teach the world Buddhism-and the treasure he specifically left the Tamshing monks. It is the life of the order, the Buddhist truth they maintain. That is one reason we have focused on Tamshing: their dances were revealed by the most famous Bhutanese saint and Tamshing alone performs the dances correctly..."*

BUDDHIST TEMPLES IN TAIWAN

Longshan Temple

The Longshan Temple is the name of at least five famous temples in Taiwan:

- Wanhua, Taipei City.
- Danshuei, Taipei County.
- Lukang, Changhua County.
- Tainan City.
- Fongshan, Kaohsiung County.

Longshan Temple at Wanhua: It was built in 1738 by settlers from Fujian, China. It served as a place of worship and a gathering place for the Chinese settlers. The temple has been destroyed either in full or in part on numerous earthquakes and fires. In the spring of 1945, it was even hit by American bombers who claimed the Japanese were hiding armaments inside. Taipei residents have nevertheless consistently rebuilt and renovated it and did so again after the close of the Second

World War a few months later. Lungshan is seen as an emblematic example of Taiwanese classical architecture.

Like most temples in Taiwan, the Temple worships a mixture of Buddhist, Taoist and folk deities such as Matsu.

Tamsui Township

Tamsui is a sea-side town in Taipei County, Taiwan Province, Republic of China. It is named after a river whose name means "Freshwater". The town is also popular as a site for viewing the sun setting into the Taiwan Strait. There are three universities in this small town: Aletheia University, Tamkang University and St. John's University.

History: Originally settled by the Ketagalan aborigines, the first major non-aboriginal settlement was established by the Spanish in the fall of 1629 with the construction of the town and mission of Santo Domingo. The Spanish occupied northern Taiwan for the purpose of securing Spanish interests in the Philippines against the Dutch, the British and the Portuguese, as well as for facilitating trade with China and Japan.

In 1641, the Spanish were expelled from Taiwan by the Dutch. The Spanish had already abandoned their settlement in Tamsui in 1638 and the Dutch built a new fort which they named Fort Anthonio (after the Governor-General of the Dutch East India Company Anthonio van Diemen). It is today known as Hung-Mao Cheng (literally, the Fortress of the Red-haired ones). In addition to "pacifying" the aboriginal tribes in the area, the Dutch also encouraged the immigration and settlement of the area by Han Chinese, as well as expanding the production and trade of sulfur, animal skins and other indigenous resources. The Dutch left Taiwan in 1661 following their defeat by Koxinga, who continued the policy of increasing Han Chinese immigration until the defeat of his descendants by the Ching Dynasty.

Because of its proximity to mainland China, as well as its location in a natural harbour, Tamsui quickly became a major fishing and trade port. The Qing naval patrol also established an outpost in Tamsui in 1808. In 1862, the Ching government opened Tamsui to foreign trade under the terms of the Treaty of Tientsin, exporting tea, camphor, sulfur, coal, opium and dyes. By the mid-19th century Tamsui had become the largest port in Taiwan, boasting a sizable foreign population as well as a British consulate at Hung-Mao Cheng.

Canadian medical doctor and missionary George Leslie Mackay arrived in Tamsui on March 9, 1872, proceeding to establish Taiwan's first hospitals in Western medicine and formal educational facilities, including Oxford College (now part of Aletheia University), the oldest higher-education institution in Taiwan by some measure.

By the time Taiwan was ceded to Japan following the end of the Sino-Japanese War, Tamsui's position as a seaport was beginning to wane due to the accumulation of sediments in the Tamsui River. By the 20th century, most of Tamsui's port operations had moved to Keelung and the local economy had switched primarily to agriculture. However, public infrastructure construction projects by the Japanese led to Tamsui's rise as a local administrative and cultural centre.

Following the end of World War II, Tamsui reverted to being a small fishing town. With the expansion of nearby Taipei City, Tamsui slowly became a centre for tourism along Taiwan's northeast coast. In the last ten years, the city has become popular as a suburb of Taipei in the local real estate market.

Following the completion of the Taipei Rapid Transit System's Danshuei Line, the town has experienced a sharp increase in tourist traffic, reflected in the completion of several riverside parks, the growth of open-air markets specializing in traditional handicrafts, the construction of a fisherman's wharf and the increase in passenger ferries traversing across and along the river.

Lukang

Lukang is a township in northwestern Changhua County, Taiwan Province of the Republic of China (latitude 24°03'N, longitude 120°26'E). The township is on the west coast of Taiwan, facing the Taiwan Strait. The township's name came from the port's trade of deerskins during the Dutch colonial period. Its old Taiwanese name was Losk-a-kang. Lukang was an important sea port in the 18th century and 19th century. It was the most populous city in central Taiwan until the early 20th century.

During the Qing Dynasty, the depth of Lukang's harbour and its proximity to Fujian province on mainland China made Lukang an important trading port. During Lukang's heyday from 1785 to 1845, Lukang's population reached 200,000. Lukang was Taiwan's second largest city after current Tainan and was larger than Bangka (now a district of Taipei), then the island's third-largest city.

The subsequent silting of the harbour and the city's refusal to allow railroads to pass through the city led to losses in trade in commerce, which, in turn led to Lukang's decline. This same decline, however, averted the modernization processes that demolished historical buildings in Tainan and Taipei, leaving Lukang preserved as it was in its heyday.

There are still many old temples in Lukang, such as Longshan Temple and Matzu Temple. The Yujhenjhai cakes are famous local specialties, as well as Lukang's Cow Tongue Cakes and oyster pancakes.

The town is also the origin of the terms e-kang and teng-kang used respectively to refer to southern Taiwan and northern Taiwan; the literal meanings of the terms are below the harbour and above the harbour.

- Area: 39.46 km^2
- Population: 85,020 people (January 2006)

Tainan City

Tainan City is a provincial city of Taiwan Province, Republic of China and is the fourth largest city after Taipei, Kaohsiung and Taichung.

Tainan was established as the capital of Taiwan in 1661 and remained capital until 1887 during the Qing Dynasty. The city is famous for her abundant historic buildings and delicious snack food.

History: Tainan was established as the capital of Taiwan in 1661 by Koxinga after he took over the island from Dutch colonial rule. In 1684, the Qing Dynasty conquered Taiwan and established "Taiwan Fu" (Taiwan Government) as the first official local government in Taiwan. This was later renamed to "Tainan Fu" in 1885 when Taiwan was established as a province. Because it was formerly the capital of Taiwan, Tainan is also called Fu-cheng (Government City).

Tainan, historically regarded as one of the oldest cities in Taiwan, began with the establishment of the Dutch port at Tayoan City (source of the name Taiwan and now called Anping) in 1624. It is also one of Taiwan's cultural capitals, as it houses the First Confucian School/Temple built 1665 on the island, the remains of the Northern and Southern gates of the old city and countless other historical monuments. The 2005 and 2006 Taiwan Lantern Festivals were also held in Tainan. Tainan is known as the city with the most Buddhist and/or Taoist temples on the island of Taiwan. Tainan City is administratively a municipality of Taiwan Province of the Republic of China. It is surrounded by Tainan County to the north and east and the South China Sea to the west and south.

Fongshan City

Fongshan City is located in southern Kaohsiung County, Taiwan Province of the Republic of China. Immediately east of Kaohsiung City, Fongshan is capital of Kaohsiung County and is home to the Chinese Military Academy. In the Qing Dynasty, Fongshan County included areas south of Tainan City (then called Prefecture City) and west of the mountains. In 1875, the southern part of Fongshan County was separated into Hengchun County. After the Japanese Colonial Government started to develop the Kaohsiung Harbour in the early 20th century, the importance of Fongshan was replaced by Kaohsiung City.

- Area: 26.76 km²
- Population: 328,878 people (2003)

BUDDHIST TEMPLES IN CAMBODIA

Angkor Wat

Angkor Wat (or Angkor Vat) is a temple at Angkor, Cambodia, built for king Suryavarman II in the early 12th century as his state temple and capital city. The largest and best-preserved temple at the site, it is the only one to have remained a significant religious centre-first Hindu, then Buddhist-since its foundation. The temple is the epitome of the high classical style of Khmer architecture. It has become a symbol of Cambodia, appearing on its national flag and it is the country's prime attraction for visitors. Angkor Wat combines two basic plans of Khmer temple architecture: the temple mountain and the later galleried temples. It is designed to represent Mount Meru, home of the gods in Hindu mythology: within a moat and an outer wall 3.6 km (2.2 miles) long are three rectangular galleries, each raised above the next. At the centre of the temple stands a quincunx of towers. Unlike most Angkorian temples, Angkor Wat is oriented to the west; scholars are divided as to the significance of this. As well as for the grandeur and harmony of the architecture, the temple is admired for its extensive bas-reliefs and for the numerous devatas adorning its walls.

According to Guinness World Records, it is the largest religious structure in the world.

Angor Wat/Vrah Vuschulok: The name Angor Wat is a misnomer from the late nineteenth century when initial European explorers mistook it for a Buddhist temple (wat). Angor was the name of a near-by village; thus Angor Wat. The building was, however, dedicated to Vishnu and its original name, however, was Vrah Vishnulok, meaning "the sacred abode of Lord Vishnu."

History: The initial design and construction of the temple took place in the first half of the 12th century, during the reign of Suryavarman II (ruled 1113-c. 1150). Dedicated to Vishnu, it was built as the king's state temple and capital city. As neither the foundation stela nor any contemporary inscriptions referring to the temple have been found, its original name is unknown. It is located 5.5 km north of the modern town of Siem Reap and a short distance south and slightly east of the previous capital, which was centred on the Baphuon. Work seems to have come to an end on the king's death, with some of the bas-reliefs unfinished. In 1177 Angkor was sacked by the Chams, the traditional enemies of the Khmer. Thereafter the empire was restored by a new king, Jayavarman VII, who established a new capital and state temple (Angkor Thom and the Bayon respectively) which lie a few kilometres to the north.

In the 14th or 15th century the temple was converted to Theravada Buddhist use, which continues to the present day. Angkor Wat is unusual among the Angkor temples in that although it was somewhat neglected after the 16th century it was never completely abandoned. Its moat also provided some protection from encroachment by the jungle. Around this time the temple was known as Preah Pisnulok, after the posthumous title of Suryavarman. The modern name, in use by the 16th century, means "City Temple": Angkor is a vernacular form of the word nokor which comes from the Sanskrit word nagara (capital), while wat is the Khmer word for temple.

One of the first Western visitors to the temple was Antonio da Magdalena, a Portuguese monk who visited in 1586 and said that it "is of such extraordinary construction that it is not possible to describe it with a pen, particularly since it is like no other building in the world. It has towers and decoration and all the refinements which the human genius can conceive of". However, the temple was popularised in the West only in the mid-19th century on the publication of Henri Mouhot's travel notes. The French explorer wrote of it:

> *One of these temples-a rival to that of Solomon and erected by some ancient Michelangelo-might take an*

honourable place beside our most beautiful buildings. It is grander than anything left to us by Greece or Rome and presents a sad contrast to the state of barbarism in which the nation is now plunged.

Mouhot, like other early Western visitors, was unable to believe that the Khmers could have built the temple and mistakenly dated it to around the same era as Rome. The true history of Angkor Wat was pieced together only from stylistic and epigraphic evidence accumulated during the subsequent clearing and restoration work carried out across the whole Angkor site. Angkor Wat required considerable restoration in the 20th century, mainly the removal of accumulated earth and vegetation. Work was interrupted by the civil war and Khmer Rouge control of the country during the 1970s and 1980s, but relatively little damage was done during this period other than the theft and destruction of mostly post-Angkorian statues.

The temple has become a symbol of Cambodia and is a source of great pride for the country's people. A depiction of Angkor Wat has been a part of every Cambodian national flag since the introduction of the first version circa 1863-the only building to appear on any national flag. In January 2003 riots erupted in Phnom Penh when a false rumour circulated that a Thai soap opera actress had claimed that Angkor Wat belonged to Thailand. Although not certain, rumors state that the actress, whose name is Suvanant Kongying (Kob), was paid large sums of money to say this. The actress was pronounced to be half Cambodian and half Thai.

Style: Angkor Wat is the prime example of the classical style of Khmer architecture-the Angkor Wat style-to which it has given its name. By the 12th century Khmer architects had become more skilled and confident than before in the use of sandstone (rather than brick or laterite) as the main building material. The Angkor Wat style was followed by that of the Bayon period, in which quality was often sacrificed to quantity. Other temples in the style are Banteay Samre, Thommanon, Chao Say Tevoda and the early temples of Preah Pithu at

Angkor; outside Angkor, Beng Mealea and parts of Phanom Rung and Phimai.

Angkor Wat has drawn praise above all for the harmony of its design, which has been compared to the architecture of ancient Greece or Rome. According to Maurice Glaize, a mid-20th-century conservator of Angkor, the temple "attains a classic perfection by the restrained monumentality of its finely balanced elements and the precise arrangement of its proportions. It is a work of power, unity and style."

Architecturally, the elements characteristic of the style include: the ogival, redented towers shaped like lotus buds; half-galleries to broaden passageways; axial galleries connecting enclosures; and the cruciform terraces which appear along the main axis of the temple. Most of the visible areas are of sandstone blocks, while laterite was used for the outer wall and for hidden structural parts. The binding agent used to join the blocks is yet to be identified, although natural resins or slaked lime have been suggested. Other elements of the design have been destroyed by looting and the passage of time, including gilded stucco on the towers, gilding on some figures on the bas-reliefs and wooden ceiling panels and doors. Typical decorative elements are devatas (or apsaras), bas-reliefs and on pediments extensive garlands and narrative scenes. Statuary is conservative, being more static and less graceful than earlier work.

The Site: Angkor Wat, located at 13°24'45?N, 103°52'0?ECoordinates: 13°24'45?N, 103°52'0?E, is a unique combination of the temple mountain and the later Chola of Tamil Nadu India. Particularly the model of the temple and the architecture was that of the Cholas, especially after Raja Chola and his son Rajendra Cholan, The work perhaps started from the early period of 12th Century, the standard design for the empire's state temples and the later plan of concentric galleries. The temple is a representation of Mount Meru, the home of the gods: the central quincunx of towers symbolises the five peaks of the mountain and the walls and moat the surrounding mountain ranges and ocean. Access to the upper areas of the temple was progressively more exclusive, with the laity being admitted only to the lowest level.

Unlike most Khmer temples, Angkor Wat is oriented to the west rather than the east. This has led many (including Glaize and George Coedes) to conclude that Suryavarman intended it to serve as his funerary temple. Further evidence for this view is provided by the bas-reliefs, which proceed in a counter-clockwise direction-prasavya in Hindu terminology-as this is the reverse of the normal order. Rituals take place in reverse order during Brahminic funeral services. The archaeologist Charles Higham also describes a container which may have been a funerary jar which was recovered from the central tower. Freeman and Jacques, however, note that several other temples of Angkor depart from the typical eastern orientation and suggest that Angkor Wat's alignment was due to its dedication to Vishnu, who was associated with the west.

A further interpretation of Angkor Wat has been proposed by Eleanor Mannikka. Drawing on the temple's alignment and dimensions and on the content and arrangement of the bas-reliefs, she argues that these indicate a claimed new era of peace under king Suryavarman II: "as the measurements of solar and lunar time cycles were built into the sacred space of Angkor Wat, this divine mandate to rule was anchored to consecrated chambers and corridors meant to perpetuate the king's power and to honour and placate the deities manifest in the heavens above." Mannikka's suggestions have been received with a mixture of interest and scepticism in academic circles. She distances herself from the speculations of others, such as Graham Hancock, that Angkor Wat is part of a representation of the constellation Draco.

Outer Enclosure: The outer wall, 1025 by 802 m and 4.5 m high, is surrounded by a 30 m apron of open ground and a moat 190 m wide. Access to the temple is by an earth bank to the east and a sandstone causeway to the west; the latter, the main entrance, is a later addition, possibly replacing a wooden bridge. There are gopuras at each of the cardinal points; the western is much the largest and has three ruined towers. Glaize notes that this gopura both hides and echoes the form of the temple proper. Under the southern tower is a statue of Vishnu, known as Ta Reach, which may originally have occupied the temple's central shrine. Galleries run between the towers and as far as two further entrances on either side of the gopura often referred to as "elephant gates", as they are large enough to admit those animals. These galleries have square pillars on the outer (west) side and a closed wall on the inner (east) side. The ceiling between the pillars is decorated with lotus rosettes; the west face of the wall with dancing figures; and the east face of the wall with balustered windows, dancing male figures on prancing animals and devatas, including (south of the entrance) the only one in the temple to be showing her teeth.

The outer wall encloses a space of 820,000 square metres (203 acres), which besides the temple proper was originally occupied by the city and, to the north of the temple, the royal palace. Like all secular buildings of Angkor, these were built of perishable materials rather than of stone, so nothing remains of them except the outlines of some of the streets. Most of the area is now covered by forest. A 350 m causeway connects the western gopura to the temple proper, with naga balustrades and six sets of steps leading down to the city on either side. Each side also features a library with entrances at each cardinal point, in front of the third set of stairs from the entrance and a pond between the library and the temple itself. The ponds are later additions to the design, as is the cruciform terrace guarded by lions connecting the causeway to the central structure.

Central Structure: The temple proper stands on a terrace raised above the level of the city. It consists essentially of three rectangular galleries rising to a central tower; with each level higher than the last. Mannikka interprets these galleries as being dedicated to the king, Brahma and the moon and Vishnu, respectively. Each gallery has a gopura at each of the cardinal points and the two inner galleries each have towers at their corners, forming a quincunx with the central tower. Because of the temple's westward orientation, the features are all set back towards the east, leaving more space to be filled in each enclosure and gallery on the west side; for the same reason the west-facing steps are shallower than those on the other sides.

The outer gallery measures 187 by 215 m, with pavilions rather than towers at the corners. The gallery is open to the outside of the temple, with columned half-galleries extending and buttressing the structure. The inner walls bear a series of bas-reliefs, depicting large-scale scenes mainly from the Ramayana and the Mahabharata. Higham has called these, "the greatest known linear arrangement of stone carving". From the north-west corner anti-clockwise, the western gallery shows the Battle of Lanka (from the Ramayana, in which Rama defeats Ravana) and the Battle of Kurukshetra (from the Mahabharata, showing the mutual annihilation of the Kaurava and Pandava clans).

On the southern gallery follow the only historical scene, a procession of Suryavarman II, then the 32 hells and 37 heavens of Hindu mythology. Glaize writes of; those unfortunate souls who are to be thrown down to hell to suffer a refined cruelty which, at times, seems to be a little disproportionate to the severity of the crimes committed. So it is that people who have damaged others' property have their bones broken, that the glutton is cleaved in two, that rice thieves are afflicted with enormous bellies of hot iron, that those who picked the flowers in the garden of Shiva have their heads pierced with nails and thieves are exposed to cold discomfort.

On the eastern gallery is one of the most celebrated scenes, the Churning of the Sea of Milk, showing 92 asuras and 88 devas using the serpent Vasuki to churn the sea under Vishnu's direction (Mannikka counts only 91 asuras and explains the asymmetrical numbers as representing the number of days from the winter solstice to the spring equinox and from the equinox to the summer solstice). It is followed by Vishnu defeating asuras (a 16th-century addition). The northern gallery shows Krishna's victory over Bana (where according to Glaize, "The workmanship is at its worst") and a battle between the Hindu gods and asuras. The north-west and south-west corner pavilions both feature much smaller-scale scenes, some unidentified but most from the Ramayana or the life of Krishna.

Connecting the outer gallery to the second enclosure on the west side is a cruciform cloister, known by the modern name of Preah Poan (the "Hall of a Thousand Buddhas"). Buddha images were left in the cloister by pilgrims over the centuries, although most have now been removed. This area has many inscriptions relating the good deeds of pilgrims, most written in Khmer but others in Burmese and Japanese. The four small courtyards marked out by the cloister may originally have been filled with water. North and south of the cloister are libraries.

Beyond, the second and inner galleries are connected to each other and to two flanking libraries by another cruciform terrace, again a later addition. From the second level upwards, devatas abound on the walls, singly or in groups of up to four. The second-level enclosure is 100 by 115 m and may originally have been flooded to represent the ocean around Mount Meru. Three sets of steps on each side lead up to the corner towers and gopuras of the inner gallery. The very steep stairways represent the difficulty of ascending to the kingdom of the gods. This inner gallery, called the Bakan, is a 60 m square with axial galleries connecting each gopura with the central shrine and subsidiary shrines located below the corner towers.

The roofings of the galleries are decorated with the motif of the body of a snake ending in the heads of lions or garudas. Carved lintels and pediments decorate the entrances to the galleries and to the shrines. The tower above the central shrine rises 43 m to a height of 65 m above the ground; unlike those of previous temple mountains, the central tower is raised above the surrounding four. The shrine itself, originally occupied by a statue of Vishnu and open on each side, was walled in when the temple was converted to Theravada Buddhism, the new walls featuring standing Buddhas. In 1934 the conservator George Trouve excavated the pit beneath the central shrine: filled with sand and water it had already been robbed of its treasure, but he did find a sacred foundation deposit of gold leaf two metres above ground level.

Angkor Wat today: Since the 1990s Angkor Wat has seen a resumption of conservation efforts and a massive increase in tourism. The temple is part of the Angkor World Heritage Site, established in 1992, which has provided some funding and has encouraged the Cambodian government to protect the site. The German Apsara Conservation Project (GACP) is working to protect the devatas and other bas-reliefs which decorate the temple from damage.

The organisation's survey found that around 20% of the devatas were in very poor condition, mainly because of natural erosion and deterioration of the stone but in part also due to earlier restoration efforts. Other work involves the repair of collapsed sections of the structure and prevention of further collapse: the west facade of the upper level, for example, has been buttressed by scaffolding since 2002, while a Japanese team completed restoration of the north library of the outer enclosure in 2005.

Angkor Wat has become a major tourist destination: attendance figures for the temple are not published, but in 2004 the country received just over a million international arrivals, of whom according to the Ministry of Tourism 57% planned to visit the temple. The influx of tourists has so far caused relatively little damage, other than some graffiti; ropes and wooden steps have been introduced to protect the bas-reliefs and floors, respectively.

Tourism has also provided some additional funds for maintenance-approximately 28% of ticket revenues across the whole Angkor site is spent on the temples-although most work is carried out by foreign government-sponsored teams rather than by the Cambodian authorities.

Bayon

The Bayon is a temple at Angkor, Cambodia. It was built in the 13th century as the state temple of king Jayavarman VII and stands at the centre of his capital, Angkor Thom. Its most distinctive feature is the multitude of smiling faces on the towers which rise up to its central peak. It also possesses two sets of bas-reliefs, which depict an unusual combination of mythological, historical and mundane events. The main current conservatory body, the JSA, has described the temple as "the most striking expression of the 'baroque' style", compared to the classical style of Angkor Wat.

History: The Bayon was the last state temple to be built at Angkor and the only one to be built primarily as a Mahayana Buddhist temple (although various local deities were also worshipped there). It was the centrepiece of Jayavarman VII's building programme and the similarity of the faces on the temple's towers to other statues of the king have led many scholars to the conclusion that the faces are, at least in part, representations of Jayavarman VII (although Avalokitesvara is another possibility). Under the reign of Jayavarman VIII in the mid-13th century the temple was converted to Hinduism. In later centuries Theravada Buddhism became dominant, before the temple was eventually abandoned to the jungle. Current features which were not part of the original plan include the terrace to the east of the temple, the libraries, the square corners of the inner gallery and the upper terrace.

In the first part of the 20th century conservation work was led by the Ecole Francaise d'Extreme-Orient, which restored the temple using the anastylosis technique. Since 1995 the Japanese Government team for the Safeguarding of Angkor (the JSA) has been the main conservatory body, holding annual symposia.

The Site: The temple is orientated towards the east and so its buildings are set back to the west inside enclosures elongated along the east-west axis. Because the temple sits at the exact centre of Angkor Thom, roads lead to it directly from the gates at each of the city's cardinal points. The temple itself has no wall or moats, these being replaced by those of the city itself: the city-temple arrangement, with an area of 9 square kilometres, is much larger than that of Angkor Wat to the south (2 km^2).

Within the temple itself, there are two galleried enclosures (the third and second enclosures) and an upper terrace (the first enclosure). The outer gallery features a series of historical and everyday scenes on its outer wall, but there is considerable uncertainty as to which historical events are portrayed and how, if at all, the different reliefs are related.

From the east gopura clockwise, the subjects are: a marching Khmer army (including some Chinese soldiers), followed by wagons of provisions; domestic scenes; in the southeast corner, a temple scene; on the south wall, a battle on the Tonle Sap between Khmers and Chams, with more domestic scenes underneath; a naval display; palace scenes; Cham boats, followed by a land battle won by the Khmers, then the Khmer victory feast; a military procession (including both Khmers and Chams); on the west gallery, unfinished reliefs show an army marching through the forest, then arguments and battle between groups of Khmers (Freeman and Jacques suggest that this may show a revolt which took place in 1182); a royal procession; on the north gallery, again unfinished, royal entertainments and more battles, one showing Khmers defeated by the Chams; in the northeast corner another marching army; and on the east gallery, a land battle being won by the Khmers.

The outer gallery encloses a courtyard in which there are two libraries (one on either side of the east entrance). 16 chapels formerly in this courtyard were demolished by Jayavarman VIII. The inner gallery is raised above ground level and has doubled corners, with the original redented cross-shape later filled out to a square. Its bas-reliefs, later additions of Jayavarman VIII, are in stark contrast to those of the outer:

rather than set-piece battles and processions, the smaller canvases offered by the inner gallery are decorated for the most part with scenes from Hindu mythology.

There is however no certainty as to what some of the panels depict, or as to their relationship with one another. One gallery just north of the eastern gopura, for example, shows two linked scenes which have been explained as the freeing of a goddess from inside a mountain (Glaize), or as an act of iconoclasm by Cham invaders (Freeman and Jacques). A nearby series of panels show a king fighting with a serpent and dying and have been connected with the legend of the leper king. Less obscure are depictions of the construction of a Vishnuite temple (south of the western gopura) and the Churning of the Sea of Milk (north of the western gopura).

The inner gallery is nearly filled by the upper terrace, raised one level higher again. On this level, the visitor is surrounded by face towers, each with two, three or (most commonly) four of the famous smiling faces. Glaize wrote that, "On the upper terrace, mystery reigns. Wherever one wanders, the faces of Lokesvara follow and dominate with their multiple presence, always countered by the overwhelming mass of the central core."

The towers are located along the inner gallery (at the corners and entrances) and on chapels on the upper terrace. Additional faces are carved on the central tower. Despite efforts to find significance in the number of towers and faces, the numbers varied from time to time as more towers were added: at one point there were up to 49 towers, although only 37 now remain. There are around 200 faces, but as some are only partially preserved there can be no definitive count.

Like the inner gallery, the central massif was originally cruciform but was later filled out, this time making it circular. It rises 43 metres above the ground. The original Buddha image from the central shrine was removed and smashed by Jayavarman VIII, but has now been restored and is displayed in a pavilion to the northeast of the temple.

Krol Ko

Krol Ko at Angkor, Cambodia, is a Buddhist temple built at the end of the 12th century under the rule of Jayavarman VII. It is north of Neak Pean.

Neak Pean

Neak Pean ("Coiled Serpents") at Angkor, Cambodia is an artificial island with a Buddhist temple at the centre of Jayatataka Baray, or Pool of Jayavarman. The name is derived from the sculptures of snakes (Naga) running around the base of the temple structure.

Preah Khan

Preah Khan is a temple at Angkor, Cambodia, built in the 12th century for King Jayavarman VII. It is located northeast of Angkor Thom and just west of the Jayatataka baray, with which it was associated. It was the centre of a substantial organisation, with almost 100,000 officials and servants. The temple is flat in design, with a basic plan of successive rectangular galleries around a Buddhist sanctuary complicated by Hindu satellite temples and numerous later additions. Like the nearby Ta Prohm, Preah Khan has been left largely unrestored, with numerous trees and other vegetation growing among the ruins.

History: Preah Khan was built on the site of Jayavarman VII's victory over the invading Chams in 1181. Unusually the modern name, meaning "holy sword", is derived from the meaning of the original-Nagara Jayasri (holy city of victory). The site may previously have been occupied by the royal palaces of Yasovarman II and Tribhuvanadityavarman. The temple's foundation stela has provided considerable information about the history and administration of the site: the main image, of the boddhisatva Avalokitesvara in the form of the king's father, was dedicated in 1191 (the king's mother had earlier been commemorated in the same way at Ta Prohm). 430 other deities also had shrines on the site, each of which received an allotment of food, clothing, perfume and even mosquito nets; the temple's wealth included gold, silver, gems, 112,300 pearls and a cow with gilded horns. The institution combined the roles of city, temple and Buddhist university: there were 97,840 attendants and servants, including 1000 dancers and 1000 teachers.

The temple is still largely unrestored: the initial clearing was from 1927 to 1932 and partial anastylosis was carried out in 1939. Since then free-standing statues have been removed for safe-keeping and there has been further consolidation and restoration work. Throughout, the conservators have attempted to balance restoration and maintenance of the wild condition in which the temple was discovered: one of them, Maurice Glaize, wrote that; The temple was previously overrun with a particularly voracious vegetation and quite ruined, presenting only chaos. Clearing works were undertaken with a constant respect for the large trees which give the composition a pleasing presentation without constituting any immediate danger. At the same time, some partial anastylosis has revived various buildings found in a sufficient state of preservation and presenting some special interest in their architecture or decoration.

Since 1991, the site has been maintained by the World Monuments Fund. It has continued the cautious approach to restoration, believing that to go further would involve too much guesswork and prefers to respect the ruined nature of the temple. One of its members has said, "We're basically running a glorified maintenance programme. We're not prepared to falsify history". It has therefore limited itself primarily to stabilisation work on the fourth eastern gopura, the House of Fire and the Hall of Dancers.

The Site: The outer wall of Preah Khan is of laterite and bears 72 garudas holding nagas, at 50 m intervals. Surrounded by a moat, it measures 800 by 700 m and encloses an area of 56 hectares (138 acres). To the east of Preah Khan is a landing stage on the edge of the Jayatataka baray, now dry, which measured 3.5 by 0.9 km. This also allowed access to the temple of Neak Pean in the centre of the baray. As usual Preah Khan is orientated toward the east, so this was the main entrance, but there are others at each of the cardinal points. Each entrance has a causeway over the moat with naga-carrying devas and asuras similar to those at Angkor Thom; Glaize considered this an indication that the city element of Preah Khan was more significant than those of Ta Prohm or Banteay Kdei.

Halfway along the path leading to the third enclosure, on the north side, is a House of Fire (or Dharmasala) similar to Ta Prohm's. The remainder of the fourth enclosure, now forested, was originally occupied by the city; as this was built of perishable materials it has not survived. The third enclosure wall is 200 by 175 m. In front of the third gopura is a cruciform terrace. The gopura itself is on a large scale, with three towers in the centre and two flanking pavilions. Between the southern two towers were two celebrated silk-cotton trees, of which Glaize wrote, "resting on the vault itself of the gallery, [they] frame its openings and brace the stones in substitute for pillars in a caprice of nature that is as fantastic as it is perilous." One of the trees is now dead, although the roots have been left in place. The trees may need to be removed to prevent their damaging the structure. On the far side of the temple, the third western gopura has pediments of a chess game and the Battle of Lanka and two guardian dvarapalas to the west.

West of the third eastern gopura, on the main axis is a Hall of Dancers. The walls are decorated with apsaras; Buddha images in niches above them were destroyed in the anti-Buddhist reaction under Jayavarman VIII. North of the Hall of Dancers is a two-storeyed structure with round columns. No other examples of this form survive at Angkor, although there are traces of similar buildings at Ta Prohm and Banteay Kdei. Freeman and Jacques speculate that this may have been a granary. Occupying the rest of the third enclosure are ponds (now dry) in each corner and satellite temples to the north, south and west. While the main temple was Buddhist, these three are dedicated to Shiva, previous kings and queens and

Vishnu respectively. They are notable chiefly for their pediments: on the northern temple, Vishnu Reclining to the west and the Hindu trinity of Vishnu, Shiva and Brahma to the east; on the western temple, Krishna raising Mount Govardhana to the west.

Connecting the Hall of Dancers and the wall of the second enclosure is a courtyard containing two libraries. The second eastern gopura projects into this courtyard; it is one of the few Angkorian gopuras with significant internal decoration, with garudas on the corners of the cornices. Buddha images on the columns were changed into hermits under Jayavarman VIII. Between the second enclosure wall (85 by 76 m) and the first enclosure wall (62 by 55 m) on the eastern side is a row of later additions which impede access and hide some of the original decoration. The first enclosure is, as Glaize said, similarly, "choked with more or less ruined buildings". The enclosure is divided into four parts by a cruciform gallery, each part almost filled by these later irregular additions. The walls of this gallery and the interior of the central sanctuary, are covered with holes for the fixing of bronze plates which would originally have covered them and the outside of the sanctuary-1500 tonnes was used to decorate the whole temple. At the centre of the temple, in place of the original statue of Lokesvara, is a stupa built several centuries after the temple's initial construction.

Ta Prohm

Ta Prohm is a temple at Angkor, Cambodia, built in the Bayon style largely in the late 12th and early 13th centuries. Located approximately one kilometre east of Angkor Thom and on the southern edge of the East Baray near Tonle Bati, it was built by King Jayavarman VII as a Mahayana Buddhist monastery and university. Unlike most of the other Angkor temples, Ta Prohm has been left in much the same condition in which it was found: the photogenic and atmospheric combination of trees growing out of the ruins and the jungle surroundings have made it one of Angkor's most popular temples with visitors.

History: Ta Prohm was one of the first temples begun in Jayavarman VII's massive building programme. The temple's modern name means "old Brahma", but the original name was Rajavihara (royal temple). It was centred on veneration of the king's family: the main image (of Prajnaparamita, the personification of wisdom, installed in 1186) was modelled on his mother, while the two satellite temples in the third enclosure were dedicated to his guru (north) and his elder brother (south). Expansions and additions continued as late as the rule of Srindravarman at the end of the 13th century. The temple's stele recorded that the site was home to more than 12,500 people, with a further 80,000 in surrounding villages helping to supply the institution. The temple amassed considerable riches, including gold, pearls and silks.

After the fall of the Khmer empire, the temple fell into neglect for centuries. When the effort to conserve and restore the temples of Angkor began in the early 20th century, Ta Prohm was chosen by the Ecole francaise d'Extreme-Orient to be left largely as it was found as a "concession to the general taste for the picturesque" (Glaize). Glaize writes that this temple was chosen because it was, "one of the most imposing and the one which had best merged with the jungle, but not yet to the point of becoming a part of it-as but one specimen typical of a form of Khmer art of which there were already other models". Nevertheless much work has been done to stabilise the ruins and to permit access, in order to maintain "this condition of apparent neglect" (Freeman and Jacques).

The Site: The basic layout of Ta Prohm is that of a typical "flat" Khmer temple, with five rectangular enclosing walls around a central sanctuary. Like most Khmer temples, Ta Prohm is oriented to the east, so the temple proper is set back to the west along an elongated east-west axis. The outer wall of 1000 by 650 metres encloses an area of 650,000 square metres that would have been a substantial town, but which is now largely forested. There are entrance gopuras at each of the cardinal points, although access today is now only possible from the east and west. Each gopura had face towers (similar to those at the Bayon) added during the 13th century, although some of these have collapsed. There were moats inside and outside the fourth enclosure.

The three inner enclosures of the temple proper are galleried, while the corner towers of the first enclosure form a quincunx with the tower of the central sanctuary. This basic plan is complicated for the visitor by the circuitous access necessitated by the temple's partially collapsed state, as well as by the large number of other buildings, some being later additions. The most substantial of these other buildings are the libraries in the southeast corners of the first and third enclosures; the satellite temples on the north and south sides of the third enclosure; the Hall of Dancers between the third and fourth eastern gopuras; and a House of Fire east of the fourth eastern gopura.

In Popular Media: The temple was used as a location in the film Tomb Raider. Although the film took visual liberties with other Angkor temples, its scenes of Ta Prohm were quite faithful to the temple's actual appearance and made use of its eerie qualities.

Ta Som

Ta Som at Angkor, Cambodia, is a small Buddhist temple dedicated to the father of King Jayavarman VII. It was built at the end of the 12th century. It is east of Neak Pean and has not been restored.

BUDDHIST TEMPLES IN SCOTLAND

Kagyu Samye Ling Monastery and Tibetan Centre

Kagyu Samye Ling Monastery and Tibetan Centre is a Tibetan Buddhist complex associated with the Kagyu school located at Eskdalemuir, near Langholm, Dumfries and Galloway, Scotland.

History: The building that now houses Samye Ling was originally a hunting lodge. The Johnstone House Contemplative Community was founded there by a Canadian Theravada monk named Anandabodhi. When the community declined, Anadabodhi returned to Canada; he was subsequently ordained in the Tibetan Mahayana tradition and enthroned as Namgyal Rinpoche by the 16th Gyalwa Karmapa.

In 1967, the Theravadins gave the centre to two Tibetan lamas and refugees named Chogyam Trungpa Rinpoche and Akong Rinpoche, who renamed it Samye Ling. Samye refers to the first Buddhist monastic university in Tibet, while Ling means a large house with grounds. Trungpa Rinpoche later left and founded further centres in the United States and elsewhere.

The centre flourished and developed under the guidance of Akong Rinpoche and his brother Lama Yeshe Losal, who served as Abbot and Retreat Master, respectively. The centre includes the first Tibetan temple to be constructed in Europe, a large stupa and accommodation for those taking a range of courses on Buddhism, meditation, spiritual development and art.

Preservation of Tibetan Art and Crafts: Under the guidance of the celebrated Tibetan artist Sherab Palden Beru, Samye Ling has also become a centre for the creation, repair and restoration of thangkas, principally in the Karma Gadri style. Since the 1970s Sherab has trained a number of western practitioners in the highly specialised techniques needed to create thangkas. The temple walls are decorated with many exquisite examples of the work of both Sherab Palden Beru and his western pupils.

Traditional deity and monumental sculpture and the creation of prayer-wheels are also carried out at the centre under the direction of resident and visiting Tibetan exp rts. The grounds of the centre feature many examples of their work, such as a statue of Nagarjuna.

BUDDHIST TEMPLES IN SINGAPORE

Fuk Tak Chi Temple

The Fuk Tak Chi Temple is the oldest Chinese temple in Singapore, built in 1824 by Hakka and Cantonese immigrants five years after the founding of the modern city in 1819. Dedicated to Tua Peh Kong, it belongs to the Shenist sect, thus catering to the religious needs of both Confucianists and Buddhists.

The small shrine later also catered to the welfare of the large Chinese community by functioning as an association. In August 1998, the building was restored and converted into a museum with artifacts on the lives of early Chinese migrants in Singapore in April 1998. In 2000, it became part of the new Far East Square development.

Hong San See

Hong San See is a Chinese temple in Singapore and is located at Mohamed Sultan Road in the River Valley Planning Area, within the Central Area, Singapore's central business district.

Hong San See Temple was constructed between 1908 and 1913, erected by migrants from Nan An town in Fujian province with materials imported from China. Built on a small hill, the temple once overlooked the sea. The temple's vicinity now mainly houses bars, restaurants and expensive apartments.

The temple is owned by the Singapore Lam Ann Association.

History: The original temple to the God of Wealth was built in 1829 on Tras Street in Tanjong Pagar and was erected by migrants from Nan An town in Fujian province of China. In 1907, the land was acquired by the government for road widening and the temple trustees were given compensation of $50,000. The temple trustees used the money to buy land on a 999-year lease on Mohamed Sultan Road from Sam Tomlimson who was the Municipal Engineer.

The name of the temple means "Temple on Phoenix Hill". Sited on the side of Institution Hill, the temple was situated on high ground with a view of the sea. According to the principles of Chinese geomancy, this is a prime spot for a temple. The construction of the temple began in 1908 with materials imported from China. The chief contractor was Lim Loh, the father of World War II hero Lim Bo Seng. The temple was completed in 1913 at the cost of $56,000. It was renovated once in 1934 and again in 1962. In 1970 renovations to the temple were not done according to restoration guidelines and several features were removed. These are to be restored to make the temple faithful to its original early twentieth century architecture. One major change, now likely to have been removed, was the addition of ornate carvings painted in gold all along the trusses of the temple.

As with some of the other Chinese temples in Singapore, its premises were used as a school for children from nearby villages. Called Nan Ming School, it was closed after ten years when it ran into financial difficulties.

Today, Hong San See has lost its view of the sea, blocked by high-rises which now surround it. However, it remains on high ground and to reach the temple, devotees have to climb a long flight of stairs.

Hong San See Temple was gazetted as a national monument on 10 November 1978.

Architecture: Hong San See is located on a hill with the entrance facing south or the yang position at the back of the complex against higher ground and the cold north that generates yin, which also has a good feng shui. There are granite plaques in the entrance hall, dated between 1868 and 1913 which list the donors who contributed to the building of the temple. There are other modern plaques on the walls commemorating donors in recent years.

The granite column on either side of the main entrance are engraved verses extolling the site's once excellent view of the sea and its wealthy neighbourhood. This view has since been blocked by high-rise development in the 1990s. There are four carved granite columns in the temple, with two at the entrance are six-sided columns with entwined dragons and other figures. Just past the entrance on either side of the courtyard are two columns with carvings of flowers and leaves.

The main door is made of double-leafed timber and painted with phoenixes. The two side doors flanking the main door are painted with door gods. The main door is usually kept barred except on important occasions. The roof ridges and eaves of the temple have chien nien ornamentation and plaster relief-work. Chen nien ornamentation is the tradition southern Chinese art of creating figures, flowers, leaves and other images with small pieces of colourful porcelain. Another key feature of traditional Chinese building is exposed structural elements. Traditionally constructed without nails, the weight of the roof is supported on the columns on which rest of the beams. Walls in Chinese temples do not bear the weight of the roof. The exposed structure shows off the ingenious carpentry. The roof of the main hall is a two-tiered xie shan roof with curved swallow tail ridge ends. In the centre of the roof ridge are two prancing dragons on either side of a blazing pearl. At the ends of the lower-tier roof are Minnan spirals.

The main hall of the temple with the altar to patron deity Guang Ze Zun Wang is raised on a nine-metre podium and opens out to the internal open-air courtyard in frong of it. The courtyard is flanked by covered corridors which lead to the side halls. At the centre of the edge of the podium is a sloping granite block with ornamental carvings. In the side hall, there is a shrine to Guan Yin. In a corner nearby is the shrine to Abbot Swee Yee. The secondary altars are dedcicated to Cheng Huang and Xuan Tian Shang Di.

These altars are positioned at the back of the main hall to the left and right of the main altar. The main hall has six solid timber columns that are convex in mid-shaft. They rest on carved granite bases. On the black columns are verses written by a Singaporean calligraphist, the late Pan Shou. The side halls have square columns set in granite bases. They are plain and without ornamentation. Nan Ming School used two halls from 1915 as classrooms. The children came from nearby villages such as Bukit Ho Swee and would not otherwise have been able to afford an education. The school closed in 1925 due to financial problems.

Kong Meng San Phor Kark See Temple

The Kong Meng San Phor Kark See Monastery, is located at 88 Bright Hill Road at Bishan. It is the largest Buddhist temple in Singapore.

History: In 1920, Venerable Zhuan Dao realised that the time was right to build a place of practice to propagate the Dharma and to provide lodging for monks, as there were many Buddhist monks who came to Singapore without lodging. In 1921, the building of Phor Kark See Monastery started as the first traditional Chinese forest monastery in Singapore. Since Phor Kark See Monastery is situated at Kong Meng San ("Bright Hill", formerly "Hai Nan Mountain"), it came to be known as Kong Meng San Phor Kark See Monastery. The Monastery grew steadily and Dharma propagation began in Singapore. In 1943, Venerable Zhuan Dao died at Putuo Monastery at the age of 72.

In 1947, Venerable Hong Choon became the monastery's abbot. With great perseverance, he progressively developed and expanded the monastery with his followers into the largest and most majestic place of practice in Singapore. Venerable Hong Choon also initiated the monthly Great Compassion Prayer and taught the Dharma to benefit many. Phor Kark See developed from a remote temple into a monastery well known to all. For the pass 20 years, more than 6000 people from all walks of life, from Malaysia and Singapore, had taken refuge in the Triple Gem here. It is also an ideal place of practice for thousands of Buddhists. News about it was soon spread overseas by the Sangha who visited the place.

In 1980, the temple began to build Evergreen Bright Hill Home with the donation of S$5.3 million from Venerable Hong Choon's followers, He Hui Zhong's family's company. In the year 1994, the then President of Singapore, Ong Teng Cheong visited the Home and praised its cleanliness, good service and well-equipped facilities.

On 25 December 1990, Venerable Hong Choon died and the monastery lost one of its most highly accomplished monks.

Venerable Yan Pei was next to take up abbotship in 1991, followed by Venerable Long Gen in 1994. The fifth Abbot of the Monastery was Venerable Sui Kim, the abbot of Xing Yuan Temple and Hwa Zhang Temple in the Philippines. He died in 2005. On 5 June 2004, Venerable Kwang Sheng became the monastery's abbot.

Sakya Muni Buddha Gaya Temple

The Sakya Muni Buddha Gaya Temple is one of the most prominent and widely visited Buddhist temples in Singapore, often referred to as the Temple of 1,000 Lights. It features a 15-metre high statue of a seated Buddha, which weighs nearly 300 tons, as well as many smaller Buddha images and murals depicting the life of Shakyamuni Buddha. The large central statue is surrounded by a stylized aura made of numerous light bulbs--often lit during evening hours--from which the temple derives its nickname.

On Vesak Day, the annual holiday celebrating the birth and enlightenment of the Buddha, devotees donate money to the temple and in exchange are allowed to place gold leaf onto a small statue of the Buddha. As the day wears on, the Buddha is almost entirely covered in a fresh layer of gold leaf.

Siong Lim Temple

Siong Lim Temple is the common Hokkien or Fukien name of the Lian Shan Shuang Lin Monastery, literally Twin Grove of the Lotus Mountain Temple. Built in 1902, the Buddhist temple is located in Toa Payoh, Singapore. The 40,000 square metres site was owned by Low Kim Pong, a wealthy Chinese Hokkien merchant and devout Buddhist.

When Low Kim Pong was sixty, he had a dream where he saw a golden light rising from the west over the sea (the west being symbolic of Buddhism which originated in India and is west of China). He took the dream to be an omen and went to the coast the next day. At dusk, he met a unusual Hokkien family arriving by boat.

The entire family had taken Buddhist vows and were on their way home to Fujian after a pilgrimage to Sri Lanka. Low, moved by their devotion, tried to persuade them to stay in Singapore and spread the faith. He promised to build a temple for their use. The head of that family, Xian Hui, eventually became Siong Lim's first abbot.

The funds used for its construction were raised by Low Kim Pong and Yeo Poon Seng, one of the saw mill pioneers during the period. In 1950s, the temple area was reduced to about 20,000 m^2 when part of the land was acquired by the Singapore Improvement Trust for public housing. Today, the temple still stands as a landmark amongst residential flats (HDB). The temple was gazetted a national monument on 17 October 1980, symbolising the social and cultural roots of the early Chinese immigrants.

In spite of being a national monument, Siong Lim was mostly neglected as the government of Singapore tried to westernize. By the 1990s, portions of the temple were in disrepair. Areas were cordoned off as being unsafe. A major renovation was started in 1994 and completed in 2002. In order to return the temple to its former southern Chinese glory, eighty carpenters, sculptors and artisans were brought in from China to work on the restoration.

The temple was originally modeled after the Xichang temple in Fujian province, but has a uniquely Singaporean style. Singapore was an immigrant society and although built by Fujian workmen, these original workmen came from different counties in Fujian. As a result, the temple has elements of Fuzhou, Quanzhou and Zhangzhou styles. The temple now boasts a seven storey gold-topped pagoda which is a replica of the 800 year old Shanfeng temple pagoda in Fujian.

Tan Si Chong Su

Tan Si Chong Su is a Chinese temple in Singapore and is located at Magazine Road in the Singapore River Planning Area, within the Central Area, Singapore's central business district.

The temple is also known as Po Chiak Keng as well as Tan Seng Haw and was constructed between 1876 and 1878. It was built as the ancestral temple of the Tan clan, in the Chinese belief that people with the same surname share a common ancestry.

History: Facing the Singapore River, Tan Si Chong Su was built in 1876 to serve the needs of the sizeable Tan clan. At the time, it sat on the banks of the Singapore River, close to a small islet called Pulau Saigon. The islet has since been dug out and a part of the river filled in so that Tan Si Chong Su is now set back from the water.

The funds needed to build the temple were donated by two men from the most prominent Tan families in Singapore-Tan Kim Ching (1824-1892) and Tan Beng Swee (1828-1884). Tan Kim Ching was the eldest son of philanthropist and businessman Tan Tock Seng, whose significant fortune he inherited. Tan Tock Seng is perhaps best remembered for his contributions to public health care. Tan Beng Swee was the son of Tan Kim Seng, also a successful businessman and a leader of the Chinese community. Of Tan Kim Seng's many civic projects, arguably the greatest was setting up of the city's first fresh water supply lines.

The temple was built as the ancestral temple of Tan clan. The Chinese believed that people with the same surname share a common ancestry. An ancestral temple like Tan Si Chong Su gives clan members a place to worship their ancestors. It is here that the soul or spirit tablets of clan members are kept and venerated. The complex consists of an entrance hall, a main hall where the patron deities are and a rear hall where the soul tablets of illustrious Tans are kept. The halls are separated by open courtyards. The first president of the temple was Tan Kim Tian. An indenture dated 28 July 1880 gave the names of the temple trustees as Tan Cheng Kiat, Tan Chew Cha, Tan Siak Kiew, Tan Mah Arang, Tan Hai Tiew and Tan Sim Boh. The temple also served as the assembly hall for the Tan clan whose members extended beyond Singapore to Malaysia.

Among some famous Tans associated with the temple was the former Finance Minister of Malaysia, Tan Siew Sin and his father Tan Cheng Lock, a founder of the Malayan Chinese Association, a political party in Malaysia. Tan Cheng Lock and Tan Siew Sin were from Malacca as were the fathers of the temple's original founders. The temple's founders, Tan Kim Ching and Tan Beng Swee, were also associated with Malacca. Another famous Tan is Tan Chin Tuan, a retired banker and noted philanthropist and one of the temple's trustees.

In 1889, a school was set up within the temple's premises; its name, Po Chiak Keng, became synonymous with that of the temple's. Tan Si Chong Su was commonly known by both names until the Japanese invasion of 1942. Shortly after the Japanese Occupation ended in 1945, Po Chiak Keng closed its doors, leaving behind about 200 students and the temple's name reverted to Tan Si Chong Su. As with many of Singapore's historic buildings, Tan Si Chong Su has been overshadowed by surrounding modern developments-in this case the Central Expressway. However, visitors to the temple will still find it an interesting place.

The Tan Si Chong Su Temple was gazetted as a national monument on 29 November 1974. The temple underwent repairs in the 1980s due to wear and tear and in 1994, the government approved of restoring the temple to its former glory. Skilled craftsman from China were brought in to restore the temple with the temple opening a few years later. In its heyday in the 1950s, Tan Si Chong Su received 1,000 visitors a day with the temple becoming very packed. By the 1990s, before its restoration, it received fewer than 100 visitors a day.

Architecture: Tan Si Chong Su is heavily decorated and filled with objects of importance. The elaborate entrance hall is dominated by three brightly painted timber double-leafed doors framed with carved granite columns. Gods, dragons and lions dance on the walls. Eight plaques bear greetings and good wishes in calligraphic script; five plaques date from 1880 and three from 1898. Beyond the entrance hall is the prayer hall, known to worshippers as Po Chiak Keng. Statues of a few major deities rest behind an antique altar, above which hangs an 1898 plaque that reads "Help the world and the people".

Behind the prayer hall is the heart of the temple-the ancestral hall. Set 90 metres back from the entrance hall, the ancestral hall is private and secure. Ancestral tablets are displayed in three glass niches and on the walls, five plaques sing the praises of revered ancestors. Because ancestral spirits occupy a very important place in the Chinese belief system, the ancestral hall is given the most important position in the temple. This layout is based on the Chinese concept of li, which means "to humble oneself to honour others".

All the original features of the temple are executed in the temple architectural style of southern China. Most typical are the graceful sweep of the curved roof ridge with upturned eaves, wooden carvings and ornamental gable eaves set in granite columns. Symbols of good luck, prosperity, wisdom, longevity and a host of other cardinal virtues are scattered throughout the temple. On the elegant curved roof, for instance, ornate ceramic phoenixes, flowers and dragons signify power and potency. A radiant pearl in the centre of the ridge speaks of celestial glory. The main entrance is flanked by a pair of fiery dragons, marking the temple's eminence. Each of the side doors is guarded by Door Gods, who protect the temple and ward off evil. Eternity is represented by circular windows.

Thian Hock Keng

Thian Hock Keng Temple is the oldest and most important Fukien, or Hoklo temple in Singapore. The main temple is dedicated to Matsu, the Taoist goddess of the sea and protector of all seamen, while a second temple at the back is a Buddhist one dedicated to Kuan Yin, the bodhisattva of mercy.

History: After the British established a trading port in Singapore in 1819, early Chinese immigrants started to arrive, crossing the hazardous South China Sea. A "joss house" was built from 1821 to 1822 for them to pray and thank the Goddess for their safe passage. Thian Hock Keng Temple was later built on the site from 1839 to 1842. The renovation cost of $30,000 was covered by donations from devotees, among them Fukien philanthropist Tan Tock Seng. It served as a temple, school and community centre. Grateful immigrants, some of whom became successful businessmen, contributed to the construction. A year after construction began, a statue of Ma Cho Po arrived from China and was installed with great ceremony in the temple's newly completed main prayer hall.

No expense was spared to obtain the finest materials and craftsmen from China. Many materials were recycled, however--the timber, stone columns and tiles were formerly ballast on Chinese junks and mosaic pieces used on the temple roof to create bird feathers, dragon scales and flower petals were broken pieces of pottery and cutlery from ships. In 1907, the temple received its most precious gift--a calligraphic panel from the Emperor of China himself, Guang Xu of the Qing Dynasty. Thian Hock Keng Temple was gazetted as a national monument on 6th July 1973.

Architecture: Constructed in the temple architectural style of southern China, Thian Hock Keng has a grand entrance with a high step in front. The side entrance gates feature brightly coloured tiles portraying peacocks, roses and the universal Buddhist swastika in green and brown. This symbol represents good luck, eternity and immortality.

Guarding the doors are tigers, lions and Door Gods, traditional sentinels of any Taoist temple. Beyond this elaborate entrance are two courtyards. Straddling the courtyards is the temple proper, comprising the shrine of Ma Cho Po. On either side of the temple are pagodas--the one on the left is a shrine of Confucius while the one on the right houses ancestral tablets of immigrants who founded the temple.

Yueh Hai Ching Temple

Yueh Hai Ching Temple is a Chinese temple in Singapore and is located at Phillip Street in the Downtown Core, within the Central Area, Singapore's central business district.

Yueh Hai Ching Temple is Singapore's oldest Taoist temple. It was constructed between 1850 and 1855 and was rebuilt in 1895. The temple holds a special significance for the Teochew community, whose way of life was closely associated with the sea. It is the only temple in Singapore to have stunningly detailed three-dimensional moulded ornaments on its roofs. Chinese Emperor Guang Xu presented a plaque to the temple in 1907.

History: Yueh Hai Ching Temple, which means Temple of the Calm Sea, is special to the Teochew community, the second largest Chinese dialect group in Singapore after the Hokkiens. The Teochews who first came here were often fishermen and sailors and dominated the early trade in seafood. The temple is known as Wak Hai Cheng Bio in Teochew. It is the only temple in Singapore to have such stunningly detailed three-dimensional moulded ornamentation on its roofs.

The temple is believed to have started in 1826 as a wood-and-attap shrine just off the seashore and was built by immigrants from Guangzhou. Reclamation of swampy land pushed the shrine inland. Like Thian Hock Keng in Telok Ayer Street, Yueh Hai Ching Temple was popular with newly-arrived migrants who came to give thanks for a safe passage over the ocean. For those who made a living from the sea, being in the good graces of water spirits was even more important.

The temple was also a meeting place for the Teochew community and remains so in the hands of the Ngee Ann Kongsi today. The present temple was built from 1850 to 1855 and rebuilt in 1895 following plans submitted by Ngee Ann Kongsi. Emperor Guang Xu presented a plaque bearing the name of the temple to the abbot in 1907, an indication of the high standing of the temple in the Chinese community. Yueh Hai Ching Temple was gazetted as a national monument on 28 June 1996.

Architecture: Yueh Hai Ching Temple shows the traditional Chinese temple structure of a walled compound with an entrance gate and a forecourt. The forecourt was originally larger but a part of it was acquired for urban redevelopment. The temple actually consists of twin temples, each with its own entrance and of similar size and arrangement but with different features. The temple to the right is dedicated to Xuan Tian Shang Di, a male deity, while the one to the left is to Ma Zu or Tian Hou, a female deity. The altar in the Xuan Tian Shang Di shrine was brought from China in 1852.

Features:

- The enclosed courtyard is characteristic of Chinese architecture. It forms a private world for the people within the buildings. Conforming to the tradition of feng shui, the open space concentrates the qi (breath) in the building complex. The wide forecourt gives a panoramic view of the temple.
- Chinese buildings and courtyards are traditionally arranged on an axis. This line can stretch north to south or, in the case of Yueh Hai Ching Temple, east to west. The length of the complex faces the main gateway.
- Unlike in traditional western architecture where pillars and walls received more attention, Chinese architecture paid a lot of attention to the roofscape. The elaborate roofscape with its heavy three-dimensional ornamentation is one of the temple's most striking and imposing features. The roofscape consists of clusters of one-and two-storey structures in miniature with human figures. They depict a Chinese town.
- The exterior walls of the two entrance halls are elaborate and richly decorated with picture panels. These picture panels can be relief plaster with drawings, relief clay with timber or relief plaster. The ornamented scenes are taken from Chinese opera. The granite lintel also has relief carvings.
- The roof ridges end in a figure which may be interpreted variously as either a dragon or a phoenix. A phoenix

is a good omen because of its symbolic value-the creature is believed to be able to spit water onto the roof if there is a fire.

- The walls between the halls are well-ventilated with large ornamented circular window openings with mouldings of dragon or phoenix.

Tian Hou Temple

- The twin temples of Tian Hou and Xuan Tian Shang Di have parallel entrance halls and shrine halls of equal size and elaborateness. They open out to each other through a small inner doorway apart from the forecourt doors.
- Behind the main halls is another smaller open courtyard. Traditional Chinese buildings are extended laterally rather than upwards by adding more courtyards and buildings to the sides or back of the existing compound.
- The temple's living quarters, utility rooms and storage space are located at the rear building.
- Yueh Hai Ching Temple has gable roofs with solid walls at the ends. This is known as renzi yin shan.
- Exposed structural elements are another key feature of traditional Chinese buildings. The timbers and brackets that hold up the huge roof with its mass of ornamentation are open to view. These exposed trusses and beams are heavily ornamented and brightly painted.
- There are two small five-tiered pagodas at either corner of the temple's front. Next to them are incense burners.
- The temple has both round and square granite columns on bases of matching shape.

BUDDHIST TEMPLES IN SRI LANKA

Gangaramaya Temple

Gangaramaya, with its imposing buildings, not far from the placid waters of Beira Lake, Sri Lanka was originally a small hermitage on a piece of marshy land.

Today Gangaramaya serves not only as a place of Buddhist worship; it is also a centre of learning. It has the main features of a Vihara (temple), the Cetiya (Pagada) the Bodhitree, the Vihara Mandiraya, the Simamalaka and the Relic Chamber. In addition, a museum, a library, a residential hall a three storeyed Pirivena, educational halls and an alms hall are also on the premises. It has also been instrumental in establishing the Buddhist temple on Staten Island (U.S.A.) the Buddhist Centre in New York, Birmingham Buddhist Vihara (U.K) and the Buddhist Centre in Tanzania, thereby helping to propagate the Dhamma in other countries. It was the home for erudite scholars such as Ratmalana Sri Dharmarama Thero, Waskaduwa Sri Subhuti Thero, Weligama Sri Sumangala Thero, Welivitiye Dhammaratna Thero and Pandit Batuwantudawe.

Kataragama

Kataragama also Katharagama,and Katirkamam is a regionally popular place of pilgrimage to Buddhist, Hindu, Muslim and indigenous Vedda communities of Sri Lanka and South India.

Current Township: Today it is a fast developing township in the deep south of Sri Lanka. But in medieval times it was only a small village. It is situated 228km south of Colombo, the capital of Sri Lanka.

Buddhist Kataragama: Some believe that it is one of the 16 principal places of Buddhist pilgrimage to be visited in Sri Lanka. According to the chronicle of Sri Lankan history the Mahawamsa, when the Bo-sapling or Pipil tree sapling under which Gotama Buddha attained enlightenment in North India was brought to the city of Anuradhapura 2,300 years ago, the warriors or Kshatriyas from Kataragama were present on the occasion to pay homage and respect. The Budhist Kiri Vehera Dagoba which stands in close proximity to the Hindu temple was built by the King Mahasena. According to the legend Lord Buddha on his third and the last visit to Sri Lanka was believed to have met the King Mahasena who ruled over the Kataragama area in B.C.580. Thus the local Sinhalese Buddhists believe that Kataragama was sanctified by Lord Buddha. The King met the Lord Buddha and listened to the Buddha's discourse and as a token of gratitude, the Dagoba was built on that exact spot where it now stands.

Hindu Katirkamam: Tamil Hindus of Sri Lanka and South India refer to the place as Katirkamam and it has a famous Hindu shrine dedicated to Lord Katirkaman. The presiding deity is popularly identified with Lord Murukan or Skandha. Saivite Hindus of South India call him also as Subramanya. Following are the other names to identify the same deity in the Hindu texts; Kandasamy, Katiradeva, Katiravel, Kartikeya and Tarakajith. Some of these names are derived from the root Katir from Katirkamam.

The deity's image is depicted either with six heads and 12 hands, or one head and 4 hands. The God's vehicle is the peacock, which is native to Sri Lanka and India. Many local Tamils undertake long pilgrimage journeys across the island to reach temple complex. There is also a related shrine called as Sella Katirkamam dedicated to Lord Ganesh nearby. The local river namely Manik Ganga or Manika Gangai (which means gem river or river of gems) functions as a place of ablution where a sacred bath is taken to remove ones sins. Native folklore tells it that one can be healed of ailments by bathing in it not only from its high gem content but also the medicinal properties of the roots of various trees that line the river through the jungle.

Pre Hindu and Buddhist Origins: The deity at Kataragama is indigenous and long-celebrated in Sri Lankan lore and legend and originally resides on the top of mountain called Wædahiti Kanda (or hill of the indigenous Vedda people) just outside of the Kataragama town. Since ancient times an inseparable connection between the God and his domain has existed. At one time the local deity was identified with God Saman, a deity that was important to the Sinhalese people before their conversion to Buddhism.

Till today the indigenous Vedda people come to venerate at the temple complex from their forest abodes. As a link to the Vedda past the temple holds its annual festival, that celebrates the God's courtship and marriage to a Vedda princess, in July to August.

Secretive shrines outside the main temple complex are also used in sorcery and cursing by local Sinhalese.

Temple of Syncretism: Kataragama is a multi-religious sacred city as it contains an Islamic Mosque within its temple complex as well.

In spite of the differences of caste and creed, all Sri Lankans show great reverence to God Kataragama. They honour him as a very powerful deity and beg divine help to overcome their personal problems or for success in business enterprises etc., with the fervent hope that their requests would be granted. They believe that God Kataragama actually exists and is vested with extraordinary power to assist those who ever appeal to him with faith and devotion in times of their distress or calamity.

Kelaniya Raja Maha Vihara

The Kelaniya Raja Maha Vihara or Kelaniya Temple is a Buddhist temple in Kelaniya, Sri Lanka, seven miles from Colombo. Buddhists believe the temple to have been hallowed during the third and final visit of the Buddha to Sri Lanka, eight years after gaining enlightenment. Its history would thus go back to before 500 BC.

The Mahawansa records that the original Dagoba at Kelaniya enshrined a gem-studded throne on which the Buddha sat and preached.

The temple flourished during the Kotte era but much of its land was confiscated during the Portuguese empire. Under the Dutch empire, however, there were new gifts of land and under the patronage of King Kirthi Sri Rajasingha the temple was rebuilt. It was refurbished in the first half of the twentieth century with the help of Helena Wijewardana.

The temple is also famous for its image of the reclining Buddha and paintings which depict important events in the life of the Buddha, in the history of Buddhism in Sri Lanka, also incidents from the Jataka tales. It is the venue for the procession each January. An 18-foot stone statue of the Bodhisattva Avalokitesvara has been erected at the temple.

Sri Dalada Maligawa

The Sri Dalada Maligawa or The Temple of the Sacred Tooth Relic is a temple in the city of Kandy in Sri Lanka. It was built within the royal palace complex which houses the only surviving relic of the tooth of Buddha, an object of veneration for Buddhists. Kandy was the capital of the Sinhalese Kings from 1592 to 1815, fortified by the terrain of the mountains and the difficult approach.

The city is a world heritage site declared by UNESCO, in part due to the temple. Monks of the two chapters of Malwatte and Asgiriya conduct daily ritual worship in the inner chamber of the temple, in annual rotation. They conduct these services three times a day: at dawn, at noon and in the evening. On Wednesdays there is a symbolic bathing of the Sacred Relic with an herbal preparation made from scented water and flagrant flowers, called Nanumura Mangallaya. This holy water is believed to contain healing powers and is distributed among those present.

The Temple has sustained damage from multiple bombings by terrorists in the past, but has been fully restored each time. On January 25, 1998, Liberation Tigers of Tamil Eelam (LTTE) terrorists committed a deadly suicide attack, killing 8 civilians and leaving 25 others injured, as well as significant damage to the temple structure.

Ceremonies: There are special religious programmes conducted in the Maligawa on every Full Moon Poya day where large numbers participate. Apart from these daily, weekly and monthly ceremonies, there are four major ceremonies held every year. They are Aluth Sahal Mangallaya, Avurudu Mangallaya, Esala Mangallaya, Karthika Mangallaya. Of these, the most important is the Esala Mangallaya.

The relic is also one of the 80 treasures featured on Around the World in 80 Treasures series presented by Dan Cruickshank.

BUDDHIST TEMPLES IN THAILAND

Wat Chaiwatthanaram

Wat Chaiwatthanaram is a Buddhist temple in the city of Ayutthaya, Thailand. It is one of Ayutthaya's most beautiful temples and a major tourist attraction.

Construction of the temple began in 1630 at the request of King Prasat Thong for the memorial of his mother's resident in that area. The temple's name literally means the Temple of long reign and glorious era. It was designed in Khmer style which popular in that time.

Wat Chalong

The most important of the 29 Buddhist temples of Phuket is Wat Chalong, located in the tambon Chalong, Mueang Phuket district. It is dedicated to two highly venerable monks, Luang Pho Chaem and Luang Pho Chuang, who with their knowledge of herbal medicine helped the injured of a tin miners rebellion in 1876.

Wat Chedi Liem

Wat Chedi Liem (originally Wat Kuu Kham) is one of the wats in the ancient Thai city of Wiang Kum Kam, now part of present day Chiang Mai. The original name means 'The temple of the Gold Chedi' and the new name means 'Temple with Angular Chedi'. Monks still live there.

History: There is no clear indication of when the wat was first built, but it was certainly in use during the Lannathai period as the new city of Chiang Mai was being built by King Mengrai.

Renovation: The current buildings are from a renovation in 1908 AD by a Burmese trader. Because of this many of the decorations of the wat are Burmese in style. For example, all but one of the monks on the chedi are wearing the yellow Burmese colourings rather than the white Thai colours.

The chedi was also renovated in 1992 AD when a number of other improvements were made to the site. Not all of these improvements were popular, nor where some needed repairs carried out. Despite its great age the wat is used in much the same way as later wats (for example, there is a weekend market there).

Architecture: The chedi is a five-tiered design common in the early Lannathai period and shows clear influence of Haripunchai design. Each corner of the chedi is guarded by a large, outward facing lion.

The main hall decorations are in very good condition both inside and out.

Wat Chedi Luang

Wat Chedi Luang is a Buddhist temple in the historic centre of Chiang Mai, Thailand. The current temple grounds were originally made up of three temples-Wat Chedi Luang, Wat Ho Tham and Wat Sukmin.

History: The construction of the temple started in the 14th century, when King Saen Muang Ma planned to bury the ashes of his father there. After 10 years of building time it was left unfinished, later to be continued after the death of the king by his widow. Probably due to stability problems it took until mid-15th century to be finished during the reign of king Tilokaraj. It was then 82 m high and had a base diameter of 54 m, at that time the largest building of all Lanna. In 1468, the Emerald Buddha was installed in the eastern niche. In 1545, the upper 30 m of the structure collapsed after an earthquake and shortly thereafter, in 1551, the Emerald Buddha was moved to Luang Prabang.

In the early 1990s the chedi was reconstructed, financed by UNESCO and the Japanese government. However the result is somewhat controversial, as some claim the new elements are in Central Thai style, not Lanna style. For the 600th anniversary of the chedi in 1995, a copy of the Emerald Buddha made from black jade was placed in the reconstructed eastern niche. The icon is named official Phra Phut Chaloem Sirirat, but is commonly known as Phra Yok.

Buildings: Also on the temple grounds is the city pillar (Lak Mueang) of Chiang Mai, named Sao Inthakin. It was moved to this location in 1800 by King Chao Kawila; it was originally located in Wat Sadeu Muang. He also planted three diptocarp tree there, which are supposed to assist the city pillar to protect the town.

In a viharn near the entrance to the temple is the Buddha statue named Phra Chao Attarot (Eighteen-cubit buddha), which was cast in the late 14th century. On the other side of the chedi is another pavilion housing a reclining buddha statue.

Wat Phrathat Doi Suthep

Wat Phrathat Doi Suthep is a Buddhist temple in Chiang Mai province, Thailand. The temple is often referred to as Doi Suthep although this is actually the name of the mountain it is located on. The temple is located 15 km from the city of Chiang Mai and is a sacred site to many Thai people. From the temple impressive views of Chiang Mai can be seen and it remains a popular destination of foreign visitors.

History: The original founding of the temple remains a legend and there are a few varied versions. The temple is said to be founded in 1383 when the first chedi was built. Over time the temple has expanded and been made to look more extravagant with many more holy shrines added. A road to the temple was first built in 1935.

White Elephant Legend: According to legend, a monk named Sumanathera from Sukhothai had a dream; in this dream god told him to go to Pang Cha and look for a relic. Sumanathera ventured to Pang Cha and is said to have found a bone, which many claim was Buddha's shoulder bone. The relic displayed magical powers; it glowed, it was able to vanish, it could move itself and replicate itself. Sumanathera took the relic to King Dharmmaraja who ruled the Sukhothai.

The eager Dharmmaraja made offerings and hosted a ceremony when Sumanathera arrived. However the relic displayed no abnormal characteristics and the king, doubtful of the relic's authenticity, told Sumanathera to keep it.

However, King Nu Naone of the Lanna Kingdom heard of the relic and offered the monk to take it to him instead. In 1368 with Dharmmaraja's permission, Sumanathera took the relic to what is now Lamphun, in northern Thailand. The relic apparently split in two, one piece was the same size, the other was smaller than the original. The smaller piece of the relic was enshrined at a temple in Suandok. The other piece was placed by the King on the back of a white elephant which was released in the jungle. The elephant is said to have climbed up Doi Suthep, at the time called Doi Aoy Chang (Sugar Elephant Mountain), trumpeted three times before dying at the site. It was interpreted as a sign and King Nu Naone ordered the construction of a temple at the site.

Wat Doi Suthep: The wat can be reached by road from Chiang Mai. From the car park, at the temple base visitors can climb 309 steps to reach the pagodas or there is a tram. Entry to the temple costs 30 thai baht for foreigners (or 50 baht if you would like a two-way tram ticket included) and is free for Thai nationals.

Once inside the temple grounds; visitors must take off their shoes. Visitors must be appropriately dressed. The original copper plated chedi is the most holy area of the temple grounds. Within the site are pagodas, statues, bells and shrines. Aspects of the Wat draw from both Buddhism and Hinduism. There is a model of the Emerald Buddha and a statue of the Hindu God

Ganesh. Views of Chiang Mai can be seen on the other side of the temple.

Wat Hong

Wat Sothornwararamworaviharn or Wat Hong is the oldest temple in Chachoengsao Province. The temple is located within the town Chachoengsao on the banks of the Bang Pakong River. The temple houses a Buddha statue named Phra Phutthasothon or Luang Pho Sothon, 1.65 m wide and 1.48 m high. The statue is highly revered locally and the target of pilgrimage. A new building housing this statue was inaugurated in 2006. According to the legend, the statue was originally floating on the river before it was placed into the temple.

Wat Phra Dhammakaya

Wat Phra Dhammakaya is a Buddhist temple (wat) in Khlong Luang District, Pathum Thani Province north of Bangkok, Thailand. It was established on Magha Puja Day, 20 February 1970, on an eighty-acre (320,000 m^2) plot of land donated by Lady Prayat Phaetayapongsa-visudhathibodi. The site, sixteen kilometres north of Bangkok International Airport, was originally called 'Soon Buddacakk-patipatthamm'. From acidic paddy fields, a woodland was created: a parkland for meditators. Buildings were kept to a minimum and emphasized finesse, easy maintenance, cleanliness and durability. The foundation stone for the main chapel laid by H.R.H. Princess Maha Chakri Sirindhorn on behalf of H.M. the King in December 1977 marked the official foundation of the centre as a temple-Wat Phra Dhammakaya.

The Main Chapel was completed in 1982 and the ceremony for the allocation of the chapel boundary (sima) was held three years later.

While the temple was under construction, the Dhammadayada ordination scheme gave training to hundreds of university students, a steadily increasing number of whom swelled the number of residents in the temple community, numbering 3,000 monks, novices, laymen and laywomen in the present day. At the same time, congregations on Sundays and major religious festivals reached 20,000, necessitating the construction of Dhammakaya International assembly Hall, presently the centre for ceremonies.

Although recognizing the importance of constructing buildings, the temple has always placed special emphasis upon training devotees. Thus, during more than twenty years since the foundation of the temple, activities at Wat Phra Dhammakaya have attracted devotees not just from Bangkok, but from all over Thailand and countries abroad.

The use of modern technology to present traditional teachings in a way that responds to the needs of those in contemporary society. Since the outset of the Dhammakaya tradition, the inner peace of meditation has reflected an aspiration to cultivate peace in the world at large. It has Dhammakaya Foundation been obvious that the work involved requires more than just a temple organized by monks. For this reason, the temple has grown together with its supporting organization, the to facilitate a broader base of activities by the public and participation by lay members of the congregation.

Activities: Presently, activities include meditation teaching and retreats, scriptual education and research, youth training, school orientations, social services and environmental conservation. Activities for devotees always emphasize working upon oneself through the practice s of charity, self-descipline and meditation.

With the expansion of the temple to one thousand acres (4 km^2) in 1985, Wat Phra Dhammakaya stands on the threshold of the development of the World Dhammakaya Centre-a resource to serve the needs of the international community.

Criticism and Controversy: Wat Phra Dhammakaya has experienced its share of controversy. In 1999 and again in 2002 the abbot, Dhammachayo, was arrested on charges ranging from fraud and embezzlement to corruption. Promenint social critic Sulak Sivaraksa criticizes Abbot Dhammachayo for promoting greed by emphasizing donations to the temple as a way to make merit. Abbot Dhammachayo is not referred to by the common title for monks, "Phra" because he has been expelled from the monastic sangha by the Supreme Patriarch of Thailand and the Sangha Council. To use this title would run foul of Thailand's laws against impersonating a monk.

"I don't understand that. The letter written by the Supreme Patriarch never reached me. It was mentioned only in the newspapers.Phra Dhammachayo said."

Apologies to Wat Phra Dhammakaya and Phrarajbhavan-avisudh (Phra Dhammachayo) were published in full after the Thai newspapers and DMC. TV channels concerned were successfully sued for slander in the period 2003-4. The apologies from mass media for examples Siamrat Newspaper, Siamrat Newspaper, Bangkokbiznews (Krungthepthurakit Newspaper) Matichon Newspaper Bangkokbiznews, (Krungthepthurakit Newspaper)

On 2006 Thailand Office of National Buddhism was declared Phrarajbhanavisudh (Abbot Phra Dhammachayo) is clear from the prosecution, because it has withdrawn an embezzlement charge against Phra Dhammachayo who now is re-holding the position of abbot of Wat Phra Dhamakaya by the appointment of Thai Supreme Sangha Council.

Wat Phra Kaew, Chiang Rai

The temple complex of Wat Phra Kaew is located on Thanon Trairat Tambon Wiang Amphoe Mueang Chiang Rai Province, Thailand.

Wat Phra Kaew was appointed the First Royal Temple of Chiang Rai on 31 May 1978 (B.E. 2521).

Before the Phra Kaew Image: The founding of the what now known as Wat Phra Kaew in Chiang Rai is obscure. The temple was known as Wat Pa Yeah, the Temple in the Golden Bamboo Forest, because it was in fact surrounded by this beautiful, useful bamboo, until 1434 (B.E. 1977) when its chedi was struck by lightning revealing the Phra Kaew Marakot image within. At that point its name changed to Wat Phra Kaew.

The Chedi: The Phra Kaew Marakot had remained at Wat Phra Kaew, Chiang Rai for 43 years before its discovery 1391-1434 (B.E. 1934-1977) and remained for two years thereafter, when it was removed to Lampang in 1436 (B.E. 1979)

Phra Jao Lan Thong Image: One of the largest and most beautiful Buddha images in Thailand is presently housed in the ubosoth at Wat Phra Kaew, Phra Jao Lan Thong. The image is made of brass and copper and is believed to be 700 years old. The image was originally housed at Wat Phra Chao Lan Thong in Chiang Rai, then moved to Wat Ngam Muang and then to Wat Phra Kaew in 1961 (B.E 2504). Thus it is now called Phra Jao Lan Thong.

The new Phra Kaew Marakot Image: A new Phra Kaew Marakot image was carved in China of Canadian jade in honour of Her Royal Highness Somdej Phrasrinkharintra, the Princess Mother's ninetieth birthday. A dedication ceremony was held in Bangkok on 20 September 1991 (B.E. 2534) and the image was installed by grand procession at Wat Phra Kaew, Chiang Rai on 19 October of the same year.

Phra Pathom Chedi

Phra Pathom Chedi is the highest stupa in the world with a height of 127 m. It is located in the town Nakhon Pathom, Thailand.

The name Phra Pathom Chedi means Holy chedi (stupa) of the beginning. The stupa at the location is first mentioned in scriptures of the year 675, however archaeological findings date a first stupa to the 4th century. In the 11th century it was overbuilt with a Khmer style prang, which was later overgrown by the jungle. The ruin was visited several times by the later King Mongkut during his time as a monk and after his coronation he ordered the building of a new and more magnificent chedi at the site. After 17 years of construction it was finished in 1870 and the population of nearby Nakhon Chai Si was ordered to move to the newly created town around the chedi.

Wat Phra That Doi Chom Thong

Wat Phra That Doi Chom Thong is located in Nakorn Chiang Rai, Amphoe Mueang Jangwat Chiang Rai, Thailand. 19°54.970'N 99°49.365'E

History: Doi Chom Thong has undoubtedly been a sacred site for a very long time. The site was surely reverenced as the home of local spirits before Buddhism arrived in the area. As in many Thai wats Spirit Houses coexist happily with the newer Buddhist shrines. Elephants are part of the lore of Doi Chom Thong. Paw Kuhn Meng Rai was said to have been following an elephant that had wandered off when he first came upon Doi Chom Thong, a solitary hill on the banks of the River Kok.

According to the Yonok Chronicle, the That or Chedi was originally built in the year 940 during the reign of Phraya Ruen Kaew, Prince of Chiang Rai, to house the Lord Buddha's relics. Those relics were originally acquired by Prince Pangkaraj of Yonok Nakpan, who divided them into three parts for the three temples of Wat Phra That Doi Tung, Wat Phra That Chomkitti and Wat Phra That Doi Chom Thong, respectively.

Later, in 1260, King Meng Rai was said to have visited Doi Chom Thong where he viewed the surrounding area and found it suitable for the establishment of a city. He then ordered the beginning of the construction of the city of Chiang Rai and had Wat Phra That Doi Chom Thong restored.

In 1992 (B.E. 2535) the City Pillar was moved from Wat Klang Wiang to Doi Chom Thong.

Phu Phek

The Pra (sat) Phu Phek or Phra That Phu Phek is a Buddhist Chedi temple ruin of Khmers, built around 1050.

It is located in tambon Na Hua Bo, Phanna Nikhom district, Sakon Nakhon Province of North-Eastern Thailand. It is about 37 km east of the town Sakon Nakhon. The temple is located within the Phu Phan National Park.

The ruins have some relevance toward sunrays. Nowadays, there's a Buddhist monastery about 100 m downhill declaring to continue the tradition of the old temple.

Wat Phra Sing, Chiang Rai

Wat Pra Singh is located on Thanon Singkhlai Tambon Wiang Amphoe Mueang Chiang Rai Province.

Wat Pra Singh was built by Pra Chao Maha Proma (P.E. 1345-1400), circa 1385 (B.E. 1928).

The Phra Singh Image: The Ubosoth contains several replicas of the Pra Singh or Pra Buddhasihing image, a cultural landmark in the history of the Lanka wong Theraveda Sect of Buddhism in Thailand.

An Ebony and Gold Image: The Pra Buddhasihing image, called the Pra Singh image in Northern Thailand, is said to have come from Sri Lanka to Nakorn Sri Thammalat to Sukhothai to Ayutthaya, Kamphaengphet, Chiang Rai and Chiang Mai before ending up in Bangkok.

A Purple Jade Image: According to the Chiang Mai Chronicles Pra Chao Maha Proma attempted to usurp the throne at Chiang Mai upon the death of his brother Pra Nue Na but failed and withdrew to the protection of the king of Ayutthaya. When he later returned to Chiang Rai he brought the Pra Buddhasihing image with him.

Other Buddha Images at Wat Pra Singh: There are several other interesting Buddha images at Wat Pra Singh, like these gathered beneath a Bodhi tree sent from India.

The Pali School at Wat Pra Singh: There has long been a Pali language school at Wat Pra Singh and a new building was dedicated on the occasion of the Queen's seventy second Phansa, on 22 July, 2005.

According to Radhika Abeysekera, the Buddha's mother, Queen Mahaa Maayaa, decided to visit her mother so that she could be with her at the time of the birth of her baby.

On the way she stopped at the Lumbini Pleasure Garden to rest. Under a sweet-scented Sala Lanka tree, on a full moon day in the month of May, in the year 623 B.C., the Prince was born.

Wat Pra Singh in Chiang Rai has a pair of Sala Lanka trees behind the chedi, in front of the kuti, or monks' quarters. They are sweet scented indeed.

The Buddha walked the earth for 80 years and passed into Nirvana in 543 B.C. The P.E and the B.E. differ by 543 years.

Wat Tham Krabok

Wat Tham Krabok is a Buddhist temple (wat) in Thailand, located in the Phra Phutthabat district of Saraburi Province.

The temple was first established as a monastery in 1958 by the Buddhist nun Mae Chee Boonruen. It was upgraded to temple status 17 years later, in 1975. The temple is majestic in its appearance, with gold pagodas marking its entrance.

Hmong Refugees: Since the end of the Vietnam War, Wat Tham Krabok has hosted Hmong refugees in a camp on its grounds, most of whom fled Laos alleging that they were persecuted by the communist government that has ruled Laos since 1975. The Hmong were United States war allies in the Secret War against the communist Pathet Lao, the Viet Cong and North Vietnam.

When several Thailand-based Hmong refugee camps closed due to a lack of financial support in the early 1990s, Hmong refugees in Thailand fled to the temple to avoid repatriation to Laos. The population at the temple quickly grew to about 16,000.

Wat Tham Krabok and its Hmong refugees drew global attention in the mid-1990s, as they became the subject of a major global political debate over their future. The United

Nations, with support from the Clinton administration, sought to repatriate the Hmong at Wat Tham Krabok to Laos. But this effort drew significant opposition from American conservatives and human rights leaders. Michael Johns, the influential former Heritage Foundation foreign policy analyst and aide to former President George H. W. Bush, helped lead opposition to the forced repatriation, labeling it a "betrayal," since many Hmong had aided the United States during the Secret War. While some Hmong were repatriated, most began to be resettled to the United States, with about one-third of them relocating to the U.S. state of Minnesota, though California, Wisconsin and other states also received significant numbers.

Drug Rehabilitation and Trafficking: Wat Tham Krabok has also gained global notoriety for its heroin and opium drug rehabilitation programme, which was started in 1959. Over 100,000 heroin and opium addicts have since gone through the unique Wat Tham Krabok detox programme, which includes Buddhist meditation, Asian herbal supplementation used for relaxation, induced vomitting and the consumption of a secret detoxification potion comprised of over 100 unknown Asian herbs.

After failing in other detox programmes, a number of prominent Western drug addicts have sought treatment at Wat Tham Krabok, including British punk rock musician and Kate Moss fiance Pete Doherty, rock music singer Christy Dignam of Aslan and American writer Patrick K. Kroupa. Because opium is commonly grown and consumed by the Hmong in the highlands of Thailand, many Hmong refugees also have undergone addiction treatment at Wat Tham Krabok.

Wat Tham Krabok also is believed to have served as a conduit for international heroin and opium trafficking and possible arms trafficking to Hmong insurgents in Laos. Responding to these concerns, the Thai military, in April 2003, deployed hundreds of troops to surround Wat Tham Krabok. Thai military and police have since fenced the entire Wat Tham Krabok compound with concertina wire in an effort to monitor and control entrance to the monastery.

Global Intrique: Wat Tham Krabok's historic role in harbouring Hmong refugees in the 1990s and its global reputation for unique Buddhist approaches to lifestyle management and detoxification, have made the temple an increasingly popular destination for foreign tourists in Thailand. Thai officials, however, have sought to keep tourists at a distance from the Wat Tham Krabok grounds, citing suspicion that the temple is a likely source of international heroin and opium trafficking. There are also concerns that Wat Tham Krabok has played a role as a conduit for weapons and military support to Hmong military insurgents, who are engaged in a military conflict against the communist Pathet Lao government in neighbouring Laos.

Tiger Temple

Tiger Temple, or Wat Pha Luang Ta Bua, is a Buddhist temple in Western Thailand which keeps numerous animals, among them several tame tigers that walk around freely once a day and can be petted by tourists.

The Theravada Buddhist temple is located in the Saiyok district of Thailand's Kanchanaburi province, not far from the border with Myanmar, some 38 km north-west of Kanchanaburi along the 323 highway. It was founded in 1994 as a forest temple and sanctuary for numerous wild animals. In 1995, it received the Golden Jubilee Buddha Image, made of 80kg of gold.

They spend most of the time in cages, being fed with dry cat food and cooked chicken to avoid giving them a taste for blood and washed and handled by monks. Once a day, they are led on leashes to a nearby quarry. Originally they would roam around freely in this area, but now with the increase in tourists will often be chained as they get grumpier in the afternoon.

A group of Thai staff and some volunteers lead tourists around by the hand to pose and pat the tigers and taking photographs of them using the tourist's camera, while the abbot and monks keep the tigers happy and under control if they get irritated. Nervous tourists may also observe this from about 10m away.

The temple collects donations for feeding and upkeep and to fund the building of a larger tiger sanctuary which would allow the animals to live in an almost natural environment all day long, with plans to release some of the animals back into the wild.

The Tiger Temple practices a different conservation philosophy than in the west. In western zoos and parks, the emphasis is on providing a natural environment for the animals. In the temple, at least until the sanctuary is completed, the animals seem to be treated more as family members. Although it may be possible for the offspring of the current generation to return to the wild, their parents will live out a life of non violence. Their conservation philosophy seems to be working, as while projects elsewhere often need to resort to artificial insemination, over 10 cubs have been born at the temple in the last three years despite having no breeding programme whatsoever.

The temple opens daily for visiters at about 1pm and the tigers are walked back to their enclosures at around 5pm. Due to the pressing need for income, the temple now charges 300 Baht admission. The most common way of visiting the temple is to go on a tour from nearby Kanchanaburi for 300 Baht per head, or to hire your own sawngthaew from the bus station for a group for less than 1000 Baht. Day trips are also available from Bangkok. Prices current as of July 2006 and do not include temple entrance fee.

World Dhammakaya Centre

The World Dhammakaya Centre (WDC.) is locate at Pathumthani Province, Thailand, was established in 1985 by Abbot Dhammachayo (Phrarajbhavanavisudh) and Khun Yay Maha Ratana Upasika Chandra Khonnokyoong. Locate on 1000 acres site. In the area There are 6 main premises in different distinguished locations, architectures, rationales and sizes...

The Dhammakaya Cetiya: The Dhammakaya Cetiya is a symbol of world peace through inner peace. Built entirely on international public contributions, it is also the embodiment of unity and love for mankind. The dome-shaped Cetiya (stupa) is the hallmark of what has become the largest venue for mass meditation and prayers for Buddhists and peace-loving people of the world.

The Grand Meditation Amphitheatre: The Grand Meditation Amphitheatre is the name of a two-storey congregation stadium built to accommodate monks, novices and peace-loving people from around the world to meditate and pray for the happiness of fellow human beings regardless of race, nationality, faith and religion.

The Dining Hall of Khun Yay Archaraya Chandra Khonnokyoong: Named after the founder of the Dhammakaya Temple, the Dining Hall of Khun Yay can seat up to 6,000 monks. Everyday, lay people come to enjoy offering food and refreshments to more than 1,200 monks and novices who reside at this temple.

BUDDHIST TEMPLES IN BANGKOK

Wat Arun: Wat Arun is a Buddhist temple (wat) in Bangkok, Thailand. The temple is located in the Bangkok Yai district, on the west bank of the Chao Phraya River. The full name of the temple is Wat Arunratchawararam Ratchaworamahavihara.

Architecture: The outstanding feature of Wat Arun is its central prang (Khmer-style tower). Steep steps lead to the two terraces. The height is reported by different sources as between 66,80 m and 86 m. The corners are surrounded by 4 smaller satellite prangs. The prangs are decorated by seashells and bits of porcelain which had previously been used as ballast by boats coming to Bangkok from China. Around the base of the prangs are various figures of ancient Chinese soldiers and animals. Over the second terrace are four statues of the Hindu god Indra riding on Erawan.

At the riverside are 6 pavilions (sala) in Chinese style. The pavilions are made of green granite and contain landing bridges. Next to the prangs is the Ordination Hall with the Niramitr Buddha image supposedly designed by King Rama II. The front entrance of the Ordination Hall has a roof with a central spire, decorated in coloured ceramic and stuccowork sheated in coloured china. There are 2 demons, or temple guardian figures in front.

History of the Temple: The temple was built in the days of Thailand's ancient capital of Ayutthaya and originally known as Wat Makok (The Olive Temple). In the ensuing era when Thonburi was capital, King Taksin changed the name to Wat Chaeng.

The Wat had a brief period as host of the Emerald Buddha, which was moved to Wat Phra Kaew in 1784. The later King Rama II. changed the name to Wat Arunratchatharam. He restored the temple and enlarged the central prang. The work was finished by King Rama III. King Rama IV gave the temple the present name Wat Arunratchawararam.

As a sign of changing times, Wat Arun officially ordained its first westerner in 2005. Sean Patrick from America.

Mythology: The central prang is symbolizing mount Meru of the Indian cosmology. The satellite prangs are devoted to the wind god Phra Phai.

The demons at the entrance way are from the Ramayana. The white figure is named Sahassateja and the green one is known as Tasakanth.

Wat Benchamabophit

Wat Benchamabophit Dusitvanaram is a Buddhist temple in the Dusit district of Bangkok, Thailand. Also known as the marble temple, it is one of Bangkok's most beautiful temples and a major tourist attraction.

Construction of the temple began in 1899 at the request of King Chulalongkorn after building his palace nearby. The temple's name literally means the Temple of the fifth King located nearby Dusit Palace. It was designed by Prince Naris, a half-brother of the king and is built of Italian marble.

Inside the Ordination Hall (Ubosot) is a Sukhothai-style Buddha statue named Phra Buddhajinaraja, cast in 1920 after the original located in Wat Mahathat in Phitsanulok. The ashes of King Chulalongkorn are buried beneath the statue. In the gallery surrounding the ordination hall are 52 buddha statues, collected by Prince Damrong Rajanubhab for his king.

Wat Bowonniwet

Wat Bowonniwet Vihara is a major Buddhist temple in Phra Nakhon district, Bangkok, Thailand. The temple is a centre of the Thammayut Nikaya school of Thai Theravada Buddhism and has been a major temple of patronage for the Chakri dynasty.

Royal Patronage: Prince Bhikku Mongkut ordained in the temple in 1836 and eventually became its abbot. He later acceeded to the throne of Siam as King Rama IV. His great grandson, King Bhumibol Adulyadej also ordained at the temple for a short period after he became King. Bhumibol's mentor, Phra Yanasangworn, eventually became abbot of the temple and the Supreme Patriarch of Thai Buddhism. King Bhumibol Adulyadej's son, Prince Vajiralongkorn was ordained at the temple for a short period, as well as several of the Prince's own sons.

Wat Paknam Bhasicharoen

Wat Paknam Bhasicharoen in Phasi Charoen district, Bangkok is a very large wat with a sizeable population of monks and nuns. Many foreigners have stayed at this temple over the years.

The temple is perhaps best known for its meditation lessons. The meditation teacher can speak some English and the junior monks are able to interpret.

The temple is located at Toed Thai Road, Phasi Charoen, Thonburi and is accessible by road or by chartered long-tailed boat from Tha Chang or Tha Saphan Phut.

Wat Pho

Wat Pho or The Temple of the Reclining Buddha, is a Buddhist temple in Bangkok, Thailand. Its official name is Wat Phra Chetuphon Vimolmangklararm Rajwaramahaviharn. The temple was created as a restoration of an earlier temple on the same site, Wat Phodharam, the work beginning in 1788. The temple was restored and extended in the reign of King Rama III and was restored again in 1982.

Wat Pho is the largest and oldest wat in Bangkok (with an area of 50 rai, 80,000 square metres) and is home to more than one thousand Buddha images, more than any other temple in the country, as well as the largest single Buddha image: the Reclining Buddha.

Made as part of Rama III's restoration, the Reclining Buddha is forty-six metres long and fifteen metres high, decorated with gold plating on its body and mother of pearl on its eyes and the soles of its feet. The latter display 108 auspicious scenes in Chinese and Indian styles.

The temple is also known as the birthplace of traditional Thai massage. Even prior to the temple's founding, the site was a centre of education for traditional Thai medicine and statues were created showing yoga positions. During the Rama III restoration plaques inscribed with medical texts were placed around the temple, while in 1962 a school for traditional medicine and massage was established.

The Wat Pho complex consists of two walled compounds, bisected by Soi Chetuphon running east-west. The northern walled compound is where the reclining Buddha and massage school are found. The southern walled compound, Tukgawee, is a working Buddhist monastery with monks in residence and a school.

Wat Phra Kaew

The Wat Phra Kaew is regarded as the most important Buddhist temple in Thailand. It is located in the historic centre of Bangkok (district Phra Nakhon), within the grounds of the Grand Palace. The construction of the temple started when King Buddha Yodfa Chulaloke (Rama I) moved the capital from Thonburi to Bangkok in 1785. Unlike other temples it does not contain living quarters for monks; rather, it has only the highly decorated holy buildings, statues and pagodas. The main building is the central ubosoth, which houses the Emerald Buddha.

Even though it is small in size it is the most important icon for Thai people. Legends hold that the statue originated in India, but it first surfaced in the vassal Kingdom of Cambodia and was given as a gift to the King of Ayuttaya in the 15th century 1434. The image disappeared when Burmese raiders sacked Ayuttaya and the image was feared lost. A century later, the 'Emerald' Buddha reappeared in Chaing Saen, after a rainstorm washed away some of it's plaster covering. It was then moved to Chiang Rai, then Chiang Mai, where it was removed by prince Setatiratt to Luang Prabang, when his father died and he ascended the throne of that Siamese vassal state.

In later years it was moved to the Siamese vassal state of Vientiene. During a Haw invasion from the North, Luang Prabang requested Siam's help in repelling the invaders. The King of Vietienne tratoriously attacked the Siamese army from the rear, so the 'Emerald' Buddha returned to Siam when King Taksin fought with Laos and his general Chakri (the later King Rama I) took it from Vientiane, which at that time had been brought to its knees by the Thai Army. It was first taken to Thonburi and in 1784 it was moved to its current location. Wat Prah Keo, in Phnom Penh, is considered by many modern Cambodians as its rightful resting place, whereas, Haw Phra Kaew, in Vientiane, is considered by many Lao people as the Emerald Buddha's rightful place.

The wall surrounding the temple area-from the outside only a plain white wall-is painted with scenes from the Thai version of the Ramayana mythology, the Ramakian. Several statues in the temple area resemble figures from this story, most notably the giants (yak), five-metre high statues. Also originating from the Ramayana are the monkey kings and giants which surround the golden chedis.

The Temple also contains a model of Angkor Wat, added by King Nangklao (Rama III), as the Khmer empire of Cambodia and the Thais share cultural and religious roots.

Despite the hot weather most of the year in Bangkok, long trousers are required to enter the wat. This rule is strictly enforced. The facility can offer the rental of proper trouser wear.

Wat Ratchanadda

Wat Ratchanaddaram is a Buddhist temple located at the intersection between Ratchadamnoen Klang and Mahachak Road, in Phra Nakhon district, Bangkok. Meaning Royal Niece, the temple was built to the order of King Nangklao (Rama III) for Mom Chao Ying Sommanus Wattanavadi in 1846.

The temple is best known for the Loha Prasat, a one of a kind in structure Thailand. The pagoda is a replica of the Loha Prasat built in India. It is 36 m high and has 37 metal spires, signifying the 37 virtues toward enlightenment. In the past, Loha Prasat was hidden behind an old movie theatre named Chalerm Thai. The theatre were demolished in 1989 as a project to improve scenery along Ratchadamnoen Road.

Wat Saket

Wat Saket Ratcha Wora Maha Wihan is a Buddhist temple (Wat) in Pom Prap Sattru Phai district, Bangkok, Thailand.

The temple dates back to Ayutthaya era, when it was called Wat Sakae. King Rama I renovated the temple and renamed it to Wat Saket. During the reign of King Rama III the Chedi

Phu Khao Thong was added to the temple. It was finished under King Rama V and then named Suwannabanphot. This building has become one of most popular the touristical places in Bangkok, however the other buildings of the temple are much less visited.

Wat Suthat

Wat Suthat Thepwararam is a royal temple of the first grade, one of six such temples in Thailand. Construction was begun by His Majesty King Rama I in 1807 (B.E. 2350). Further construction and decorations were carried out by King Rama II who helped carve the wooden doors, but the temple was not completed until the reign of King Rama III in 1847 (B.E.2390).

This temple contains the Buddha image Phra Sri Sakyamuni which moved from Sukhothai province. At the lower terrace of the base, there are 28 Chinese pagodas which mean the 28 Buddhas born on this earth. Was Suthat also contains Phra Buddha Trilokachet in the Ubosot (Ordinary Hall) and Phra Buddha Setthamuni in Sala Kan Parien (Meeting Hall).

Wat Mahathat, Bangkok

Wat Mahathat Yuwarajarangsarit Rajaworamahavihara is a Buddhist temple in Bangkok, Thailand. It is one of the 6 royal temples of the highest class. Built during Ayutthaya period, the temple was then known as Wat Salak. Soon after Bangkok was established as the capital of Siam, the temple became strategically situated in between the newly-built Grand Palace and Front Palace (residence of the vice-king). As a result, the temple was used for royal ceremonies and funerals. Throughout the past two centuries, the temple has been renovated and elevated in status by many Thai kings and royalties. It became the Wat Mahathat of Bangkok in 1803 and was given its current name in 1996.

Mahachulalongkornrajavidyalaya University, Thailand's oldest higher education institute for Buddhist monks, is located within the temple.

Wat Pathum Wanaram

Wat Pathum Wanaram is a Buddhist temple in Bangkok, Thailand. At the temple is the Phra Meru Mas, a reconstruction of the crematorium late Princess Mother of Thailand. Folllowing her cremation at Sanam Luang in March 1996, her remains were transferred to these grounds in an elaborate procession. The crematorium is a rare example of ancient craftsmanship featuring ornate stencils and lacquered sculptures.

BUDDHIST TEMPLES IN THE UNITED KINGDOM

Buddhist Temples in England

Kadampa Buddhist Temple: Located in Ulverston, England and consecrated in July 1997, the NKT-Kadampa-Temple is the main meditation hall at Manjushri Kadampa Meditation Centre and the location of annual Spring and Summer Festivals attended by New Kadampa Tradition (NKT) Buddhists from all over the world.

According to the NKT Temple site:

> *"The International Temples Project was established by Venerable Geshe Kelsang in the early nineties. The vision is to build a Kadampa Temple for World Peace in every major city in the world."*

Different NKT Temples are currently under construction in various countries

Wat Buddhapadipa

Situated in Wimbledon, the Buddhapadipa temple was the first Buddha temple to be built in the UK. It is home to monks and nuns, but welcomes visitors of any faith to view the grounds and temple as long as they are respectful. Its white exterior walls are put into contrast by the red and gold colours of the roof and decorations of the frames of the windows and doors.

Inside the temple hall though, the walls are covered with paintings showing the life of the Buddha-from his birth to his death. There are pictures of his birth in Lumbini (Nepal), his renunciation, his enlightenment and finally his death. The main doorway leading out from the shine room has a grand painting of the Buddha meditating to reach enlightenment, directly above it. On the right side of the Buddha are angry Mara, trying to disrupt the Buddha and distract him from reaching enlightenment.

On the left side of the Buddha are the Mara looking more subdued and respectful. Mara means the evil one. They are like this because the Buddha has reached enlightenment and they could not distract him. There are two sides of the Mara shown and this is reflected below, where on the left side of the doorway an angry eye can be seen, with a mouth that looks evil. On the right side of the doorway, there is an eye that looks more gentle and not so mad and the mouth does not curve in such a way that it looks angry.

It symbolises that when you go out into the world, you are entering a world full of evil and you are leaving a spiritual world. Also in the room, is a great shine built for the Buddha. There are three statues of the Buddha in it; the back one is black, the middle statue is gold and the front statue is green and smaller than the other two. The green statue is only a copy of a much more valuable statue-the Jade Buddha.

The gold statue is not real gold, because that would prevent the Buddhists from touching it; if they did it would break the tenth precept of refraining from touching gold; this is 20 to 30 years old. Lastly, the black statue is the most valuable of the three; it is 800 to 900 years old. These statues are surrounded by candles and other decorations. Also within the grounds are a house, pond and several bridges. In the gardens signs are stood, each sign giving a message of wisdom to those who stop to read them.

BUDDHIST TEMPLES IN SCOTLAND

• ***Kagyu Samye Ling Monastery and Tibetan Centre:*** Kagyu Samye Ling Monastery and Tibetan Centre is a Tibetan

Buddhist complex associated with the Kagyu school located at Eskdalemuir, near Langholm, Dumfries and Galloway, Scotland.

History: The building that now houses Samye Ling was originally a hunting lodge. The Johnstone House Contemplative Community was founded there by a Canadian Theravada monk named Anandabodhi. When the community declined, Anadabodhi returned to Canada; he was subsequently ordained in the Tibetan Mahayana tradition and enthroned as Namgyal Rinpoche by the 16th Gyalwa Karmapa.

In 1967, the Theravadins gave the centre to two Tibetan lamas and refugees named Chogyam Trungpa Rinpoche and Akong Rinpoche, who renamed it Samye Ling. Samye refers to the first Buddhist monastic university in Tibet, while Ling means a large house with grounds. Trungpa Rinpoche later left and founded further centres in the United States and elsewhere.

The centre flourished and developed under the guidance of Akong Rinpoche and his brother Lama Yeshe Losal, who served as Abbot and Retreat Master, respectively. The centre includes the first Tibetan temple to be constructed in Europe, a large stupa and accommodation for those taking a range of courses on Buddhism, meditation, spiritual development and art.

Preservation of Tibetan Art and Crafts: Under the guidance of the celebrated Tibetan artist Sherab Palden Beru, Samye Ling has also become a centre for the creation, repair and restoration of thangkas, principally in the Karma Gadri style. Since the 1970s Sherab has trained a number of western practitioners in the highly specialised techniques needed to create thangkas. The temple walls are decorated with many exquisite examples of the work of both Sherab Palden Beru and his western pupils.

Traditional deity and monumental sculpture and the creation of prayer-wheels are also carried out at the centre under the direction of resident and visiting Tibetan experts. The grounds of the centre feature many examples of their work, such as a statue of Nagarjuna.

Tourist Attraction: Listed as a tourist attraction by VisitScotland, the centre attracts visitors who come simply to see a spectacular gilded temple, stupas and gardens with statues of bodhisattvas and Buddhas.

BUDDHIST TEMPLES IN THE UNITED STATES

Bodhi Manda Zen Centre

The Bodhi Manda Zen Centre, founded in 1973 is a Myoshin-ji Rinzai Zen Buddhist centre in Jemez Springs, New Mexico, in the United States. It was once part of a Catholic monastery, but has been converted to suit Buddhist monastic practices. While the Bodhi Manda Zen Centre is Japanese in origin, led by Kyozan Joshu Sasaki Roshi, all of its members are English-speaking. Formal training is offered in the spring and fall and is open to everyone on a first-come-first-serve basis. Check the website below for more information. The Zen Centre also has several hot springs which are open to the public during certain times of the year, though a donation of $10 per person is suggested. The name 'Bodhi Manda' means the same thing as 'Bodhi Mandala,' which the centre was once called and roughly translates to 'sacred space' or 'the place of awakening.'

Byodo-In Temple

The Byodo-In Temple is a non-denominational Buddhist temple located on the island of O'ahu in Hawai'i at the Valley of the Temples. At 47-200 Kahekili Highway, the Byodo-In Temple is a replica of a 900-year-old Buddhist place of worship at Uji in Kyoto prefecture of Japan. Inside the Byodo-In Temple is a nine-foot (3 m) Lotus Buddha, the largest wooden Buddha carved in over 900 years. It is covered in gold and lacquer. Outside is a three-ton, brass peace bell. Surrounding the temple are large koi ponds that cover a total of two acres (8,000 m^2). Around those ponds are lush Japanese gardens set against a backdrop of towering cliffs of the Ko'olau mountains. Sparrows are often seen fluttering about and playing in the garden trees while peacocks strut about displaying their beautiful feathers.

The Byodo-In Temple is visited and used by thousands of worshippers from around the world. It welcomes people of all faiths to participate in its traditions. Apart from worship, the temple grounds are also used for weddings and office meetings.

Origins

Ancient Japan: Byodo-In Temple is a full-scale replica of the Byodo-in Temple, a United Nations World Heritage Site near the ancient city of Kyoto, originally a monastery founded by Fujiwara no Yorimichi in 1052 of the Heian period. It was famous for its Dainichi Nyorai, a female Buddha. The statue was lost and replaced in 1053 with a large wooden Amida Buddha called the Amitabha Tathagata, a national treasure of the Empire carved by the Japanese artisan Jocho. Amida Buddha stands in the midst of the Phoenix Hall or Hoodo, an artistic reproduction of Amitabha Tathagata's heavenly palace in what was called the Pure Land. It is called Phoenix Hall in reference to the two phoenixes stretching their wings upon the temple roof. 52 wooden images of Bodhisattvas surround the Amida Buddha, dancing and playing musical instruments on floating clouds.

Since 2001, Byodoin Temple has undergone restoration that will continue through 2007 in the spirit of preservation of Japan's ancient heritage.

Modern Hawai'i: Byodo-In Temple was commissioned and built in 1968 at its present location in the Valley of the Temples to celebrate the centennial anniversary of the arrival of Japanese culture to Hawai'i. It was dedicated by Governor John A. Burns, a favorite of the Japanese community for his long service for the cause of Japanese rights during the state's territorial years. Japanese immigrants entered the Kingdom of Hawai'i and later Territory of Hawai'i to labor in the sugarcane and pineapple plantations. They joined the Chinese, Filipino, Korean, native Hawaiians and Portuguese.

Valley of the Temples: Byodo-In Temple is situated in what is now called the Valley of the Temples, a vast area of lush, rolling green hills at the foot of the Ko'olau mountains on the Windward side of O'ahu. It overlooks the sleepy town of Kane'ohe. Valley of the Temples is a memorial park where thousands of Buddhist, Christian and Shinto residents of Hawai'i are laid to rest, side by side. Also on the grounds are large Roman Catholic statues depicting the Stations of the Cross, a non-denominational chapel, crypts and mausoleums of some of the most influential people in Hawai'i. Most notable of those interred at the mausoleums of the Valley of the Temples is Walter F. Dillingham, Hawai'i entrepreneur and statesman. For a time, former Philippine President Ferdinand E. Marcos was interred at a private mausoleum overlooking the Byodo-In Temple.

Chua Bo De

Chua Bo De is a Buddhist Temple located just outside the New Orleans area.

History: The Chua Bo De Buddhist Temple was built in 1983 following traditional Vietnamese design and decoration. The temple's design and lush setting make it unique to New Orleans since it reflects the look of a Southeast Asian temple. The temple is named after the Bodhi Tree, the tree that Buddha sat under when he reached enlightenment.

Activities and Schedule: The temple holds regular services on Saturdays at 7:30 p.m. and Sundays at 11:00 a.m. Chua Bo De also offers Sunday school classes for children to learn the Vietnamese language and the fundamental teachings of the Buddha. The classes are preceded by by a short prayer at 9:45 a.m. A service at noon is for lay people and it is regularly preceded by a community meal. Special ceremonies are held in connection with the "Phat Dan Sanh" or the Buddha's birthday and "Phat Thanh Dao", the day marking the Buddha's enlightenment.

Description: The area around the temple is largely undeveloped. In addition, the landscaping around the temple is manicured carefully and provides several benches for people to relax on. The Chua Bo De Temple is a single story, square building about the size of a four-bedroom home. The temple has a double door entrance and a five-foot porch. The temple is guarded by two lions, traditional ornaments, to ensure the temple's protection. The interior of the temple is comprised of one large prayer room, a large room for classes and social events, a kitchen and two small prayer rooms dedicated to the worship of ancestors and Quan Cong. There is also an attached living quarter for the resident monk. The temple serves as a community centre for the local Vietnamese population although a few non-Vietnamese New Orleanians are active.

Location: The Chua Bo De temple is located just outside of New Orleans in the Belle Chase area. It is approximately a twenty-five minute drive from uptown New Orleans to the temple. It is located on Woodland Highway near the English Turn golf course.

Hsi Lai Temple

Hsi Lai Temple is a traditional Chinese Buddhist mountain monastery. It is located on the foothill region of Hacienda Heights, California, USA, a suburb of Los Angeles. The name "Hsi Lai" means Coming West, by which they mean the "Great Buddhadharma Coming West."

The temple is affiliated with Taiwan's largest religious organization, the Fo Guang Shan Buddhist order, founded by Venerable Master Hsing Yun. It is one of the first branch temples the order has built. Hsi Lai was the site of the founding of Buddha's Light International Association, which was established in 1991. The temple, like its mother temple in Taiwan, follows the Rinzai Zen school of Buddhism and also follows the Pure Land School.

The current abbot of the temple is Venerable Hui Chi and the current deputy abbot is Venerable Hui Sheng.

History: In 1976, Master Hsing Yun represented a Buddhist group from Taiwan to participate in America's bicentennial celebration. Many American friends asked Master Hsing Yun to build a monastery in the US. Therefore, Fo Guang Shan asked the Venerable Tzu Chuang (Upon the inception of the temple, became the founding and first abbess of Hsi Lai Temple) and Yi Heng to plan and organize the construction of the temple in the Greater Los Angeles area. It was officially registered under the name of International Buddhist Progress Society. Until the temple was complete, Ven. Tzu Chuang bought an old church building, which was to be Hsi Lai's temporary headquarters. The original temple, located in the city of Maywood was called Bai Ta (White Pagoda) Temple.

The planning and construction of the temple in the 1980s was met with suspicion and resistance from local residents outside of the Asian/Buddhist community, many of whom knew little about Buddhism or had negative attitudes. Some main reasons for resistance against the building of the temple was the promise of weekly services, heavy traffic and noise.

Originally, they had planned to build the temple in the South Bay, Los Angeles area, but was blocked from acquiring land. They also tried to acquire Pyrenees Castle in Alhambra (formerly the residence of Phil Spector), but to no avail. The building of the temple survived six public hearings and 165 explanatory sessions. Finally in 1985, the temple was finally granted a building permit. The groundbreaking ceremony was held the following year and was completed on November 26th, 1988.

The temple was finished at a cost of $10 million. Such negative feelings about the building of Hsi Lai have diminished as the general level of awareness has been raised and as the temple and its residents have proven to be good neighbours. In addition, when the temple opened, the Master blessed the land from the highest point on the property and some believe that the blessing brings good fortune and will raise property values. Immediately after its opening, Hsi Lai was the venue of many important events. The 16th General Conference of the

World Fellowship of Buddhists and the 7th conference of the World Fellowship of Buddhist Youth was held from November 19th to the 26th, an international Triple Platform Full Ordination Ceremony for monastics was held for over a month and a Liberation Rite of Water and Land, the first of its kind in North America, was held prior to the temple's opening.

University of the West: In 1990, in conjunction to the completion of Hsi Lai Temple, Master Hsing Yun founded Hsi Lai University, one of sixteen Buddhist colleges and universities operated by Fo Guang Shan. The university was relocated in Rosemead, California in 1996. It is one of the first Buddhist colleges in the United States.

There are departments for Bachelor of Arts and Master of Arts in Buddhist studies, comparative religious studies and a Master of Business Administration programme is also offered.

In 2004, the university changed its name to the University of the West and appointed Dr. Lewis Lancaster, a religion professor at UC Berkeley and longtime member of Fo Guang Shan, as president. Dr. Roger Schmidt became Lancaster's successor in 2006.

Sites

- *The Bodhisattva Hall:* The first shrine before entering the temple. It is a large hall that honours five Bodhisattvas, Samantabhadra (Puxian), Ksitigarbha (Dizang), Maitreya (Míle), Avalokitesvara (Guan Yin) and Manjushri (Wenshu). Outside the shrine, on each side, honours the Bodhisattvas Skanda (Weituo) and Sangharama (Qielan).
- *The Arhat Garden:* Located on the left of the temple, it contains 18 statues of the earliest known disciples of the Buddha.
- *The Avalokitesvara Garden:* Located on the right of the temple, it is also known as the "Salvation Garden". It contains the acolytes of Avalokitesvara (Guan Yin) and statues of the Four Heavenly Kings.

- *Founder's Statue:* A statue of Venerable Master Hsing Yun. It is a bronze effigy of the master in a very lifelike pose, stepping forward with a heroic stride. The statue is behind the Bodhisattva hall, facing the main shrine.
- *Main Shrine:* The heart of the temple's activities. It contains the statues of the historical Sakyamuni Buddha (Shijiamounifo), Amitabha Buddha (Omituofo) and Bhaisajyaguru Buddha (Yaoshifo). Thousands of niches containing an image of the Buddha can be seen on the walls. Outside, a large bell and drum can be seen on either side. Traditionally in many Chinese Ch'an temples, they are played daily to ready monastics for daily practice. Hsi Lai does not use these instruments regularly because of their loud volume when played and there are residential areas at the foot of the temple. The bell and drum are only used to mark special occurrences.
- *Requiem Pagoda:* Located at the summit of Hsi Lai, it honours those who have died. In the past, it was also a mausoleum, but since there was no more room for urns to be interred, the urns were moved to a new Buddhist mausoleum built by Hsi Lai Temple in 1999, located at Rose Hills Memorial Park in Whittier. The Requiem Pagoda is now for people who entered their loved one's names in the pagoda and can only be accessed by request.
- *Meditation Hall:* Located on the back of the main shrine and next to the monastic dorm rooms, meditation classes are held here.
- *Dining Hall:* Vegetarian buffets are served here every day for lunch only and sometimes dinner on special days. Each person can make a voluntary donation for their lunch.
- *Translation and Publishing Centre:* The Fo Guang Shan International Translation Centre and Buddha's Light Publishing are located on the very top of the temple

complex cross facing to the Requiem Pagoda. BLP was established to publish Buddhist books translated by F.G.S.I.T.C. as well as other valuable Buddhist works. BLP is committed to building bridges between East and West, Buddhist communities and cultures.

Attraction and Services Offered

Because of the temple's beautiful surroundings and various facilities, Hsi Lai is a popular venue for tourists interested in knowing more about Chinese culture and Buddhism, even being coined the "Forbidden City of America". Over the years since its foundation, Hsi Lai has been a favorable site for school field trips, business trips, organization meets and a centre for interreligious dialogue. The temple facilities have been utilized for over ten thousand occasions and group activities with favorable feedback.

Not only does Hsi Lai have workshops on Buddhism, the temple also holds workshops on a wide range of topics including taxation, legal issues, education, immigration, marriage, family discipline, etc. Many of the temple's invited speakers or members are experts in their respective fields who are willing to share their knowledge for the benefit of others.

Dharma Services: Regular Dharma services are held on some Sunday and weekday mornings, usually chanting various sutras such as the Diamond Sutra or the Amitabha Sutra. Meditation sessions, retreats and Buddhism classes, are held on some days of the week, which are offered in both English and Chinese. Monks and nuns who reside at the temple speak a variety of languages besides Mandarin, primarily English and Cantonese, are available to perform weddings or funerals services.

Many larger services Hsi Lai holds annually mostly revolve around filial piety, the Buddhist and Taoist philosophy of love and respect for one's parents and ancestors. In the spring, they hold a large service in commemoration of Ching Ming, a traditional Chinese festival where many pay respects to deceased relatives by cleaning their graves. In the summer, they hold a large service in commemoration of Ullambana. During this time, they also hold a ceremony known as Sangha Day, where devotees gather to honour the monastics by offering food to them, as well as offer a public cultural performance, performing classical and traditional Chinese music or elegant solo dances.

Annually, they also have retreats and services for those who wish to take refuge in the Triple Gem, retreats and services for those who wish to receive the five precepts and even offer a short-term monastic retreat.

Larger Dharma Functions Held

- *Water Repentance Service:* A one day repentance service for filial piety. Held during the Qingming Festival.
- *Emperor Liang Repentance Service:* A week long repentance service held during Ullambana.
- *Amitabha 7-day Retreat:* Seven days of mindful recitation of the Amitabha Sutra and Amitabha's name.
- *Yogacara Flaming Mouth:* A Tantric ceremony inviting and feeding sentient spirits. Held in the afternoon after Sangha Day and at the end of the Emperor Liang Repentance service.
- *Great Compassion Repentance Service:* Monthly service held in the evening on the second Friday. A popular service at Hsi Lai, it involves the recitation of the Great Compassion Mantra, elaborate bowing, offering and circumbulations.
- *Grand Offering to Celestial Beings:* A ceremony of Taoist origin. Pays homage to the deity Sakra (Otherwise known as the Jade Emperor in Chinese mythology). Held on Chinese New Year's eve and Chinese New Year day.
- *Bathing the Buddha Ceremony:* Celebration of the Buddha's Birthday held outside Hsi Lai and is hosted by other temples in Southern California.

- *Thousand Buddha Repentance Service:* Bowing to a total of 3,000 Buddhas; held during the Chinese New Year celebrations.
- *Waterland Dharma Function:* The largest Buddhist ritual in Chinese Buddhism. Held every four years, Hsi Lai last held this service in 2000 to celebrate the millennium. However because of lack of staff, Waterland has yet to have been initiated and planning of the ceremony was postponed several times. This service involved the invitations of beings of the higher realms to help the beings in the lower realms get out of their sufferings.

1996 Presidential Election Controversy: During the 1996 presidential campaign, Vice President Al Gore held a fundraiser at the Hsi Lai Temple. The temple fundraising luncheon attended by Gore was organized by Democratic National Committee fund-raisers John Huang and Maria Hsia. It is illegal under U.S. law for religious organizations to donate money to politicians or political groups due to their tax-free status.

The U.S. Justice Department alleged Hsia facilitated $100,000 in illegal contributions to the 1996 Clinton-Gore re-election campaign through her efforts at the Temple. Hsia was eventually convicted by a jury in March 2000. The Democratic National Committee eventually returned the money donated by the Temple's monks and nuns. Twelve nuns and employees of the Temple refused to answer questions by pleading the Fifth Amendment when they were subpoenaed to testify before Congress in 1997.

Claims of the Largest Monastery in the Western Hemisphere: Since 1988, members of Hsi Lai and others have claimed that their temple is the largest temple in the Western Hemisphere. However, the City of Ten Thousand Buddhas situated in Talmage, Northern California has over 80 acres of built-up land on 488 acres of property as compared to Hsi Lai Temples' 15 acres, but rather than a temple complex as is Hsi Lai Temple, the City of Ten Thousand Buddhas is more of an entire community with several large buildings clustered together. Therefore, it is unclear which is the largest, as there is a significant difference between the structure and location of the two Buddhist organizations.

Past Abbots and Abbesses of Hsi Lai

- 1978-1989: Ven. Tzu Chuang (1st term)
- 1989-1993: Ven. Hsin Ting
- 1993-1994: Ven. Tzu Chuang (2nd term)
- 1994-1995: Ven. Yi Kung
- 1995-2000: Ven. Tzu Jung
- 2000-2003: Ven. Hui Chuan (1st term)
- 2003: Ven. Yi Heng (acting abbess)
- 2003-2005: Ven. Hui Chuan (2nd term)
- 2005-Present: Ven. Hui Chi

Pao Fa Temple

Pao Fa Temple is one of the largest Buddhist monasteries and Buddhist temples in the United States. It is located in the upscale suburb of Irvine, California. It mainly attracts Chinese American and Vietnamese American Buddhists, including many who are students at the University of California, Irvine.

The Taiwan-born Venerable Jen-Yi is the founder and abbot of Pao Fa Temple. In 1990 he accepted the advice from the Venerable Master Hsuan Hua of the City of Ten Thousand Buddhas to build the temple in Irvine. At a cost of $5 million, the temple was built on a former site of a Pacific Bell building and it was opened in late 2002. Pao Fa Temple is the host of many Buddhist activities, including celebration of the Buddha's Birthday, various offerings and many other ceremonies including chanting and meditation. It is also a host of a summer camp.

Wat Mongkolratanaram

Wat Mongkolratanaram is a small Thai Buddhist temple located in Berkeley, California. It mainly attracts Thai American

Buddhists, including many who are students at the University of California, Berkeley, but it also draws in many local, non-Buddhists who come searching for authentic Thai food on Sundays or attend its frequent cultural events. The temple is home to a Thai school for San Francisco Bay Area youth, as well as Berkeley's Thai Cultural Centre. The Thailand-born Ajahn Manat is the current abbot of Wat Mongkolratanaram.

Wat Nawamintararachutis

Wat Nawamintararachutis is a working Thai Theravada Buddhist temple or "wat" in Raynham, Massachusetts. It is one of only a handful of Thai Buddhist temples in the United States with actual Thai Buddhist monks in residence. Constructed on 35 acres previously occupied by a farm, it opened its doors to the public in 2006.

Zenshuji

Zenshuji Soto Mission, established in 1922 in the Little Tokyo section of Los Angeles, California, was the first Soto Zen Buddhist temple in North America. Today, it is the North American headquarters for Soto Zen, under the guidance of Sotoshu Shumucho (the headquarters of Soto Zen in Japan) and is a direct branch of Eiheiji and Sojiji (the two head temples in Japan).

Temple Practice: Zenshuji follows the 2,500 year old teachings of Gautama Buddha as passed down by Koso Dogen Zenji (1200-1253) and Taiso Keizan Zenji (1268-1325) who are recognized as the founding patriarchs of Soto Zen. The essence of Soto Zen was transmitted during the Kamakura Period in Japan approximately eight hundred years ago by Dogen Zenji. Keizan Zenji further enhanced the School and significantly increased its accessibility and popularity with lay people. In 1244, Dogen Zenji established Eiheiji Temple in present-day Fukui Prefecture. Later, in 1321, Keizan Zenji established Sojiji Temple in present-day Kanagawa Prefecture. Today, Eiheiji and Sojiji still serve as the head temples/monasteries for the Soto Zen school of Buddhism.

Temple History: In 1922, a few years after attending the Pan-Pacific International Exposition in San Francisco, Rev. Hosen Isobe established the Zenshuji Soto Mission in a Los Angeles apartment. Anti-immigration laws at that time made it extremely difficult for people of Japanese descent to purchase land in the United States. Nonetheless, in 1923, land was purchased and construction of a temple was eventually completed in 1926. In 1927, Zenshuji was recognition as a non-profit organization by the United States. In 1937, Zenshuji formally became the North America Headquarters for Soto Zen and a direct branch of Eiheiji and Sojiji.

During World War II, all Japanese in the United States were sent to detention camps and Zenshuji was temporarily closed. Returning from a detention camp in May 1945, Bishop Daito Suzuki began working energetically to restore Zenshuji. During this time, the temple served as a temporary shelter for members coming home from the camps. Bishop Suzuki's contributions were significant to the temple's history and are remembered with appreciation and gratitude. The popularity of Zen Buddhism boomed in America during the 1950s and 1960s. Many influential figures in Zen have been affiliated with Zenshuji. Rev. Taizan Maezumi (1931-1995), who devoted his life to establishing a foundation of Zen Buddhism in America, was a priest at Zenshuji from 1956 to 1966. Rev.

Maezumi later established Zen Centre Los Angeles in 1967 and wrote numerous books on Zen. Rev. Dainin Katagiri (1928-1990) served as a priest at Zenshuji from 1963 to 1964 before moving to San Francisco where he assisted Rev. Shunryu Suzuki at the Sokoji Temple and Zen Centre San Francisco. Rev. Katagiri went on to become the first Abbot of the Minnesota Zen Centre in 1972. Rev. Koun Yamada served as Bishop of North America at Zenshuji for almost four years prior to his return to Japan to become president of Komazawa University and eventually abbot of Eiheiji.

Another priest that served at Zenshuji during the 1960's was Dr. Wako Kazumitsu Kato. Dr. Kato went on to teach and hold academic positions at San Francisco State University, University of California, Berkeley, California State University, Los Angeles and University of California, Los Angeles. He also served as Dean of International Studies at the Nagoya University of Foreign Studies for seven years. Dr. Kato is still actively involved at Zenshuji. Bishop Kenko Yamashita is also a key figure in Zenshuji's history; having served as general supervisor for 26 years from the late 60's through the mid 80's.

Zenshuji Today: Rev. Gengo Akiba (Bishop of North America since 1987) keeps an office at Zenshuji and frequently presides over various ceremonies and services at the temple, though his responsibilities require him to travel often. Rev. Shumyo Kojima and Rev. Myoshin John Lang are chartered with Zenshuji's ongoing mission to offer the ethnically diverse area of Los Angeles guidance in the practice of Soto Zen to those interested in satisfying a spiritual, intellectual, or social need.

Located in the Little Tokyo district of Los Angeles, Zenshuji is a stimulating mix of traditional and contemporary practices and activities. Dr. Wako Kato, a priest, professor and author of numerous books and articles (in both English and Japanese) holds monthly lectures on Buddhism in English. Zazen, the Zen practice of seated mediation, is also held at various times throughout the week in a traditional Japanese Zendo (meditation hall). English and Japanese Buddhist services are conducted on a regular basis in a Hondo (main hall). In addition to the serving the spiritual needs of community, Zenshuji offers its Sangha (congregation) activities that help to preserve popular aspects of Japanese culture such as Taiko drumming, Shakyo (writing sutras in calligraphy), Ikebana (flower arranging) and Sado (tea ceremony).

BUDDHIST TEMPLES IN JAPAN

Buddhist temples in Japan are varied, yet there are certain generalizations that can be made and general rules or guidelines that are followed.

Along with Shinto shrines, Buddhist temples are the most numerous, famous and important religious buildings in Japan. The Japanese word for a Buddhist temple is tera and the same kanji also has the pronunciation ji, so temple names often end with-ji or-dera. There are a number of other variations such as-in. Famous temples in Japan including Enryaku-ji, Kiyomizu-dera and Kotoku-in illustrate the naming patterns.

Layout and Geomantic Positioning: The Horyu-ji in Nara, which claims to include the world's oldest wooden buildings, serves as a perfect example of the standard layout of a Buddhist temple/monastery complex. There are three essential buildings in any temple complex: a pagoda (typically three or five stories), a Great Hall (often called kondo or honden) and a monastic study hall kodo.

The arrangement of the major buildings (garan haichi) changed over time. An early pattern had a gate, tower, kondo and kodo in a straight line from south to north. Corridors extended east and west from the flanks of the gate, then turned north and finally joined north of the kodo, forming a cloister around the pagoda and the major halls. This pattern, typified by Shitenno-ji in Osaka, came from China, through Baekje; the Chinese style of Buddhist temples, though altered somewhat by its passage through Korea, ultimately was based on that of Chinese palaces and this is evident in many of the basic design features which remain today in the temples of all three countries.

A Buddhist temple complex in Japan generally follows the pattern of a series of sacred spaces encircling a courtyard and entered via a set of gates. These gates will typically have a pair of large guardian statues, called Nio.

In addition, many of the morc important or powerful temples are built in locations which are favorable according to the precepts of Chinese geomancy. For example, Enryaku-ji, which sits atop Mount Hiei to the north-east of Kyoto, is said to defend the city from evil spirits by being placed in that direction. The arrangements of mountains and other geographic features in particular directions around the temple play important roles as well. This custom continued for a long time. Eight centuries after the founding of Enryakuji, the Tokugawa shogunate established Kan'ei-ji in a similar direction for the protection of their castle in Edo. Its mountain-name, Toei-zan, takes a character from Hiei-zan (Mount Hiei) and can be interpreted as meaning "the Mount Hiei of the East."

In addition to geomantic considerations, Buddhist temples, like any other religious structures, need to be organized in order to best serve their various purposes. The most primary space in any Buddhist temple complex is the sacred space, where images of Buddhas and bodhisattvas are kept and where important rituals are performed. This area is always separated off from the areas accessible to the lay worshippers, though the distance between the two and the manner of their separation is quite varied. In many temples, there is little more than a wooden railing dividing the sacred space with that of the laypeople; but in many others, there is a significant distance, perhaps a gravelled courtyard, between the two. Another structure or space of great importance accommodates the physical day-to-day needs of the clergy. Spaces for eating, sleeping and studying are essential, particularly in those temples that serve as monasteries.

Architecture: The architecture of Buddhist temples, like that of any structure, has changed and developed over the centuries. However, while the particular details may vary, the general themes and styles have strong similarities and common origins.

Most, if not all, Buddhist temple buildings exhibit the same basic design elements as other traditional Japanese buildings. Tall thick wooden columns serve as the load-bearing and stabilizing element of the structure. Each column sits atop a single large stone, anchoring the building. The walls, floors and complex bracketed roof structure are then built around these columns. There is great diversity in the style and appearance of roofs, but most follow the basic concept of a tiled sloping roof. The roofs of many older temples, designed more directly on mainland forms, have upturned flaring corners. Meanwhile, newer temples that are based more on native Japanese styles will have smoother, flatter roof corners.

The Horyu-ji already mentioned was one of the first, if not the first, Buddhist temple built in Japan. Its primary structures represent the style then current in 6th century Sui dynasty China. The Konden (Golden Hall) is a double-roofed structure, supported by thick, strong pillars and giving a feeling of boldness and weight.

Antai-ji

Antai-ji is a Buddhist temple that belongs to the Soto Zen school. It is located in northern Hyogo prefecture, Japan, where it sits on about 50 hectares of land in the mountains, close to a national park on the sea of Japan. It accepts visitors in the summer months, but is inaccessible during the winter.

Kyoto: Antai-ji was founded in 1923 by Oka Sotan as a monastery for scholars to study the Shobogenzo. At that time it was located in northern Kyoto and many leading scholars studied there. Vacated during the second world war, in 1949 Sawaki Kodo (1880-1965) and Kosho Uchiyama (1912-1998) moved into Antaiji and made it a place for the pure and simple practice of sitting Zazen. During the late sixties, the name of this small temple became known both in Japan and abroad for its practice of Zazen and formal begging.

Northern Hyogo: The increase of visitors and the many new houses being built around the temple created much noise, which made it difficult for the practice of Zazen to continue at the Kyoto location. Therefore the following abbot, Watanabe Koho (1942), decided to move Antaiji to its present location in northern Hyogo.

Together with the quietude of the mountains, he was looking for a new life style that would bring Zen back to self sufficiency. The former abbot Miyaura Shinyu (1948-2002) protected this quiet life of Zazen while putting the ideal of a self sufficient monastery into practice, until his sudden death in the snow in

February of 2002. His disciple, the German monk Muho Noelke (1968-), continues as the present abbot.

Chionin Temple

Chionin Temple is the headquarters of the Jodo Shu (Pure Land Sect) founded by Honen (1133-1212), who proclaimed that sentient beings are reborn in Amida Buddha's Western Paradise (Pure Land) by reciting the nembutsu, Amida Buddha's name. The vast compounds of Chion-in include the site where Honen settled to disseminate his teachings and the site where he died.

History: The original temple was built in 1234 by Honen's disciple, Genchi (1183-1238) in memory of his master and was named Chion-in. Numerous buildings in the complex were burnt down in 1633, but were entirely rebuilt by the third Tokugawa Shogun Iemitsu (1604-51) these are the palatial structures that stand today.

Architecture: The colossal main gate, San-mon Gate, was built in 1619 and is the largest surviving structure of its kind in Japan. Chion-in has a large and small guest houses in the Irimoya roof style called Ohojo and Kohojo that are designated Important Cultural Heritages. Both guest houses were built in 1641.

There are two interesting features to note about Chion-in. First, the roof beams are all carved with the family crest of the Tokugawa family: three hollyhock leaves. Another feature is the umbrella found stashed in the rafters outside the main temple. One of the architects who helped rebuild the temple placed the umbrella in the rafters to help bring rain (and thereby ward off fire).

Lastly, an interesting feature inside the temple are the very squeaky boards. The wooden boards where built with metal ends that would rub against the metal joints they were attached too, created a piercing noise as people step on them. This was intentionally done so that when the Tokugawa family stayed at the temple, they could detect unwanted intruders at night.

Daitoku-ji

Daitoku-ji is a Rinzai Buddhist temple located in Kyoto, Japan. The temple complex has the mountain-name Ryuho-zan, literally meaning "dragon treasure mountain." It was established in 1319 by Shuhomyocho who is also called Daito Kokushi.

Daitoku-ji was frequented by Emperor Go-Daigo and was counted as one of the five sacred mountains (temples). But after the Ashikaga shogunate was established, it was removed from the list and the shogunate chose to ignore it in favor of other temples that had not openly opposed them. It then decided to stay away from meddling in politics and to focus on Buddhist teachings through Zen practices. During the Onin War, some of its temples were burned down and it was subsequently rebuilt by rich merchants of Sakai. After the Ashikaga shogunate fell, many daimyo donated and supported Daitoku-ji.

Many of Daitoku-ji's temples were constructed before and early Edo period. The karamon of Daitoku-ji is believed to be a remnant of Toyotomi Hideyoshi's richly decorated palace, Jurakudai and is a national treasure of Japan. The first of three gates was constructed in 1526. The temple has such national treasures as Kannon Enkaku-zu and Daito Kokushi Gazo. There are also six temples constructed by various daimyo and patrons.

- Obai-in -Constructed by Kobayakawa Takakage
- Shinj-uan -Believed to be constructed by Ikkyu. The garden by Murata Tamamitsu and wall paintings by Soga Dasoku and Hasegawa Tohaku
- Daisen-in -The main temple is a national treasure. Also with a rock garden
- Juko-in -The wall painting by Kano Eitoku
- Ryoko-in -Constructed by Kuroda Nagamasa. The tea room Mittan is widely known
- Koho-an -Constructed by Kobori Enshu. The tea room Bosen is widely known

Ikkyu and Sen no Rikyu are two of the many famous people who had been influenced by Daitoku-ji. A rumor has it that Sen no Rikyu completed two of Daitoku-ji's three gates in 1589 and this was his undoing. It is said that he chose to have a statue of himself in the chamber at the top of the second gate. Toyotomi Hideyoshi, who also frequented Daitoku-ji, realized that he and everyone else who pass through the gate to enter will be looked down on by the statue. He commanded that the offending statue be removed and ordered Sen no Rikyu to commit seppuku. While it is true that Sen no Rikyu did commit seppuku, the reason for it is not known.

Eihei-ji

Eihei-ji is one of two main temples of the Soto sect of Zen Buddhism. Eiheiji is located about 10 km east of Fukui City in Fukui prefecture, Japan. Its founder was Eihei Dogen.

Eiheiji is the main training temple of Soto Zen. The standard training for a priest in Eiheiji is a two year period of practice.

Zenshuji Soto Mission is a direct branch of Eiheiji, located in North America. In addition, the San Francisco Zen Centre, founded by Shunryu Suzuki Roshi, is officially associated with Eiheiji.

Over the years, several of San Francisco Zen Center's students have spent time practicing at Eiheiji. In 2005, the son of Suzuki Roshi, Hoitsu Suzuki, became Abbot of Eiheiji. His frequently visits San Francisco Zen Centre, have further solidified relations. In addition, Sojun Mel Weitsman, abbot of San Francisco Zen Centre and Berkeley Zen Centre, received dharma transmission from Hoitsu Suzuki.

Engaku-ji

Engaku-ji is one of the most important Zen Buddhist temple complexes in Japan. It is situated in the city of Kamakura, in Kanagawa prefecture to the south of Tokyo. It is very close to the Kita-Kamakura railway station on the Tokyo to Yokosuka line and indeed the railway tracks cut across the formal entrance to the temple compound, which (showing Chinese influence) is by a path beside a pond which is crossed by a small bridge.

The temple was founded in 1282 by a Chinese Zen monk at the request of the then rule of Japan, the regent Hojo Tokimune after he had repelled a Mongolian invasion in the period 1274 to 1281. Tokimune had a long-standing commitment to Zen and the temple was intended to honour those of both sides who died in the war, as well as serving as a centre from which the influence of Zen could be spread. According to the records of the time, when building work started a copy of the Engaku-kyo, the sutra on Perfect Enlightenment, was dug out of the hillside in a stone chest during the initial building works, giving its name to the temple.

The fortunes of the temple have waxed and waned over the centuries. Its present form is owed to the Zen priest Seisetsu, who reconstructed and consolidated it towards the end of the Edo era. In the Meiji era, Engaku-ji became the chief centre for Zen instruction in the Kanto region; Kosen Roshi and Soyen Shaku were successively abbots in this period and Daisetz Teitaro Suzuki was a student under them. Zazen courses are still held in the temple. Fire has damaged many of the buildings at different times and the dates given below refer to the building of the structures currently seen. From the entrance, the buildings of the temple rise up a wooded hillside, with the major buildings in a straight line in the Chinese style; the austere buildings and the trees blending in a satisfying overall composition. There are altogether 18 temples on the site. Among the buildings and other monuments are:

- the two-storied main gate, San-mon (1783), with framed calligraphy by the Emperor Fushimi;
- a large modern Buddha Hall or Butsu-den (1964);
- Shari-den, built in the sixteenth century in the style of the Chinese Song Dynasty, which houses what is claimed to be a tooth of the Buddha;

- the thatched Butsunichi-an which is the burial site of Hojo Tokimune;
- Obai-in, a small thatched temple containing a statue of Kannon;
- Ogune (1301), at 2.5 metres tall the largest of all the many temple bells of Kamakura.

Of these, Shari-den and Ogune have been designated as Japanese national treasures.

There is a small charge (as of 2005, 200 yen) for visitors to enter the temple complex and additional similar charges to enter a few of the buildings. Booths selling tourist items are located near the entrance, below the San-mon and there are refreshment facilities in the garden of the Shari-den and at the platform where the Ogune bell is located, from where there are extensive views across the valley to other temple complexes in the Kita-Kamakura neighbourhood, such as Jochi-ji and Tokei-ji.

Engyo-ji

The Shoshazan Engyo-ji is a temple of the Tendai sect in Himeji, Hyogo, Japan. It was founded by Shoku Shonin in 966. The complex of buildings is at the top of Mt Shosha and can be reached by cable car and is often visited by pilgrims. Scenes from The Last Samurai were filmed here.

Gango-ji

Gango-ji is an ancient Buddhist temple in Nara, Japan. It is part of a group of temples, shrines and palaces in Nara that UNESCO has designated as a World Heritage Site. The Gangoji complex includes three historic sites. The Gokurakubo is a well-preserved structure that is one of those sites. It and the Zen room, are national treasures.

Gokoku-ji

Gokoku-ji is a Buddhist temple in Tokyo's Bunkyo-ku. It was established by the mother of the Shogun Tokugawa Tsunayoshi.

In 1873, Emperor Meiji declared Gokoku-ji the Imperial mausoleum and several of his children are buried there, as well as Emperor Meiji himself. It remains the Imperial mausoleum today.

Gokoku-ji is also famous as the central temple that oversees the practice of Japanese tea ceremony in all the country's temples.

Gokuraku-ji (Kamakura)

Gokuraku-ji is a Buddhist temple of the Jodo-shu sect, located in Kamakura, Japan. It was founded in 1259 and has been restored and rebuilt many times since then.

Gyoran ji

Gyoran ji is a temple which exists in 4-chome, Mita, Minato, Tokyo in Japan.

It is located in the mountain side of Gyoran zaka of Tuki. The formal name is Suigetuin Gyoran."

Origin of the Name: Since the principal image is Gyoran Kanzeon, this name was attached.

There is a tale of the following times of Tangnu in China. The Buddha appeared in a beautiful maiden's figure, selling the fish put into the bamboo basket and spread Buddhism. The sculpture was made based on this wonderful story.

Hase-dera

Hase-dera is the main temple of the Buzan sect of Shingon Buddhism. The temple is located in Sakurai, Nara, Japan.

Heirin-ji

Heirin-ji is a Japanese Buddhist temple located in Niiza city on the outskirts of Tokyo. It is the largest Zen Buddhist temple from the Rinzai school in the Kanto area. The temple was built in 1375 by Sekishitsu Zenkyu, the founder of other temples including Shofuku-ji, Engaku-ji and Tenryu-jiLike many other Zen temples the principal buildings are arranged in a straight line.

Heirinji differs from many other temples in the Tokyo area in the lack of a temple market. Also there are no public festivals held at the temple. Rather the temple remains a training ground for monks. The monks can often be seen working in the grounds.

The grounds of the temple preserve a stretch of the Musashino woodlands. Many creatures, such as Raccoon Dogs that are now not often seen in the city are found here. The grounds also provide a roost for a large colony of Jungle Crows.

The gardens are notable for the maple trees in autumn and the Ume blossoms in early spring. The bell, with the Ume blossom was the inspiration for one of Toshi Yoshida's wood block prints.

Honno-ji

Honno-ji is a temple of the Nichiren branch of Buddhism located in Kyoto, Japan. Its honzon is mandara-honzon from Nam Myoho Renge Kyo.

Honno-ji is most famous for the Incident at Honnoji. Oda Nobunaga lodged there before his invasion of the west. However on the morning of June 21, 1582, the traitorous forces of Akechi Mitsuhide surrounded the temple and set it on fire. Knowing there is no way out for him, Nobunaga commited suicide.

The rebuilt Honno-ji stands on a different site in Kyoto, near Kyoto Shiyakusho-mae Station. The Honno-ji is also used in the game Onimusha 3: Demon Siege. The name of the main character, Samanosuke Akechi and the name of the final boss Nobunaga Oda are the same as the ones in history. It is believed that the game's script is based on the true story.

Horyu-ji

Horyu-ji (lit. Temple of the Flourishing Law?) is a Buddhist temple in Ikaruga, Nara Prefecture, Japan. Its full name is

Horyu Gakumonji, or Learning Temple of the Flourishing Law, named as such because the site serves as a seminary as well as a monastery. The temple is widely acknowledged to have some of the oldest wooden buildings existing in the world. While there are older and more important temples, Horyu-ji is the most celebrated temple in Japan. In 1993, Horyu-ji was nominated as a UNESCO World Heritage Site and the Japanese government lists it as a National Treasure.

History: The temple was originally commissioned by Prince Shotoku, using the construction firm Kongo Gumi; at the time it was called "Ikaruga-dera". This first temple was completed in 607. Horyu-ji was dedicated to Yakushi, the Nyorai of healing and in honour of the prince's father. Excavations done at the present site of the temple confirmed that Prince Shotoku's palace occupied the eastern part of where temple sits today. Also discovered were the ruins of a temple complex which was south of the prince's palace and not within the modern temple complex. The temple was hit by lightning and burned to the ground in 670. From 670 to 700 the temple was reconstructed in its original style but reoriented in a northwest position. The temple has been repaired and reassembled in the early twelfth century, in 1374 and 1603. It is estimated that only fifteen to twenty percent of the Kondo contains materials from the original reconstruction.

The Soga clan defeated Shotoku's family in a power struggle and Shotoku's family was summarily exterminated. It is a testament of the respect of the prince that a rival family, the Soga, permitted the reconstruction of a temple for a rival and powerless family.

The temple later became a major religious centre for Hosso Buddhism.

Fire Controversy: Although, the majority consensus view is that the current temple is a reconstruction from the fire of 670, there is still a debate as to whether the fire actually occurred. Proponents of the theory that there was no fire point out the absence of proof of a fire based on soil samples of the temple complex, the fact that the temple measurements were based on the Goguryeo shaku instead of the Tang shaku and the archaic style of the temple that is incongruent with architectural styles of the early eighth century...

Proponents of the fire theory point out that the Nihon Shoki states that there was a massive fire in 670 in which not a single building was left standing; the biography of Prince Shotoku states that there was a temple fire in 610. The excavations that uncovered the older temple site is accepted as conclusive proof that there was an original temple that burned down and that the current temple was a reconstruction.

Architecture: The current temple is classified into two areas, the western Sai-in area and the eastern To-in. The western part of the temple contains the kondo (Golden Hall) and the temple's five-story pagoda. The To-in area holds the octagonal Yumedono Hall (Hall of Dreams) and sits 122 metres east of the Sai-in area. The complex also contains monk's quarters, lecture halls, libraries and dining halls.

While most early Japanese temples were arranged like their Korean and Chinese prototypes, the reconstructed Horyu-ji breaks from those patterns by arranging the kondo and pagoda side-by-side in the courtyard.. The statue of Yakushi of the original temple was saved during the fire of 670.. While the temple was being rebuilt the Shaka Triad was commissioned or had been already cast. Because the temple builders wanted to honour both statues equally, the kondo and pagoda were set next to each other creating a unique arrangement.

Excavations at Yamadadera shows discrepancies between a temple dated to 643 and the Horyu-ji suggesting that the oldest buildings of the temple are not representative of the pure Asuka style.

The temple architecture was strongly influenced by the Korean kingdom of Baekje, with whom Wa (Japan) enjoyed close relations and gives clues as to what Baekje architecture would look like. There is evidence that Baekje architects, craftsmen and artisans provided the technical expertise to help the Japanese build the Horyu-ji, as the Japanese at the time were likely to have lacked skills to undertake such a massive structural enterprise.. Baekje artisans helped build the first Japanese Buddhist temple, Hoko-ji (Asuka-dera) at the end of the sixth century. Additionally, the bracket work of a Baekje gilt bronze pagoda matches the Horyu-ji bracket work exactly. In the book of Samguk Sagi concerning the affairs of Baekje, it is recorded that the Yakushi was created by a Baekje craftsmen by Prince Shotoku to assist the recovery of his father, who, as it turned out, passed away before the completion of the temple complex.

Pagoda: The five-story pagoda stands at 32.45 metres in height (122 feet) and is widely regarded as one of the two oldest wood buildings in the world. It is likely of Baekje Korean or Tang Chinese style and was probably completed in 700. The brackets and railings of the pagoda are almost identical to those of the kondo. Of note is the probable existence of a reliquary or sarira casket underneath the pagoda. The massive foundation stone, set three metres into the ground, contains a hollow for relics. Unfortunately, because of the weight of the pagoda itself, the treasures will probably never be retrieved.. Visitors are not allowed to enter the pagoda and far from having a function is designed to inspire people.

Kondo: The kondo is widely regarded as the other oldest wood building extant in the world. The hall measures 18.5 metres by 15.2 metres. It is based on Chinese and Korean prototypes. The hall is double roofed with curved corners and the original Kondo roof had to be held up with extra posts because they extended more than four metres past the building.. Repair work on the roof structure and upper part of the hall was stopped during the Second World War because of the damage being done to the famous wall murals in the interior of the temple. During this renovation, on January 26, 1949, a fire broke out in the temple because of a heating pad and severely damaged the remaining portion of the structure and the wall murals. Because the fire had singed the wood to a depth of three centimeters it was determined that the burnt areas would have to be rebuilt with new wood.. The charred leftovers of the original reconstruction are now housed in a fire-proof warehouse where only a select few are allowed to study them and glean information about ancient building techniques. The hall also holds the famous Shaka Triad.

Yumedono: It is believed that Prince Shotoku resided in this hall to study the Buddhist scripture. The present incarnation of this hall was built in 739 and repaired in the ninth century. The hall also contains the famous Yumedono or Guze or Kuze Kannon; which is only displayed at certain times of the year.

Treasures: The treasures of the temple are considered to be a time capsule of Buddhist art from the sixth and seventh century. Much of the frescoes, statues and other pieces of art within the temple, as well as the architecture of the temple's buildings themselves show the strong cultural influence from Korea, China and India and demonstrated the international connection of the countries of East Asia.

Murals: The Korean monk Tamjing (Doncho in Japanese) from Goguryeo is credited as the painter of the famous murals on the walls of the Kondo.

Kudara Kannon: The Kudara Kannon is a statue of Kannon and made of gilded camphor wood. It is 210 centimeters in height and therefore very tall.. The statue is very thin which also creates the illusion of height. The word Kudara is the Japanese for the Baekje Kingdom. The statue is unique in Japanese art.. Some art critics believe it to be a Korean creation. Another source suggests that the statue was carved in Japan but does not describe its origins.

Yumedono (Guze) Kannon: This Kannon is a statue that supposedly is the representation of Prince Shotoku. It is approximate six feet and one inch and some sources believe that Shotoku was that height. It is 197 centimeters in height. The kannon is made of gilded wood. It is suggested that the statue was made to assuage the dead prince's spirit based on the fact that the halo was attached to the statue by a nail driven through the head.. The statue bears a close resemblance to extant portraiture of the prince..

The Kannon retains most of its' gilt. It is in superb condition because it was kept in the Dream Hall and wrapped in five hundred metres of cloth and never viewed in sunlight. The statue was held to be sacred and was never seen until it was unwrapped at the demand of Ernest Fenollosa, who was charged by the Japanese government to catalogue the art of the state and later became a curator at the Boston Museum.

Fenellosa believed that the Kannon was Korean. Additionally, it is suggested that the Kannon is a Korean synthesis of Northern and Southern Chinese influences. However, other art historians suggest that this figure is based on the Tori style.

Shaka Triad: Tori Busshi is credited with the casting of this massive Buddhist statue. It is a triad and so the centre Buddha is attended by two other figures. The figure is dated to 623 and the style originates in Northern Wei art.. The style of the statue is also known as Tori style and is characterized by the two-dimensionality of the figure and the repetitive pattern-like depictions of the cloth the triad sits upon..

Hoko-ji

Hoko-ji, also known as Asukadera, was one of the first Buddhist temples to be built in Japan. It is located near to Hamamatsu. It was completed in 596 under the orders of Soga no Umako.

According to Nihongi and the Suiko section of Fuso-ryakuki (compiled by the monk Koen during the early thirteenth century), the records say that, on January 15, 593, when relics of Buddha were deposited inside the foundation stone under the pillar of a pagoda at Hokoji, the Great Minister Soga Umako, together with a hundred people, had appeared wearing

Paekche clothes and the spectators were very much delighted. Buddhism was very new to Japan at the time and so the first two abbots of the temple were Koreans.

During the Taiko's Sword Hunt at the end of the 16th century, the Taiko, Toyotomi Hideyoshi, claimed that all confiscated weapons would be melted down to create a new Buddha statue for the Hokoji.

The current abbot of the temple is Oi Saidan Roshi.

Iiyama Kannon

Iiyama Kannon is a Buddhist temple in the city of Atsugi, Kanagawa Prefecture, Japan. The temple is nearly 800 years old. Its cherry blossoms are known throughout the area.

Jinrakuji

Jinraku-ji is a Buddist temple in Nara, Japan. It is located in Tawaramoto near Kasanui Station. It was commissioned by Prince Shotoku in the 5th century and built by Hata Kawakatsu. The Great Hall contains a Bodhisattva while outside there is also a Shinto shrine with a torii and a pond in the shape of a Chinese character.

Kofuku-ji

Kofuku-ji is a Buddhist temple in the city of Nara, in Nara Prefecture, Japan. The head temple of the Hosso sect, it traces its origin to the Yamashina quarter of Kyoto. That temple was moved first to Fujiwara and then to the permanent capital at Nara at the beginning of the Nara period in 710. Kofuku-ji, along with several Buddhist temples, Shinto shrines, the remains of the Heijo Palace and other sites in Nara, received the distinction of being named a UNESCO World Heritage Site.

Kotoku-in

Kotoku-in is a Buddhist temple of the Pure Land sect in the city of Kamakura in Kanagawa Prefecture, Japan.

The temple is renowned for the Great Buddha, a monumental outdoor bronze statue of Amida Buddha which is one of the most famous icons of Japan. The statue stands at 13.35 metres high and weighs approximately 93 tons and is the second largest monumental Buddha in Japan after Todaiji in Nara.

The statue probably dates from 1252, in the Kamakura period, when temple records report the construction of a bronze statue. However, it is unclear whether that is the present statue. The statue was built inside a wooden temple but that building washed away in a tsunami sometime during the Muromachi period in the late fifteenth century. The statue remains. The statue is referred to as 'The Buddha at Kamakura' in several verses that preface the initial chapters of the novel Kim by Rudyard Kipling, 1901.

The Great Buddha: The Great Buddha of Kamakura is a monumental outdoor bronze statue of Amida Buddha in the Kotoku-in Temple in Kamakura, Kanagawa Prefecture, Japan.

It is believed that the statue was originally cast in 1252, following an idea by the priest Joko, who also collected donations to build it. The sculptors were One-Goroemon and Tanji-Hisatomo.

The statue is approximately 13.35m tall and weighs approximately 93 tons. The statue is hollow and visitors can view the interior for a mere 20 Yen a person.

Kuonji

Kuonji is the major temple in Yamanashi Prefecture, Japan. It is the head temple of the Buddhist sect, Nichren-shu. Locally it is referred to as the Minobu-san Temple, after the mountain upon which it is built.

It is famous for its 287 steps of stone stairs known locally as the steps of enlightenment which are climbed by chanting pilgrims regularly each year. The golden dragon painted on the black ceiling of the main temple is a notable feature usually pointed out by monks at the temple as the dragon has five toes, making it a Japanese dragon. The blossoming of thousands of cherry trees, including the hundred-year-old weeping cherry tree in the garden, also makes this temple a popular tourist destination.

Over 1.5 million people visit the temple annually. It is reached by bus or car and then climbing the 287 steps, or alternatively scaling the sloping road which curves around the back of the temple. Behind the temple proper is a cable car which takes tourists and pilgrims up to the top of the mountain and further temple buildings.

Kofuku-ji (Nagasaki)

Tomeizan Kofuku-ji is an Obaku Zen temple in Nagasaki, Japan. It is an important cultural asset designated by the government.

Mibu-dera

Mibu-dera is a Buddhist temple in the Japanese city of Kyoto. The temple was established in AD 991 by the monk Kaiken.

Mii-dera

Mii-dera, formally called Onjo-ji, is a Buddhist temple located at the foot of Mount Hiei, in the city of Otsu, in Shiga Prefecture. It is only a short distance from both Kyoto and Lake Biwa, Japan's largest lake. The head temple of the Tendai Jimon sect, it is something of a sister temple to Enryakuji, at the top of the mountain and is one of the four largest temples in Japan. Altogether, there are 40 named buildings in the Mii-dera temple complex.

History

Founding and Feuds: In the year 672, Onjo-ji was founded, following a dispute over Imperial succession. Emperor Tenji had died and his son was killed by Tenchi's brother, who was then enthroned as Emperor Temmu. Temmu founded Onjouji in honour and memory of his brother. The name "Mii-dera," literally 'Temple of Three Wells,' came about nearly two centuries later. It was given this name by Enchin, one of the earliest abbots of the Tendai Sect. The name comes from the springs at the temple which were used for the ritual bathing of newborns and in honour of Emperors Emperor Tenji and Emperor Temmu and Empress Jito, who contributed to the founding of the temple. Today, the Kondo, or Main Hall, houses a spring of sacred water.

Under Enchin's guidance, from 859 to his death in 891, Mii-dera gained power and importance, eventually becoming (along with Todaiji, Kofuku-ji and Enryakuji) one of the four chief temples charged with the spiritual guidance and protection of the capital. It was during this time also that Enryakuji & Mii-dera split away from one another, developing two branches of the Tendai sect, called Jimon and Sammon.

For the most part, this was more a geographic rivalry than an ideological schism, but it was an intense one nonetheless and only grew more severe after Enchin's death. The rivalry turned violent in the second half of the 10th century, over a series of official appointments to other temples and similar slights.

The zasu of Enryakuji in 970 formed the first permanent standing army to be recruited by a religious body. Mii-dera can be assumed to have established one very soon afterwards. In 989, a former abbot of Mii-dera by the name of Yokei was to become abbot of Enryakuji; but none of the monks of Enryakuji would perform services under his direction. He soon resigned. But in 993, the monks of Mii-dera took revenge, destroying a temple where Ennin, founder of Enryakuji's Sammon sect, had once lived. The monks from Enryakuji retaliated, destroying more than 40 places associated with Enchin.

In the end, over 1,000 monks of Enchin's Jimon sect fled permanently to Mii-dera, cementing the split between the two Sects. Over the course of the 10th, 11th and 12th centuries, there continued to be similar incidents, over the appointment of abbots (zasu), involving many sohei, or warrior monks. Mii-dera was burned to the ground by the sohei of Enryakuji four times in the 11th century alone. There were, however, times that the two united against a common enemy, including an attack on the Kofukuji in Nara in 1081 (avenging the burning of the Mii-dera by Kofukuji monks that same year) and a united attack on Nara once more in 1117.

The Genpei Wars: At the end of the 12th century, the attentions of the monks of Mount Hiei were turned towards a greater conflict: the Genpei War. The Taira and Minamoto families supported different claimants to the Chrysanthemum Throne and in June of 1180, the Minamoto brought their claimant, Prince Mochihito, to the Mii-dera, fleeing from Taira samurai. Mii-dera asked for aid from Enryakuji, but was denied. The monks of the Mii-dera joined the Minamoto army and fled to the Byodoin, a Fujiwara clan villa, which had been converted to a monastery by Mii-dera monks. (see Battle of Uji (1180).) Angered at the Mii-dera/Minamoto alliance, Taira no Kiyomori ordered the destruction of Mii-dera and of many of the temples of Nara. The monks of Mii-dera figured once more in the Genpei War, fighting alongside Taira sympathisers against Minamoto no Yoshinaka, who invaded Kyoto in 1184, setting fire to the Hojujidono Palace and kidnapping the Emperor Go-Shirakawa.

Following the Genpei War, there was a long period of relative peace, as the temples of Kyoto and Nara, including the Mii-dera, were rebuilt. As the temples regained strength, rivalries reappeared, though little to no violence actually erupted between Mii-dera and Enryakuji. In 1367, when a novice from Mii-dera was killed at a toll barrier established by the temple of Nanzenji, warrior monks from Mii-dera set out to attack Nanzenji; when the Shogun's forces were sent to quell the rebellion, they discovered Mii-dera's monks to be supported by sohei from Enryakuji and Kofukuji as well. A year later, another battle erupted, over comments made by the abbot of Nanzenji; the monks of Mii-dera, along with their allies, defeated the Shogun's forces once again.

Sengoku Period and Beyond: In the late 16th century, Mii-dera, along with many of the other nearby temples, sought alliances, for military (defensive) strength, as well as military power. The territories of the Asai and Asakura families were closest to Mount Hiei, but these families, as well as others the temples had allied with, were rivals of Oda Nobunaga. These two families suffered heavy defeats at the hands of Nobunaga and his chief general Hideyoshi Toyotomi, so in 1571 they sought a stronger alliance with the temples. That same year, Nobunaga set to destroying everything on Mount Hiei, starting with the town of Sakamoto at the foot of the mountain and setting his sights on Enryakuji at the summit. Much of Mii-dera was destroyed, as the warrior monks failed against Nobunaga's large and highly trained samurai army.

Following these attacks, the monks of Mount Hiei were finally granted a reprieve and rebuilt their temples once more. Mii-dera has never been attacked or destroyed since then.

Halls and Treasures: Within the Kondo and Hondo (the Main Hall and Buddha Hall) of Mii-dera, there are at least six statues of the Buddha, sacred personal possessions of various Emperors, including Emperor Tenji, which are hidden away and shown only on rare, special occasions, as well as one large statue of the Miroku, or Maitreya, Buddha in the centre of the Hall. The Kondo was built in 1599 and is a replacement for the original, built in 672 and destroyed by the Taiko Hideyoshi Toyotomi. Mii-dera also has a Kannon-do, built in 1072, a hall dedicated to Kannon, Bodhisattva of Compassion. Mii-dera is the fourteenth temple in a Pilgrimage of 33 Temples devoted to Kannon in the Kansai area.

Nanzen-ji

Zuiryusan Nanzen-ji is a Zen Buddhist temple in Kyoto, Japan. Emperor Kameyama established it in 1291 on the site of his previous detached palace. Nanzenji is one of the Five Great Zen Temples of Kyoto. It is also the headquarters of the Nanzenji branch of Rinzai Zen.

Narita-san

Narita-san is a Buddhist temple located in central Narita city, Chiba prefecture, Japan. This temple is one of the most well known in the Kanto region of Japan and is only surpassed in visitors during the O-shogatsu period (lit: New year period) by the Meiji Shrine in Tokyo. The temple grounds are comprised of a main gate, a steep stairwell and the main buildings (including a couple five-story pagodas) and a garden area with large pond. A very small zoo is also within the temple grounds.

The mail hall is a Buddhist worship area. The interior is based on Indian Buddhist design but has a distinct Japanese impression. Throughout the day visitors come to sit and to pray aloud.

Tourism: Travelers leaving Japan via Narita International Airport commonly stop by to visit. The temple is within 10 minutes walking from either the JR Narita Station or the Keisei Narita Station and both paths offer many small shops selling Japanese snacks and other foodstuffs and also Japanese good-luck charms such as Daruma dolls.

Special Events: At the beginning of the year locals flock to Narita-san for the O-shogatsu holidays to pray. In spring the Taiko festival occurs at Narita-san. One can observe taiko drum play and dancing at this time.

Ofuna Kan'non

The Ofuna Kan'non or Muga sozan Ofuna Kan'nonji is a Buddhist temple in Kamakura, Kanagawa, Japan. The outstanding feature of the temple is a 25 metre tall 1,900 ton reinforced concrete statue of Kan'non which is dedicated to the bodhisattva Kan'non or Kuan Yin. Construction of the Temple began in 1929 by the Soto(Zen) Buddhist sect. The outline of the statue was complete by 1934 but work was suspended at the outbreak of the Pacific War. The Ofuna Kan'non Society continued construction work in 1954 and the Temple was finally completed in 1960.

The Kan'non incorporates stones from ground zero of Hiroshima and Nagasaki to commemorate those who died in the explosions of the atomic bombs. A fire originating from the atomic fires of Hiroshima burns in a mushroom-formed statue.

Provincial temple

Emperor Shomu of Japan established provincial temples in each province of Japan. Todaiji, the provincial temple of Yamato Province, served as the head of all these kokubunji and Hokkeji held that duty for the kokubun niji.

The words "kokubunji" and "kokubun niji" gave rise to many place names that continue to today, including:

- Kokubunji, Kagawa
- Kokubunji, Tokyo
- Kokubunji, Tochigi

Saidai-ji

Saidai-ji is a Buddhist temple in the city of Nara, Nara Prefecture, Japan. The temple was established in AD 765 and it is the main temple of the Shingon Ritsu sect of Buddhism. It is the counterpart to Todai-ji. Its name means "west great temple."

Senju-ji

Senju-ji, also known as Takadayama, is the chief Buddhist temple of the Takada branch of Jodo Shinshu, a Japanese sect of Buddhism. Originally founded by Shinran in 1226, it was later named an imperial temple. Though the temple's central sacred mountain is located in Tsu city, Mie prefecture, where Senju-ji was originally founded, today the head temple is in Takata, Ninomiya town, in Tochigi prefecture. The temple is named after the prayer chant senju-nenbutsu and as a result of the fact that another branch built a temple called Senjo-ji; thus, a similar but different name was chosen. Named an imperial temple in 1477, Senju-ji was later elevated further, to the classification of Monzeki-dera in 1574.

Senso-ji

Senso-ji is an ancient Buddhist temple located in Asakusa, Taito, Tokyo. It is Tokyo's oldest temple and one of its most significant. Formerly associated with the Tendai sect, it became independent after World War II. Adjacent to the temple is a Shinto shrine, the Asakusa Jinja. Senso-ji is the focus of Tokyo's largest and most popular matsuri (Shinto festival). This takes place over 3-4 days in late spring and sees the surrounding streets closed to traffic from dawn until late evening.

Dominating the entrance to the temple is the kaminari-mon or "Thunder Gate". This imposing Buddhist structure features a massive paper lantern dramatically painted in vivid red-and-black tones to suggest thunderclouds and lightning. Within the precincts stand a stately five-story pagoda and the main hall, devoted to Kannon Bosatsu.

Many tourists, both Japanese and from abroad, visit Senso-ji every year. Catering to the visiting crowds, the surrounding area has many traditional shops and eating places that feature traditional dishes (hand-made noodles, sushi, tempura, etc.). Nakamise-dori, the street leading from the Thunder Gate to the temple itself, is lined with small shops selling souvenirs ranging from fans, ukiyo-e (woodblock prints), kimono and other robes, Buddhist scrolls, traditional sweets, to Godzilla toys, t-shirts and cell-phone trinkets. These shops themselves are part of a living tradition of selling to pilgrims who walked to Senso-ji.

Within the temple is a quiet contemplative garden kept in the distinctive Japanese style.

History: The temple is dedicated to the bodhisattva Kannon. According to legend, a statue of the Kannon was found in the Sumida River in 628 by two fishermen, the brothers Hinokuma Hamanari and Hinokuma Takenari. The chief of their village, Hajino Nakamoto, recognized the sanctity of the statue and inshrined the statue by remaking his own house into a small temple in Asakusa so that the villagers could worship the

Kannon. The blessings of the Kannon gradually received a high reputation throughout Japan and people near and far flocked to Asakusa to venerate the statue.

Shinshogokuraku-ji

Shinshogokuraku-ji or Shinnyo-do is a Buddhist Tendai temple in Kyoto. It was established in 984 AD by Kaisan Shonin.

Shitenno-ji

Shitenno-ji is a Buddhist temple in Osaka, Japan.

The prince Shotoku constructed this temple in 593, using the construction firm Kongo Gumi. It is the oldest officially administered temple in Japan, although the temple buildings have been rebuilt over the centuries. It is also home to a major flea market on the 21st of each month. Access to Shitennoji is via a 10 minute walk from Tennoji station, on the JR, Midosuji and Tannimachi train lines.

Shoso-in (Todai-ji)

The Shosoin is a structure at Todai-ji in Nara, Japan. The building is in the azekura log-cabin style, with a raised floor. It lies to the northwest of the Daibutsuden (which houses the Great Buddha). The Shosoin houses artifacts connected to Emperor Shomu (701-756) and Empress Komyo (701-760), as well as arts and crafts of the Tempyo period of Japanese history. It was formerly a storehouse belonging to Todai-ji, but after the Meiji Restoration, it came under the administration of the national government and since World War II has been under the administration of the Imperial Household Agency. It is on the UNESCO register of World Heritage Sites as one of the Historic Monuments of Ancient Nara. It is also a national treasure of Japan.

One of the treasures of Shosoin is an ivory one-shaku ruler.

Shosoin

Shosoin, or treasure houses, are sections of Buddhist temples and Shinto shrines used to house collections of Japanese art.

Although locations range from northern Honshu to Kyushu, the largest number of these treasure houses are in the Kansai region in the Kyoto-Nara-Osaka area.

While these collections are not open to the public, selections from the Nara National Museum are shown once a year in autumn.

The following shosoin in Nara have notable collections:

- Horyu-ji Great Treasure House-opened in 1939
- Kofuku-ji Treasure House-opened in 1959
- Toshodai-ji Treasure House-opened in 1970
- Todai-ji Treasure House

The Horyu-ji Treasure House houses famous Buddhist sculptures, which date from the Asuka period through the Kamakura period. Among the objects are the Kudara Kannon and the Tamamushi Shrine.

The Kofuku-ji Treasure House has sculpture dating from the 7th century through the Kamakura period. There are pieces attributed to Kamakura sculptors such as Jokei, Unkei and Koben. In addition, temples on Mount Koya in Wakayama Prefecture preserves and displays objects in its Koyasan Treasure House.

The following shosoin in Kyoto have notable collections:

- Daigoji Treasure House-opened in 1935
- Koryuji Treasure House-opened in 1922
- Chion'in Treasure House

The Itsukushima Shrine on Miyajima in the Inland Sea had a treasure house as early as 1896. This shosoin housed Heian and Kamakura armor and Noh masks. The Kamakura National Treasure House also holds a fine collection of Japanese art and sculpture.

Shunko-in

Shunko-in, in Kyoto, Japan, is a Buddhist temple established in 1590 by the daimyo Horio Yoshiharu.

Shoren-in

Shoren-in is a temple in Kyoto, Japan. Also known as the Awata Palace, it was built in the late 13th century. Shoren-in was formerly the temple of the imperial abbot of the Tendai headquarters on Mount Hiei. After the Great Kyoto Fire of 1788, it was used as a temporary imperial palace. The main hall was rebuilt in 1895.

Soji-ji

Soji-ji is one of two main temples of the Soto sect of Zen Buddhism. The temple was originally founded in 740 in Noto, but was totally destroyed by fire in 1898. It was rebuilt over a period of several years and reopened in its present location at Tsurumi, Yokohama in 1911.

Zenshuji Soto Mission is a direct branch of Soji-ji, located in North America.